THE
WINNING
CONTEST
PLAYER

THE
WINNING CONTEST PLAYER

Inside the Minds of the World's Greatest Horseplayers

Peter Thomas Fornatale

Published by
Daily Racing Form Press
708 Third Avenue, 12th Floor
New York, New York 10017

ISBN: 978-1-932910-32-2
Library of Congress Control Number: 2013954761

Cover, jacket, and text designed by Chris Donofry and Meg Price
Jacket photos by Barbara D. Livingston
Printed in the United States of America

Statistical data and related information provided by:

C O M P A N Y
The Thoroughbred Industry's Official Source for Racing Information
www.equibase.com
821 Corporate Drive Lexington, KY 40503-2794

For Cary Fotias and Jeff Sotman,
I'll miss you, you magnificent degenerates.

EPIGRAPH

"He doth nothing but talk of his horse."
—William Shakespeare, *The Merchant of Venice*, Act 1, Scene 2

CONTENTS

Foreword by Harvey Pack

I was allegedly in charge of promotions at NYRA, and my immediate boss, Pat Lynch, wanted me in charge of the toilets. So he really pushed me aside and had me in charge of important matters like what we should do with the parking lot at Aqueduct. I ended up renting the lot out to the Jehovah's Witnesses. Another client was a flea market, which I thought at the time was the biggest joke in the world, but the guy ended up staying there ten years and making a million bucks. But my heart was always still in promotions. I wanted to do a handicapping contest, because to me, handicapping was the backbone of the sport. It was the best way we had to create new fans.

We had money then. And I came up with the concept of a free contest open to everyone, with people entering on their way into the track. We'd give them a coupon, and they'd have to pick all the winners that day, and the top ten would advance to the finals. The finals would be a two-day Saturday-Sunday contest. It was almost like the NHC is today, only we didn't charge anything to play. We put up $5,000 in prize money, and it was a big deal.

The problem we had was people playing multiple entries. Some of these guys would try to put in 50 entries, and it wasn't fair to everybody else. So I set out to conquer that. My friend Fred Lief in the marketing department in particular became obsessed with making sure people took only one entry. We had a good staff, and over time we modified the rules and procedures so that couldn't happen.

What really helped the contest pick up steam was our first winner. He was named Marty Blum. It was as if I'd gone to Central Casting and said, "I want a nut to win the contest." And that was Marty. He wore a ten-gallon hat, and we called him the Kosher Cowboy. He came from the Bronx. He wasn't a very good handicapper, but under the rules that first year, he was able to make just one big bet. That's what he did and he won. But it worked out great for us because we were on the news and in all the papers.

I had stolen the idea of a handicapping contest from a guy named Kelso Sturgeon, who was the head of publicity at Penn National. But Penn National charged people to enter—and they did something even worse than that: they invited the press to play for free to compete with the people who'd won their way in through the preliminaries. The idea was that they'd be more likely to write about it if they got a free roll. We didn't want to do it that way. We'd do a separate contest for the press with a token prize where they could qualify for the finals like everybody else. And I wish to point out that several of them did— though none of them ever finished in the money.

As the years went by, we changed the rules to make it harder for somebody to stab and win, more like it is in today's contests, with odds caps. The second year, a guy named Tony DiMucci won. And what do you know? He was a nut, too. I tell the story in my book, *May The Horse Be With You*, of how DiMucci was so happy with Jean Cruguet's ride that led him to victory that he sent the jockey a case of fine Champagne. Later that day, Tony went down to the paddock to thank Jean in person. Jean was riding the seven, but he held up three fingers for Tony to see. Tony, degenerate that he was, raced to the windows to put all the money he had on the three horse, who promptly finished last. Tony went to find Jean again after the race and asked him why he'd held up three fingers. Cruguet replied, "Three of the bottles were broken."

After we modified the rules, better players started winning: Ragozin players, people who knew what they were doing. But people still loved it and it was great.

Then I had another idea. This contest was working great with no entry fee and getting us lots of attention. What if we had a for-pay contest where we could offer a purse of $1 million? My vision was for 1,000 entries putting up $1,000 apiece, and people could enter as syndicates if they wanted. We'll put up a million bucks and even the newspapers that hate racing would have to cover it.

I went to our attorney, Marty Lieberman, and I explained it to him. He thought it was a good idea, but being a lawyer, he needed to make sure it was legal. "I have to run it by the Attorney General of New York State," he said. I told him, "By all means, ask away."

The Attorney General at that time was a guy named Louis Lefkowitz. And I thought we were going to be golden because this guy Lefkowitz liked racing—he was out at the track a lot. It turned out that the key legal issue was whether handicapping was a game of luck or skill. If he ruled it was skill-based, we'd be okay. If not, the contest would be an illegal lottery under state law. I figured since Lefkowitz spent time at the track, he'd know the effort that goes into picking winners.

Guess what? I was wrong. Lefkowitz came back and told Lieberman that handicapping was a game of chance. That infuriated me. Maybe it was a game of chance to Lefkowitz because he didn't know what he was doing and lost. But obviously it's a game of incredible skill for the hardworking people who do it every day and have made sure that handicapping contests are alive and well into the 21st century. But the "million-dollar" contest got dropped. And it's bothered me ever since.

I had a friend named Steve Wolfson who owned Happy Valley Farm with his brother. The original Dick Dutrow, the father of Anthony Dutrow and Rick Dutrow Jr. was their trainer. At some point, Steve got a job in Vegas at the Mirage Hotel. He was a fraternity brother of Steve Wynn's at the University of Pennsylvania. He was a misfit in Vegas because he's a class guy. He didn't belong there, but he was there. And the first idea he came up with? A handicapping contest. This was in 1991, right around the time of the first Gulf War. And he came up with an idea that is now all over Vegas—a real, for-pay handicapping contest. He called me up and said he thought it would give his contest a lot of pizzazz if I were to host. I told him it would be my pleasure. As an afterthought I asked, "Are you going to pay me?" He gave me $5,000 and a first-class round-trip to Vegas for my wife, Joy, and me, along with a suite at the Mirage with room, food, and beverage. It was the full high-roller package, something I knew nothing about because I only bet $5 at blackjack. The whole thing was just unbelievable. The players had a great time. Bombs may have been dropping over Baghdad, but all they cared about was who they liked in the double.

I went out there and I thought it went great, and Steve thought so too. A lot of people I knew came out, and it was a real success. I said to Steve afterward, "Are we going to do this again next year?" He said, "I can't see any reason why not." And sure enough, a year later, he called me and told me we were back on, same deal as before. I was thrilled.

So the next year, I get out there and Steve tells me that Steve Wynn has decided to put blackjack and dice tables in the contest room with the players. He wants to make a little extra money and see how much these guys will bet. I told him, "Don't let him do that."

He told me, "Well, there's not much I can do. He's the boss and he wants to do it."

I said, "Does he honestly believe anybody good enough to be competing in this contest is going to go and play dice in the middle of it? Plenty of these guys will play it all night in the casino after the contest is over, but not while it's going on. It's going to be terrible, and we're going to look bad, and he's going to kick us out."

But they did it anyway. And nobody played. And that was the last contest we ever had at the Mirage. Still, it was the best gig I ever had. Steve Wolfson left the Mirage, but I'm happy to report that he was way ahead of the curve. And both he and his son have not only done well in all kinds of contests, but they've won them. When I did my book, Steve called me up after and said, "Hey, you told me the Mirage was the best gig you ever had. Why wasn't it in the book?" It was an oversight. But now I think we've made up for it.

I'm extremely proud to have been there when Steve Wolfson put on his first contest. Sometimes I wonder what would have happened if he hadn't forgotten the "Golden Rule": don't ever put gambling paraphernalia in front of a horseplayer when he's handicapping.

HOW TO USE THIS BOOK

This book, based on a series of interviews I have done with successful contest players over the past five years, is meant to be a resource for anyone interested in getting involved in betting on the horses, specifically via contest play. I hope new players will get a lot out of it, and I've covered some basic ground and included a glossary for their benefit.

I also hope the book will be of great interest to players already active, even abundantly successful, on the contest scene. No matter your skill level, you'll get to read the thoughts of many of the greatest contest players—several of whom are also the greatest professional gamblers—in the country. Forget about anything I might bring to the table: how can you not learn something just by listening to them?

The book is organized in four parts: the Basics, Strategy, Handicapping, and Applications. There are also a few appendices: two contain walk-throughs of entire tournaments; one is an in-depth glossary in case you encounter any unfamiliar jargon along the way.

The book is meant to be read straight through, but readers, especially readers with contest experience, should also feel free to jump around to parts that suit their particular interest. Many of the discussions in this book are interrelated, and I've included cross-references wherever possible so you can gain additional insights without my having to be too repetitive. Last thing: I want to follow Michael Beychok's lead and pledge a portion of the proceeds of this book, as well as any future contest winnings, to racehorse rescue, retirement, and re-training organizations. I encourage you to join me in the latter. See the back of the book for a list.

May you win all your photos,
Peter Thomas Fornatale

THE PLAYERS

Michael Beychok won $1 million in the 2012 National Handicapping Challenge (NHC) and is a respected advocate for equine rights. He is also one of the featured players on Esquire Network's *Horseplayers* reality TV show. For more from him, check out www.beychokracing.com.

Matt Bernier is a new face on the contest scene and another one of the players who can be seen on Esquire Network's *Horseplayers* reality TV show.

Scott Carson is founder of *DRF* PublicHandicapper.com—the largest NHC qualifier on the Internet. He has qualified for the NHC six times and has finished as high as 23rd in that contest.

Roger Cettina is a five-time NHC qualifier who is a vice president of Tishman Construction Corp., in New York. His biggest contest score to date was his second at the NHC in 2013 when he took home $200,000. He lives in Rumson, New Jersey.

John Conte won the NHC in 2009. He is a respected veteran on the contest scene and part of the *Horseplayers* TV show.

Kevin Cox, aka The Brooklyn Cowboy, is *that* guy. He is a former mounted police officer and jockey agent who had an impressive rookie year playing contests in 2013, highlighted by his big win in the Belmont contest. He is also part of Esquire Network's *Horseplayers* TV show and writes for www.saratogabets.com.

Dennis Decauwer has qualified for the NHC eight times. Here's the amazing thing: between him and his playing partner, Don Beardsworth, they ran second two years in a row, in 2008 and 2009.

John Doyle won the 2011 NHC. He is a former IBM executive who now is the spokesperson for Derby Wars. As he once told me, "Let's put our money up and compete!"

Dave Gutfreund is a racing media personality, contest veteran, and partner in Derby Wars. His biggest win came in 2012 at the Players Challenge at Bettor Racing OTB in South Dakota, where he took home $65,000.

Patrick McGoey is a two-time winner of the Breeders' Cup Betting Challenge, in 2011 and 2012. Rarefied air, indeed.

Mark McGuire is a restaurateur, *Daily Racing Form* loyalist, and four-time NHC qualifier. His biggest payday to date was a second in the Wynn contest that netted him $45,000.

Mike Maloney is one of the biggest bettors in America and a force to be reckoned with at any contest held at Keeneland.

Don Marr is an independent valuation analyst with a background in logistical and tactical operations from his time in the United States Navy and the United States Army 10th Mountain Division. He's another *Daily Racing Form* fanatic who has made a mark in his brief time on the contest scene, particularly in pick-and-pray contests online.

Ken Massa is the founder and owner of Handicapping Technology and Research (HTR) software and online services. HTR clients include many of the top tournament players in North America. Massa finished second at the NHC in 2007 and has several other top-10 finishes in Vegas competition over the years. He lives in Yorba Linda, California.

Duke Matties comes from a racing family. He is a professional gambler and noted tournament player with a specialty in live-bankroll events. He has moneyed in the Breeders' Cup Betting Challenge and won the Santa Anita live-bankroll contest. He has qualified for the NHC 11 times.

Noel Michaels is the author of *The Handicapping Contest Handbook* and an excellent contest player in his own right. He is a four-time NHC qualifier and won the 2011 Public Handicapper Challenge.

Eric Moomey is fairly new to the tournament circuit but quickly became one of the most consistent contest players in the online world. His biggest score so far came in April 2013 when he won the

Xpressbet Showdown.

Brian Nadeau replaced me as the handicapper for the *Saratoga Special* sometime back in the last decade. These days, when he's not handicapping tennis, he bets horses and writes for The Horse Player Now website.

Michael P. Ryan is a Thoroughbred racing enthusiast and owner who has been active in the online contest world over the past three years, where he's had a lot of success, especially in survivor tournaments on Derby Wars. He lives in Northern Virginia with his wife and family.

Joe Scanio is a nine-time NHC qualifier who has had success in tournaments from coast-to-coast. His best finish was coming in first in a tournament at the Meadowlands in 2004 for $25,000.

Frank R. Scatoni, the former editor of *The HorsePlayer Magazine* and co-author of *Six Secrets of Successful Bettors*, is a relative newcomer to the serious contest scene, but he qualified for the NHC for the first time in 2013 and is hooked on the challenge.

Garett Skiba is a graduate of the University of Notre Dame and holds a University of Chicago MBA. He is a two-time NHC qualifier and has played in more than 250 head-to-head contests online. Currently, while not playing the horses, he is the vice president of finance & business intelligence at Pharos Innovations.

Hank Seaman has an impressive body of handicapping work that is there for all to see on PublicHandicapper.com. He also wrote a guest piece for my personal blog (www.unbearablebetting.com) about his dad and Kelso that's worth seeking out.

Matt Shifman is a correspondent for HorseRacingNation.com where he covers racing at Aqueduct, Belmont Park, and Saratoga in his blog, "New York State of Racing." Shifman began training for survivor tournaments at an early age when he and his father wagered on show parlays at Monmouth Park.

Paul Shurman is an attorney and a highly successful tournament player who has qualified for the NHC 12 years in a row. His career highlights (so far) were winning the 2011 NHC Tour as well as third and sixth place finishes in the NHC.

Brent Sumja was a very successful trainer in Northern California who now gambles on horses full-time. His meteoric rise has impressed the contest world.

Brian Troop won the NHC in 2010. He may not be the most emotive guy on the contest scene, but he might be the nicest.

Judy Wagner won the second-ever NHC in 2001, and she hasn't rested on her laurels since—she's an 11-time NHC qualifier. She and her husband, Bryan, are fixtures on the scene.

Maury Wolff is a horseplayer who was an active tournament player in the `90s. He finished second in the very first NHC.

Steve Wolfson, Jr., is a high school social studies teacher who lives in Florida. He won the NHC in 2003.

Steve Wolfson, Sr., directed the breeding operations for his father's Harbor View Farm from 1965 to 1972. He also owned and managed, with his brother, Happy Valley Racing and Breeding stable from 1970 to 1990. Then in 1991 Wolfson Sr., created and conducted Thoroughbred Challenge handicapping tournaments I, II, & III at Mirage Resorts in Las Vegas and has competed on the NHC Tour trail since its inception.

Cara Yarusso is a chemical engineer in the food industry and a contest enthusiast. She has qualified for the NHC four times and has numerous cashes in tournaments ranging from the Orleans' contests to NHC qualifiers.

Ricky Zimmer, the "Quiet Assassin," works in information technology for The Walt Disney Company. He's qualified for the NHC seven times, and his biggest contest victory was capturing the Wynn Handicapping Challenge in 2011.

1 The Pleasures of the Track

*"The race is not always to the swift nor the battle
to the strong—but that's the way to bet.*
– Damon Runyon

WHY DO YOU LIKE GOING TO THE TRACK?

At the top of the list for me is to be around the horses, incredible athletes that they are, unmatched in their beauty and grace. Without them, there is no sport. End of story.

If you asked most horseplayers why they like the game, they might cite the action. When you're playing the races and things are going well, you don't think about anything else for six hours. You're completely engaged and in the moment, making good decisions and feeling the rush as your horses hit the wire first. It doesn't happen every time you play, but it happens enough to keep you coming back. That's action in a nutshell.

A great many horseplayers love the intellectual exercise. I firmly believe that there's no greater game in the world, no better puzzle to solve, than piecing together what's going to happen in a horse race. There are many ways to put it together, but all methods come down to the same basic thing: they are all different ways to try to help us win at this challenging game.

People who love numbers are drawn to the pen-and-paper aspect—and increasingly the computer aspect—of handicapping. Just as people can look at various metrics and stats to help pick everything from stocks to elections to the winner of the NCAA tournament, one can also use computers and numbers to help you win at the track.

And speaking of winning, that competitive spirit must be noted as well. As Harvey Pack has said many times, "It's not just making money. It's not just picking winners. It's about being able to hold up your ticket to the guy next to you and saying, I had that winner and you didn't."

Then there's the camaraderie. I've made many of the greatest friends I have through the track—guys who've been with me through the highest highs and lowest lows of my life. These are guys—and girls—I'd share a foxhole with.

The final reason people go to the track is to make money—or have a lot of fun trying. You can go to a ball game and buy two decent tickets, get a couple of hot dogs and a few rounds of beers and a giant foam finger, and be out $300. Maybe you saw the Mets pull one out in the bottom of the ninth, and that's great. But at the end of the day, there are no two ways about it: you're paying for your pleasure. At the racetrack, you might see a performance like any one of Zenyatta's races or one of Wise Dan's big wins that gives you tingles, and once in a while, maybe more if you work really hard, you'll leave with more money than you came in with. You try that at the ballpark and you end up at Rikers.

This brings us to handicapping contests. The great thing about contests is that they allow you to enjoy all of the things that are best about the track—only more so. The single-track Santa Anita contests—both the weekly low-roller and the live-bankroll—allow you to get up-close and personal with the horses before you have to bet.

Action? I recently played in a $20 online qualifier that started in the first race at Saratoga, won that, and ended up alive in the big tournament in the last race at Del Mar for all the money. I didn't win, but I played for seven hours on $20, and was up to bat to win $4,000: how's that for action?

No matter what contest you're in, you'll always have the intellectual challenge of trying to find the right winners at the right prices. You don't need math beyond the third-grade level to succeed, but math-oriented players will have a field day applying different formulas and using game theory to increase their odds of winning.

You want competitive? It doesn't get more competitive than sitting in the same room with the people you're playing against, rooting your selections in, and watching your name rise up the leaderboard.

Camaraderie? Check. So many of the players I interviewed for this book listed camaraderie as the number one reason they play in tournaments that after a while I stopped recording their answers—I had way too much material on the topic!

And then there's the money. Just ask John Conte, Brian Troop, John Doyle, or Michael Beychok, all of whom I interviewed for this book, all of whom took home $500,000 (or more) for their National Handicapping Challenge (NHC) scores.

How about this for a reason to play in contests? They might make your cash game better.

Michael Beychok: "I became a successful bettor when I started playing the tournaments. As a cash player, I was always trying to pick winners, regardless of value: 6-5, 5-2 ... It didn't matter to me. I just wanted to impress the people around me, consistently picking winner after winner. And I don't know anyone who can make money that way.

"That's how I played in contests at first, and I wasn't playing enough to realize that this method was a failure. When I realized how the winning contest players did it—picking fewer winners but with greater value—I started doing what they did. Then I took that idea of demanding value to my cash play, and it improved my game tremendously. It got me totally off of just straight picking winners. To me, value is the name of this game. When you think a horse is 3-1, and you are getting 6-1, you have to bet."

I share this belief that contests are a great way for players to improve their game.

Joe Scanio: "Mythical-money contests eliminate the most difficult things for the unsavvy gambler. They take out the exotics. All they have to do is pick some winners. They don't have to worry about who is going to finish second or third, who is going to win the next race or the race after that. These types of contests are a great way to educate players."

I recently read an interview with Mark Midland, CEO of the contest website Derby Wars (www.derbywars.com), and he talked about this very issue. He said, "Playing the races is great, too—but you might put $120 into a trifecta only to have it pay $100. In contests, the prize is clear."

Mike Maloney: "Contests are a good, simple starting point, especially the win-and-place contests. They're not overwhelming, and it's not impossible for a novice to do well in them. They level the playing field. The biggest advantage that I can see is there are so many people playing online now, and they don't get that physical experience of playing live at the track, listening to the mentors who hang around there—whether they're good or bad.

"My generation learned to play the horses from our dads or our uncles or from some guy at the track who liked to talk. Now it's harder to get that. But contests are a good way to replicate that, a good way to meet people who might know a little more than you. I would encourage new players to ask a lot of questions, to make a lot of new acquaintances. Most guys are like me: you get them started talking about this stuff and they'll go on forever. And there's some good information you're going to get from almost anyone who has been around this game and survived long enough to still be playing in a contest.

"Even if you don't agree with what's being told, it's good to listen, because part of the money on the tote board is being represented by that line of thought. The more you can understand what makes those lights blink on the tote board, the more you'll know about all the different philosophies and what the game is all about."

Maury Wolff: "It's difficult to know how much equity there is in handicapping tournaments. It's a question every player has to answer for themselves. But here's one thing I know for sure: whatever the equity in tournaments might be, it is better being in a 100 percent payback tournament than playing into a 20 percent takeout pool at the track every day."

WHY DO YOU PLAY IN CONTESTS?

Two-time Breeders' Cup Betting Challenge winner Patrick McGoey had this to say about the thrill of playing the horses.

Patrick McGoey: "I have been playing fantasy football and poker with my buddies for 20 years and racing just for 10. There really is no comparison between the games. While you can play all three from the comfort of your home, horse racing is so much more exciting than pulling for football players to score or catching a card on the river. Nothing is better than watching your horse come down the stretch and win a close race. And the payouts for a winning bet in horse racing can be tremendous."

Let's take a look at what the rest of our panel of players had to say about why they play contests. As referenced above, by far the number one reason is camaraderie. I'll just share a few representative quotes.

Cara Yarusso: "There is camaraderie among players that I have never seen before. I've played competitive billiards, and players become catty and rude to each other in the heat of competition, and I've taken a stab at poker and hate the eerie silence that comes with a good game of cards. With horses, you are competing against your friends. Some of them are your dearest friends who you look forward to seeing at each event, and some of them are friends who you haven't yet had a chance to meet. The friendships run at the heart of the whole experience though.

"After a little more than ten years of tournament play, I have met the most amazing group of people who I ever could have imagined. I count these people as the best friends I have ever had. I can't wait to get to the next tournament just to see everyone. While we're competing against each other, we're rooting for each other as well. If you're not doing well, you're hoping your friends are winning. You cheer each other's horses home. The only thing more fun than the tournaments themselves is the people who you get to spend time with along the way."

Dennis Decauwer: "I'm an old-fashioned people-person. I know everybody practically when I'm there and everyone knows me, and it's a friendly rivalry with just about everyone. I love that part of it."

Judy Wagner: "This is a hobby my husband and I developed together. We would travel everywhere from River Downs, Saratoga, Del Mar, Santa Anita, dog tracks, wherever. We began to see a lot of the same people, and from there, we developed some very close friendships. The camaraderie with the handicapping contest group is great. In 2011, I developed some serious health problems and complications, and the emails, the well wishes, the concern and encouragement came in from all over. Some people I might not even recognize, but I knew their names from the tournaments."

Brent Sumja: "I've played poker, but I found that poker was being taken over by a younger group of people who had a big clique. There was never a feeling of camaraderie at the table when I was playing poker. With horse racing tournaments, you can relate to every single person there from a 25-year-old male to a 75-year-old female.

"I've met an amazing group of people. In all walks of life you hear people say things along the lines of 'If I don't win, I hope you win.' And most of the time, it's not really believable. But when you hear someone in this tournament group say that, he actually means it. It's genuine. Everyone is welcoming. And because of this common interest of loving horse racing, it's easy to make friends quickly. I've made a bunch of friends and if I'm not going to win, I really, really want them to win. Even when you're out of it, you'll see these names you know on the leaderboard and you still have people to root for. It's almost like it's you."

Mark McGuire: "I own a restaurant and see thousands of people a day. I play competitive softball all around the United States. I've played golf and travelled around for that. Nowhere are there people like the horseplayers in these contests. They are the most fun people. In golf and softball, people just can't be nice if they're losing. In racing, there are people who will root for you even to their own detriment."

I asked McGuire what accounts for the bond among horseplayers.

Mark McGuire: "I think contests are like that because horse racing— because it's gambling—has always had a negative stick to it. Most people don't go around telling people they play horses. You can tell someone you play the stock market and people will think you're a genius. I tell people I play the horses, and they look at me cross-eyed. Everyone in these contests has been looked at that way, so I think they go out of their way to be positive when they're together, to help each other."

This quote of McGuire's reminded me of Mike Maloney once telling me about how being a professional gambler creates a certain amount of socially awkward moments: you go to the neighborhood cocktail party and get seated next to the drug dealer.

Paul Shurman: "I like being around other people who get what you're doing, who appreciate it when you do well, who commiserate with you when you don't do well. I hate the online tournaments. You win and you yell, 'Yay! I won!' And you look around and there's no one there. I used to do crosswords a lot, and I liked the challenge, putting the pieces together. All my friends at work, they know I play in tournaments and they are still confused and think I'm a poker player. They don't get it. But when I go to a tournament, these are my people. The people I see at these tournaments are my closest friends."

Is it hard to compete against the very people you're preparing with?

Paul Shurman: "It's a game we should all enjoy together. It's tremendous to work together. We go through things from our different perspectives, help each other remember what's coming up. Sometimes you miss something that someone else catches. After a race closes, we tell each other who we've bet. We root for each other. Of course you want to win. Some people don't like you to know their strategy, but I'll tell people which horse I bet."

The number two reason players love contests is the competition.

Joe Scanio: "The real thing all these people have in common is they're competitive. Don't buy how it's all so friendly and everybody roots for each other. The real truth of it all is it's a competitive game and that's what the motivation is. You want to beat the other guy. You want to qualify. You want to be in Las Vegas. "

Dennis Decauwer: "I feel the competitiveness much more in a live tournament, and I think that's one of the biggest attractions."

Roger Cettina: "I really like competing against the other guys in the room, more so than just betting through the windows. Instead of trying to beat the house, you're just trying to beat the other people. There's a good energy when you're competing in a contest, trying to be the best. It's a better experience."

Mike Labriola: "If you've ever talked to someone who is more of a tournament player than a cash player, he could tell you we're definitely a subspecies. There's a competitive aspect that appeals to us. We all know that with pari-mutuel wagering, we're playing against everybody else, but in a tournament, it's a lot more obvious. Very often the players are right there in the same room with you; there's a leaderboard. If you have that kind of a competitive inclination, tournaments get their hook into you.

"In the first tournament I played in, I didn't get anything in terms of remuneration, but I knew that eventually I would. I loved that tournaments took the betting mistakes part of horse playing out of the equation. It was all about who could pick winners and who could pick longshot winners, and I knew that was me."

John Doyle: "Day-to-day wagering is like being on an island. You're not even sure who you're competing against. During tournament play, I met the competition and realized they are really smart. These people are the best. Being in a room competing against them really got my juices flowing. And I think we could do more to play that up. And tournaments are also a great way around the takeout—let's put our money up and compete."

Judy Wagner cited both making money and the puzzle-solving aspect of horse racing as secondary reasons why she likes contests.

Judy Wagner: "If you had asked me the same question back when I first started, I would have said that I played to win the prize money. And of course it still is a big factor, but now you have so many contests, especially the online ones, where there is not always a check in your pocket. You just qualify for something else. I have a competitive spirit; I want to qualify for the NHC, and I want to see my name at the top of the leaderboard. This is something that my husband and I both enjoy, and that we can enjoy together. Contests make me feel rewarded and challenged. Some people like to solve puzzles to stay sharp as they age. I like handicapping races."

This is a major appeal to amateur players as well.

Don Marr: "I call them horse-word puzzles. Even if I don't have time to handicap a whole card, I might pick out a few races on a Saturday night and go through them and do a drill-down analysis. There's nothing more fun to me than trying to pick a winner."

Then there's the numbers aspect of the game, yet another way in for some players.

Don Marr: "Being an operations analyst has helped me a lot being a horse-racing analyst. I can look at a gazillion numbers and I feel like numbers talk to me. And I feel like I can get the story out of them."

Matt Bernier: "As a kid, I collected baseball cards and I loved reading the numbers on the back and figuring out what everything meant. So when I first looked at the *Daily Racing Form*, even though I had no idea what any of it meant, it felt familiar to me in a way, and I wanted to learn more about it."

I asked John Doyle about the future of contests after his NHC win back in 2011.

John Doyle: "If you get them to be bigger and you get them to be richer, you'll attract younger people. When I go to the track, I don't see many young people, obviously. But at the NHC, there were some young folks, and let me tell you, they are competitive.

They got mad when they lost. Where some of the older guys kind of took the losses in stride, they didn't. And I think that's great. We need more of that type of energy, more of that young blood. I think tournaments are a great way for younger players who maybe don't have bankrolls that big to get in on the action and make a big score—especially if we could increase the visibility of tournaments and the players in general the way ESPN has done for poker."

Doyle's words have proven to be prophetic, judging by the success of Matt Bernier, a 20-something racing fan and star of the *Horseplayers* TV show who qualified for the NHC for the first time in 2012.

Matt Bernier: "The first time I walked into the NHC I was like, 'Whoa. Half these guys are old enough to be my father ... and the other half are old enough to be my grandfather.' But as I got to know them, they were a great, welcoming bunch of guys who were always very friendly."

Just because the majority of players are in a certain demographic doesn't mean new players aren't welcome. Unfortunately, that was not always the case. There's a funny story about this that William Murray, author of *The Wrong Horse* and many other wonderful books about racing and life, used to tell all the time. One of the gang brings a date to the box at Del Mar. The day proceeds as normal, and everyone seemingly has a great time. But at the end of the day, the guy asks the box owner what he thought of his date. "She's a lovely girl," the box owner said. "Don't bring her again."

But those were the bad old days. Today, there are women who can legitimately handicap circles around 90 percent of the men, including the three women who helped me with this book. I asked Judy Wagner about being a successful woman in such a predominantly male world.

Judy Wagner: "There are more and more women coming into it and more and more women who are doing their own handicapping. It's not a hang-up with me. There was one incident once. After I won the NHC, I went to a contest. I almost left in tears. I went in, sat down, and then my husband walked in a few minutes later. Some old codger said, 'Here comes the real handicapper; I knew she couldn't do it by herself.' Other than that rude person, I have been treated with the utmost respect. I don't feel out of place at all as a female."

THE LUCK-TO-SKILL RATIO

Another great aspect of handicapping contests is the opportunity for newer players to compete against—and even defeat—the biggest names in the business. I met a young contest player, Emily Gullikson, aka "Mayhemily," at Saratoga, and told her I was interviewing Michael Beychok for this book. She was respectful of Beychok's accomplishments and told me she was very proud of the fact that she'd actually finished ahead of him in tournaments a couple of times. How cool is that that a third-year player can test her mettle against a guy who has won $1 million in a single tournament? Gullikson added, "That's the great thing about tournaments: on any given day, any level of player can step up and beat the best players in the world."

This concept came up with me as well. When I interviewed Steve Wolfson, Sr. and Jr., Steve Jr. remembered seeing my name (briefly) atop an online NHC qualifier tournament the weekend before. As I'm studying these players, I'm also competing against them, almost as if TNT commentator Craig Sager dropped his microphone, tore off the pink-and-aqua-checked sport coat, and ran out on the court to try to guard Kevin Durant. It's an absurd concept in sports, but it's · possible in horse-racing contests, in part because of the luck-to-skill ratio involved.

Maury Wolff: "I recently read a book by Michael Maboussin, *The Success Equation*, that has something to offer to this conversation. He mentions a guy who never loses in Chinese checkers. So in that game, skill is everything because the best player never loses. On the other hand, he discusses a major stock-picking competition in which some Hooters girls won against a bunch of Wall Street types. What does that tell you about the role of luck in stock-picking contests? There is a tremendous amount of luck involved.

"In horse-racing tournaments, the ratio of luck to skill is enormous. This isn't you playing tennis against Roger Federer. You'd have no chance. But you could sit down in a head-to-head tournament with the best horseplayer in the world, and you'd have a fair chance.

It's not that skill doesn't matter; it's the ratio. I'm not saying it's all luck. The good players have better longshots than the bad players, absolutely. But maybe the good players' 20-1 shots win seven percent of the time and the weaker players' 20-1 shots win only five percent, so over the course of a couple of days, guess what? Anybody employing correct strategy can win. This is the attraction to the novice. This isn't you against the biggest bettors in the country every day at the windows. You lose, they win. The difference between the best guy and you is much less in tournaments."

Brent Sumja: "You have to know going in that you're going to look like a genius one day and a complete moron the next. Even the best players who qualify for the NHC every year, it's not like they have a stronghold you can't overcome. This isn't LeBron James in the NBA. In theory, you could pick names and possibly win. There is a lot of luck involved."

Sumja agrees with Wolff that the skill portion of the equation rises in everyday play.

Brent Sumja: "I've gone to the track with new players picking by the color of the jockey silks or something like that. Perhaps they have a winning day and I have a losing day. And they ask me, 'If you're a professional, how come I don't know anything and I can win and you still lost?' I explain it this way: they have a 50-50 chance of beating me for a day. They have a decent chance of beating me over three days. But over a period of months, they have no chance. That's how I explain racing to them. Anybody can get lucky for a little while. In the end, you have to have some kind of education behind what you're doing or you're in serious trouble."

No discussion of the role of luck in handicapping contests would be complete without a shout-out to Audrey Louise-Sellers. The year was 2000. The place was Reno. Sellers, in town as a babysitter for her nephew, was entered into the Flamingo Reno Challenge.

Audrey Louise-Sellers: "I don't know anything about horse racing. I don't know anything about [*Daily Racing Form*]. I pick up some sheets with the horses' names on it [overnights], and I bet the names I liked. There was also one jockey who I kept betting because we have the same name, [Shane] Sellers."

With logic like that, you might as well bet on the horse with the longest tail! And yet, against a field that included many sharpies, Sellers had a solid day one before unleashing hellfire on her competition on day two and quintupling her bankroll. She bested all comers and took home more than $50,000.

The point is, if Audrey Louise-Sellers can get lucky when the money is on the line, why can't we, especially if we've done the work and handicapped the cards? Baseball Hall-of-Famer Lefty Gomez said it best: "I'd rather be lucky than good." As contest players, we need to be both lucky and good. At the end of the rainbow, you might find a pot of gold, or in this case, a life-changing score.

2 Different Contest Types

"I been gamblin' hereabouts for ten good, solid years,
If I told you all that went down it would burn off both of your ears."
– Robert Hunter

Let's take a look at some of the different tournament formats that are out there. The full variety of contests is too myriad to list. Most contests span just one day, but there are many notable exceptions. The NYRA contests are two-day affairs. Many Vegas contests, like the big ones at the Orleans, can last three days, and there is at least one contest, the Public Handicapper Challenge, that spans over six months. Later in the book, we will come back to some of the more common formats and get into specific strategy for each type of contest, but for now, I just want to lay out the basics.

Dave Gutfreund: "One thing that's happening more and more in tournaments generally, and is especially something we're trying to do at Derby Wars, is to offer different types of games, like head-to-head games and survivor games where people can get involved in tournaments for a lot less money. We used to think we were in the tournament business, but we're in the entertainment business. It's a different way to get people interested in horse racing."

OPTIONAL RACES VERSUS MANDATORY RACES

Contest play doesn't get more basic than this. An optional race is one you choose yourself, usually out of a select group of tracks and/or races, though occasionally, like in the Orleans contests, you might have up to seven full cards from which to choose your 10 or 12 races. A mandatory race, as the name suggests, is one that the contest director chooses for you. Many contests, like the NHC, offer a mix of optional races and mandatory races. The idea here is that a mix provides the best test for handicappers. They can't just pick the races where they are most proficient; they must know how to look at dirt sprints, turf routes, and synthetic first-time starters alike. But they also don't just get to have all the races handed to them. They also need to choose the right races to play in the optional races. What makes a race the "right" one to pick? One where you can pick the longshot winner. This topic will be covered extensively later in the book.

FIXED–BANKROLL TOURNAMENTS

By far, the most popular format involves a certain amount of fixed bets, usually $2 win and place. The goal in a fixed-bankroll tournament is simply to accumulate the highest score. Within this format there are variations. You might see what I would call an optional-heavy format, a contest where there are three contest tracks and you need to make ten mythical $2 win/place bets on any ten races at these three tracks.

What is a mythical bet? It's a bet that exists in the vacuum of the contest. That is, it counts for the contest but the money doesn't hit the track pool. You can hit a $50 winner, but you don't get to keep that money in a mythical-wager contest—the mutuel payout is used to determine the number of points you get for that winner.

However, there are also fixed-bankroll contests where you do bet live money. In these, you get to keep the winnings from your contest plays.

NYRA Format

In the NYRA contest model (a personal favorite), you need to make ten mythical win, place, or show bets over a two-day span. Nine of the bets are $20; one is $40. There are no mandatory races per se, but half of your bets (five) must be made on the host track's races.

NHC

As I mentioned above, the NHC is a blend of mandatories and optionals. You make 15 bets a day: eight mandatory and seven optional. It's $2 win/place. In 2014, a third day of competition was added to ratchet up the drama, where 50 players will advance and eventually be winnowed down to a final table of ten, including ties. For more about the NHC, keep reading. We'll discuss various aspects of the contest throughout the book.

Bullet Formats

Online sites like NHCQualify.com, Derby Wars, and HorseplayersQualify.com offer what are known as "bullet" contests where all the races are chosen for the contestants, who must make $2 win/place selections in however many designated contest races there are (I've seen as few as six and as many as twelve). I love bullet contests because I can focus all my energy on finding value and picking winners in these races and not drive myself crazy trying to figure out which races to play in the first place.

Head-To-Head

Another type of contest I find appealing is the head-to-head format. This is popular on Derby Wars. There was a great line on the Derby Wars blog about them.

Mark Midland: "It reminds me of one of my favorite competitive stories, which goes like this: Two men are walking through an African game reserve when they come across a lion. One of the men calmly puts down his backpack and slips on the running shoes he has been carrying. The other man chuckles and says, 'You'll never outrun a lion.' To which the other man calmly responds, 'I don't need to outrun the lion; I just need to outrun you.'"

Indeed, you only have to beat one other player in a head-to-head, which follows the bullet rules described above. The game theory aspect of knowing your opponent becomes huge in this format. Most players are creatures of habit, and if you can block them—or avoid being blocked—by playing the same horse, you can get an edge. I am convinced that if head-to-heads continue to grow, they could make a great TV product for horse racing.

Survivor

Another great format, especially for, but not limited to, beginners is the Survivor/Showvivor one. The idea in these is that you just have to pick one horse to show. Sometimes you must survive over a series of races in just one day; other times you'll have to pick one race a day in which to survive throughout a whole race meet. In either case, it's not as easy as it sounds. It's a war of attrition. These are definitely a fun way for new players and more experienced ones to sharpen their skills at finding horses that run consistently well. Later in the book you'll hear from two players who have had a lot of success in this unique format.

Pick-and-Pray/Lockdown

The final format I want to discuss is the pick–and-pray or lockdown format. These are the simplest and, in at least one respect, the most pure contests—nobody can pick a horse because of what price he is because, except in the first race, nobody knows the prices. There are a certain number of races chosen, you put in your mythical $2 win/place bets before the first race goes off, and you watch—the highest score at the end of the day wins. If you're just interested in pure paper handicapping, these are the races for you. If, like me, you make your selections more based on how the horses look and/or you want to know what price they will be before betting them, these can be awful, frustrating affairs. I also love the in-contest tournament strategy that is lost in these games. But there are certain players for whom these tests of winner-picking ability are the absolute best.

LIVE–BANKROLL TOURNAMENTS

In live-bankroll contests, you typically have a buy-in that goes to the contest payout pool and a live-money bankroll. There are some smaller live-bankroll contests, like Monmouth's, where you can buy in for $100. In other instances, you'll need a bunch of money to play live money: $3,000 for Santa Anita, $5,000 for Del Mar, or even $10,000 for the Breeders' Cup Betting Challenge. The rules vary greatly from contest to contest, and you'd be wise to know them like the back of your hand before you arrive. In rare instances, there is no minimum number of races you need to play. More typically, you might have to make ten bets of at least a certain dollar amount.

It's important to understand the distinction between a live-bankroll contest and a live-money contest: in a live-bankroll contest, the key thing isn't whether your money hits the pool; it's the idea that you can reinvest your initial bankroll if your bets win. Let's say you have a $100 starting bankroll and you bet it all on a 5-2 shot. You get back $350. Now you can bet any of that $350 you wish. This differs from live-money/fixed-bankroll contests where you get to keep the money you win, but you cannot reinvest it beyond your initial bankroll. In fixed-bankroll contests, you bet the specified amount ($2 win/place, for example) and that's it.

The big advantage for some players is that you can play your vertical exotics in a live-bankroll tourney, so exactas and trifectas—even sometimes superfectas—are at your disposal. I have even seen one or two where the horizontal exotics (doubles, Pick-3s, Pick-4s) come into play. You can also create de facto horizontal exotics by manually making parlays—bet your whole wad on one horse, then if it wins, bet the whole amount back in the next race, etc.

ODDS CAP

It was the fall of 2012. Saratoga was over and I was feeling sour—mostly because the meet was over but also a little bit because I felt burned. I had put my heart and soul into an unofficial online handicapping contest—think fantasy football or your office NCAA pool, but for horse racing. This was the famous "Huddie" pool, enjoyed by Saratoga locals, industry insiders, and gambling degenerates alike. I was steamed because I felt there were a couple of results that summer that unfairly skewed the entire tournament because there was no odds cap limiting the mutuel payouts of longshots. I took to Twitter to vent. Like Amanda Bynes, I discovered this probably wasn't the best idea.

Really, I was just being a baby, and when I interviewed Dave Hudson, "Huddie" founder, while doing some background research for this book, I admitted as much. In a meet-long tournament with 44 picks over seven weeks, especially one that's meant to be more for fun than any test of handicapping skill, it's okay to not have an odds cap. But in your average day-to-day tournament play, I believe a cap is the right way to fly, particularly when it comes to fixed-bankroll, mythical-money tournaments. Contests should never be won by one horse. Lady Luck is always going to have an invitation to the party in any handicapping contest, but you don't have to let her sit at the head of the table.

John Conte: "The reason they cap the odds is because years ago, people used to sit back and play only longshots. There could have been an old lady who saw a gray horse with blue eyes, and he's 50-1. But she takes a shot and she's not a real handicapper, but the horse wins and it's a $100 horse. It's one of her only winners, and she wins the contest. That's not handicapping. So now they cap 20-1 on win, 10-1 on place. So if you hit a $100 horse, you're only getting $42 on it on the win end. It's an excellent, excellent idea."

Dave Gutfreund: "Caps are a necessary evil in any contest that involves mythical money. Caps have to exist or else you'll always have people shooting for 100-1s at the end of the tournament. You'd have a replay of what happened in Connecticut in that infamous tournament. This was in the mid-'90s, in the Hutcheson at Gulfstream. Frisk Me Now won and paid like $200. This was at the end of the tournament, and all 20 people who ended up cashing in the tournament had that winner. If you weren't just stabbing at that winner, you didn't have a chance. The rest of the tournament didn't matter."

Maury Wolff: "I can remember being in Connecticut at the Auto-tote tournament when Frisk Me Now came in, and 20 people had it, and I realized that times were changing—people had learned the correct way to play in a tournament with no odds cap. Somebody came up with a phrase I thought was beautiful: 100-1 on the board and 6-5 in the room."

The idea is to ensure a fair contest and limit the role of luck. Part of the theory behind the cap is that while it certainly takes skill to pick a 35-1, it doesn't take appreciably more skill than it does to hit a 15-1, and yet the rewards are outsized for hitting the longer shot. Plus, especially at the ends of tournaments, there's no handicapping involved at all for players down the ladder. All they need to know is that a 30-1 will get them to the lead and—presto!—they have a pick, with no other handicapping knowledge necessary.

Typically, caps on the win end are either 15-1 ($32), 20-1 ($42), or 25-1 ($52). Place payoffs are typically capped at 10-1 ($22), 12-1 ($26), or 15-1 ($32), and show payoffs, in the rare instances they are used, are typically capped at 5-1 ($12). There are also some formats, like the Orleans contests, that offer a compromise solution. In those, where the base bet is a mythical $100, the contest pays out $20 of the $100 on full track odds and caps the other $80 at 20-1. I see the point as this gives you a little extra credit for really catching a bomb, but I don't like that it forces me to do extra math.

I asked Dave Gutfreund what he thought about the idea of a no-cap tournament.

Dave Gutfreund: "If a tournament is long-term enough, you could do it without a cap. If a tournament had 200 picks or 300 picks, then maybe, or you can do uncapped until the last ten days of the tournament. Personally, as long as the rules are the same for everyone and they don't change, I'm fine with that. At Derby Wars, we cap at 15-1 and 8-1. But we have a lot of eight- and ten-race tournaments. The more races in the tournament, the higher the cap can be. The logic of the cap is to not have one individual race skew the event too much. The more races, the higher odds threshold you can have where one race is going to determine who wins the tournament."

Maury Wolff: "In the absence of a cap, you can't avoid playing these ridiculous longshot horses because one or two of them are going to come in, and that's going to tip the whole tournament. But day in, day out, if you play those same types of horses, most people are going to lose 30 or 40 cents out of every two dollars. If you have a cap at 20-1 and you can't get beat by an $80 horse, then it's fine to play a 12-1 shot."

I wanted to ask a professional player about the difference between picking a 15-1 and a 40-1.

Maury Wolff: "Can you handicap an $80 horse? All of us have bet 40-1 shots that we thought were going to win. They usually don't.

But that doesn't mean you don't have a real reason to like them. So you can handicap them. But in some sense that doesn't really matter because too many people are going to be playing the horse just because it's an $80 horse, and if it wins, they win."

And to me, that's why you really need to have a cap in any contest that fancies itself a serious test of handicapping skill. But there's another way of looking at it where having a cap doesn't exactly solve the problem anyway, especially if the cap is too low.

Duke Matties: "The problem with some contests, say the cap is 15-1, everybody looks for a 10-1 to 15-1 shot, and that's all they do. So a lot of players are not truly handicapping; they're just looking for horses in that range to play."

Scott Carson: "We have a 30-1 odds cap on *DRF* Public Handicapper, which is pretty generous, and I do think you need an odds cap of some kind, because a 100-1 horse can really skew the results. But you can hit a nice 30-1 and still be catchable. But at the same time, it pays so well that it is a huge advantage to have. So I do think that odds caps are okay; I just don't want them to be too low. To me, a 15-1 cap is too low. You're not getting enough of a reward for picking a 'have-able' longshot."

I knew Carson had finished second in a recent NYRA contest, so I asked him if the 15-1 cap had cost him the win.

Scott Carson: "There are so many cappers that come in, that if everybody counted and said, 'Oh, I would've actually made another $16 if it weren't for that friggin' cap,' then everybody would be griping, you know? You don't even think about it; you're just happy if you hit it."

And that's the thing. Noel Michaels says in his *Handicapping Contest Handbook* that cap horses are the Holy Grail, and I can't improve on that metaphor. Yes, you can win a contest without hitting a capper, but it's a lot easier if you do.

BUY-INS AND PRIZES

Before we proceed, I want to discuss buy-ins, prizes, and field sizes. Buy-ins and prize structure vary wildly from contest to contest, and you need to be aware of exactly what it is you are paying for and playing for. Some online contests are only qualifiers—that is, you don't win any actual money, only an entry into another tournament. Typically in on-site contests, known as brick-and-mortars, you are putting up money that goes to a prize pool. Sometimes 100 percent of the prize-pool money gets paid out and then some, like in the NYRA contests; other times there is a takeout.

You want to know what the takeout is in each tournament because that might well make the difference for you in deciding whether it's worth it to travel to different places to play. Maybe it makes sense to fly to Saratoga to get the VIP treatment for two days but not to fly to Reno to play at some random biker casino with a 20-cent rake. It's easy to figure out what a tournament's takeout is: you just need to ascertain how much money is going in and how much money is coming back out. For example, if it's a 200-player contest with a buy-in of $100, then there is $20,000 (200 x $100) going into the pool. If the prize money exceeds $20,000, well, then you're in great shape because the contest has positive expected value. If the prize money is less than $20,000, say, $17,500, you simply divide the $17,500 (the money going out) by the $20,000 (the money coming in) and you get .0875. Multiply that by 100 and you get 87.5, meaning 87.5 percent of the money gets paid out. Subtract 87.5 from 100 again to determine the takeout, in this case 12.5 percent.

Many of the best tournaments around the country will offer both cash prizes and qualifying seats to other tournaments like the NHC, the Horse Player World Series, or the Breeders' Cup Betting Challenge. These are the most likely places where you might actually find a contest with positive expected value; for example, between the prize money being paid out and the value of the seats being given away, NYRA is actually paying out more money from the contest than what goes into the contest from the entry fees. Why do they do it then, you might ask? It's still a huge win for them because the contest brings in so many high-rolling players to play on-track that their handle gets a boost. This is why I like contests so much—everybody wins.

Steve Wolfson, Sr.: "Harvey [Pack] told you about the contests I did for the Mirage in the early nineties. One of the big pushes for the casinos to hold tournaments was to get the handle up. I told them people would be betting. And our three-day handle at the Mirage went from $500,000 to $1.4 million because of the handicappers who were there."

Some online tournaments do offer cash prizes with reasonable takeout, but, as mentioned above, many online tournaments, largely due to legal issues, are only offering up qualifying seats to other tournaments. That can absolutely be okay. I estimate an NHC seat to be worth about $5,000, and it's easy to see exactly what other qualifying tournaments are worth (i.e., the value of the buy-in of the bigger tournament).

John Doyle: "When online qualifying tournaments came in, it made it much more convenient. Even if you have to pay a fee and there isn't any prize money, they are still a lot more cost-effective for me than going to travel somewhere. That made it much easier for me to get involved."

With all the different formats that are available, it's critical to pick one that suits your lifestyle and the way you play. This topic will be fully explored in Chapter 8: Game Selection.

The Cream of the Crop: Six Can't Miss Contests

NHC

Held in February in Las Vegas, the NHC is an invitation-only event (i.e., one must qualify for it to play). It is a three-day event with eight optional and seven mandatory races. First prize is $750,000 as of this writing. There are qualifying tournaments for the NHC all over the country and the Internet (see www.ntra.com for full lists), but the two best places to qualify online are www.NHCQualify.com and www.publichandicapper.com.

BREEDERS' CUP BETTING CHALLENGE

A live-bankroll contest held annually over the two days of the Breeders' Cup. Contestants are required to put up $10,000, $2,500 of which goes into a prize pool (to which additional money is added), and $7,500 of which represents your bankroll and can be bet in any of the vertical pools on any Breeders' Cup race. The purse totals $500,000 with $210,000 to the winner. The best place to qualify is www.BCQualify.com.

HORSE PLAYER WORLD SERIES

The HPWS is held at the Orleans in Las Vegas and is a three-day, fixed-bankroll, mythical-money tournament where players must make 12 optional plays per day over a large variety of tracks. The 2012 winner took home over $300,000. For more information about qualifying events or the contest in general, call 1-888-566-7223 or check out www.orleanscasino.com/

PLAYERS CHALLENGE

Held in Sioux Falls, South Dakota, and co-sponsored by HorsePlayersQualify.com and Bettor Racing, the Players Challenge is held each September. It's a two-day live-bankroll format with four tracks where contestants must play between five and ten races each day. A $10,000 buy-in includes travel and expenses with $4,500 going to a prize pool that gets paid back 100 percent, and the remaining $4,000 as a live bankroll. Seats to both the NHC and Breeders' Cup Betting Challenge are offered to the top finishers as well. In 2013, the winner got $130,000 and the total purse was $335,000. Players can qualify via www.HorsePlayersQualify.com. Check there for more information or call 1-877-600-8676.

THE WYNN

The Handicapping Challenge at Wynn Las Vegas takes place in early August and uses only Saratoga and Del Mar. Entries cost $2,000 and players must make 14 mythical $2 win-and-place wagers plus one $4 win-and-place bet each day. A $100,000 payoff is guaranteed for overall top scores. The top two finishers also get NHC seats. The Wynn phone number is (702) 770-7000.

SARATOGA BETTING CHALLENGE

As described elsewhere in the book, The Saratoga Betting Challenge is a two-day, fixed-bankroll contest where players must make ten bets a day across three selected tracks, with five of those races being at the home track. Nine of the ten bets are $20 win, place, or show, the tenth bet is $40 win, place, or show. The total purse is over $200,000 and the winner's share is $100,000.

3 THE NHC

"If you wanna be the man, you gotta beat the man."

— Ric Flair

The most prestigious tournament in the country is the National Handicapping Challenge, referred to throughout this book as the NHC. As Ricky Zimmer has said, "Anybody who wants to be crowned the best wants to play in the NHC."

There are several reasons for the NHC's prominence in the contest world. It is a true championship event, and it's the one contest where you can't buy your way in—you must qualify by playing in another event first. This creates a special vibe, not just at the NHC tournament itself but also at all the tournaments across the country all year long.

> **Joe Scanio:** "The first question all of these guys ask each other when they see each other at one of these contests is: 'Did you qualify yet?' They don't care what you've won or how much you've made, it's, 'Are you qualified?'"

One of the perquisites of winning the NHC is that you get an automatic entry into next year's event to defend your title. I love picturing the stereotypical contest player in Scanio's quote above winning the NHC and being more excited about qualifying for next year than winning the big money for first place. But there is no doubt that the money is another thing that makes the NHC special.

The very first NHC started with a total purse of $200,000, and over the years that number has grown to nearly $2 million with the winner walking away with $750,000. The seven-figure prize is super significant, something I refer to all the time. Throughout the writing and researching of this book, a couple of non-racing-fan friends (yes, I tolerate a few) had asked me what I was working on. I then had to explain what handicapping contests are. I always started with the poker analogy—handicapping contests are to racing what poker tournaments are to cash games. But then I'd throw in, "And there's a national championship event where you can win in for as little as free and play for more than $1 million." It's that last bit that piques their interest.

You know how when somebody says, "It's not just the money" how that usually means, "It's just the money"? That's not the case with the NHC. It isn't *just* the money. In addition to getting an invite to the coolest party of the year and the chance to play for a small fortune, NHC contestants also play for the title of "Handicapper of the Year" and the actual Eclipse Award that comes with it. So if you win, you join company with the likes of Paul Mellon, Bobby Frankel, Angel Cordero, Jr., Secretariat, and Zenyatta as recipients of racing's highest award.

It was *Daily Racing Form* chairman and publisher Steven Crist who came up with this last, brilliant idea. As he was quoted in Noel Michaels' *Handicapping Contest Handbook*, about a conversation he had with then-NTRA commissioner Tim Smith: "He asked me for suggestions on the Eclipse Awards dinner, and I said, 'How about honoring an actual horseplayer?' To me, that's the greatest thing about the NHC. Whoever wins it gets a trophy at the Eclipse Awards, and the industry will be saying something it needs to say more often: 'You, the fan, are as important to this business as the owner, the breeder, the trainer, and the jockey.'"

In addition to the NHC itself, there is also now an NHC Tour, where players earn Tour points for tournament finishes at various qualifying events held around the country and online. The Tour is an evolving animal, and something I intend to cover more thoroughly in my *Daily Racing Form* column and on my contest blog.

Paul Shurman: "Other tournaments might offer better value, but the NHC isn't about value: it's about being the best. When you get out there and you're in that room with all those people, you'll understand, and you'll want to be back every year."

I asked relative NHC newcomer Mike Maloney what he thought it would take to win the big one.

Mike Maloney: "What I've learned about the NHC is just how important preparation is. If you don't take the time to watch all the videos and do all the legwork on the trainer research, then you're operating at a huge disadvantage.

"The first year I played in it, I flew in the day before the contest and the night before I was down in the race book playing Mountaineer and Charles Town until 11 o'clock at night. Then I went back to my room and pulled the *Form* out and thought, 'Okay, I'll look at tomorrow.' I had no shot. I treated it like it was just another day at the races, and it's not. If you're going to compete with those guys, you're going to have to take more time than that and prepare properly."

Any recommendations?

Mike Maloney: "Getting out there two or three days in advance is a good idea. You need to acclimate and get the Vegas rush out of your system. This way you'll have time to focus and really do the work. Most people reading this book can probably figure all that out on their own; they're probably smarter than I was the first time. But I have a hard time walking by a race book with lights on. You probably have to be there once and go through it before you can focus properly."

For Paul Shurman and his playing buddies, the NHC is an annual excursion.

Paul Shurman: "I have four people or so I play in tournaments with when we are lucky enough to be together: my brother, Bill; Steve Wolfson, Sr., and Steve Wolfson, Jr.; and Mitch Schuman among them. We've qualified for the NHC just about every year. We go to Vegas on Tuesday and start handicapping for Friday. The goal always is to finish up the Friday races by Thursday morning so then

49

we can start looking at the Saturday cards. We don't want to have to handicap all of Saturday after the Friday races. But of course, it never works out that way."

The 2011 NHC champ, John Doyle, took a similar approach and felt like that gave him a significant advantage over the race-to-race players.

John Doyle: "I did all my prep work ahead of time, and that let me spend the two days making final adjustments. It seemed to me like I had more stamina than a lot of the field. It seemed to me like a lot of people were still doing their handicapping at the event. I was able to focus on when I wanted to use my optional races, tweaking my strategy based on odds and how the various tracks were playing."

And what did his prep work consist of specifically?

John Doyle: "I started on Monday with the early entries. I didn't worry about trying to handicap every race at every track. I have three tracks I play on a regular basis: Fair Grounds, Gulfstream, and Santa Anita. I look at all those races anyway. I decided to just handicap those cards, knowing that at least four or five mandatory races were going to fall out of those three tracks. For the other tracks, I planned to just focus on the mandatory races when they came out. That's what I did, and I felt ready."

Another guy who knows the importance of preparation is 2013 runner-up Roger Cettina.

Roger Cettina: "I study for hours and days before contests. I'll go through almost every race for a given contest. For a contest like the NHC, I'll get there Wednesday and start studying for Friday's races. And by the middle of the day Thursday, I'm done with Friday and I'm looking at Saturday. If there's a track I don't like that I'm not going to do the whole card for, I'll just pick out races with big fields.

"Each day there are eight optional bets. So I took the races I thought I might be interested in, maybe 16 total, and I put them in order of post time, and for each one I tracked the odds, and if

I didn't like the odds I was getting on the contenders, I'd just pass and move on to the next one. I try not to narrow things down to one or even two horses in a race. I'd rather narrow it down to four or five contenders."

That's a great point generally, not just for the NHC. If it suits your own handicapping style, then it can be a great advantage to pick races that interest you, not just horses. It's so hard to predict what the tote board will do, and a race-focused approach will give you more options without increasing your overall workload.

WE ARE THE CHAMPIONS

I was fortunate enough to interview six past NHC winners for this book. I asked them all about their experiences.

Judy Wagner: "The biggest thing for me was being able to be consistent for two days in a row. In spite of what some people will say, you can win the NHC without hitting a capper. It was only three years ago when I hit my first capper in the NHC. The year I won, on the first day I had five winners and four seconds; the second day I had four winners and five seconds. The longest-priced horse I had paid $37. The only reason I had that horse was because I had liked another horse who had scratched, and there I was with only two races left until the end of the contest. The track was wet, sloppy, and there were tons of scratches, but I had to put in a play. I scanned the Tomlinson numbers, and I picked the one with the highest number, Hoovergetthekeys. He went off as the longest shot. That was the horse that won the contest for me."

Brian Troop went the other way, but with the same result. Back at NHC XI, Brian Troop put up the biggest one-day score of all-time—$232.60—and dared the rest of the field to come get him. No one could.

Brian Troop: "Once I got to $187 on the Friday, I tried to widen my lead. I knew I'd be a target on Saturday and that people would be gunning for me. I figured the further I got ahead, the better off I'd be. People say, 'He didn't do that well, he only got $34 on Saturday.' That's true, but you have to remember, too, that a lot of favorites came in on Saturday, and I knew favorites couldn't hurt me unless somebody could string six or seven of them together."

We'll get more into the specifics of Troop's day two strategy in our Endgame Theory chapter. I also asked him about his previous tournament success in our interview, and he told me something that was both fascinating and encouraging.

Brian Troop: "I had three seconds in contests before but had never won. I broke my maiden in a Grade 1, which doesn't happen too often."

Consistency was also an issue the year John Doyle won, when two players opened up big leads on day one. I asked him how he dealt with that.

John Doyle: "I felt a little discouraged. The NHC I won was the first tournament I ever played in for money. I tried to qualify the previous year online and didn't. And then I qualified early that year and didn't play any more tournaments. So I didn't have a lot of experience to rely on. But I just said to myself, 'I know these guys are way ahead, but I'm just going to stick with my plan and play the horses that I want to play. It usually takes a final bankroll of about $250 to win the thing, and I have $91. Let the chips fall where they may.' I thought it would be a bad strategy to start stabbing early. There were a lot of 5-1s and 6-1s that I thought had good chances of winning, so I just played them and I got on a roll."

Obviously, that was a great plan. But how was Doyle able to stick to it?

John Doyle: "I had a conversation with the gentleman sitting next to me. He said, 'I can't play this horse because it's not enough of a price.' But my attitude was: you can't get off winners. I wanted to have a shot going into the last race, even if it meant that I'd have to play a 20-1 shot. And I wouldn't have been able to be in that position by picking losers. It's very difficult to pick horses that are longer than 10-1. It's much easier to pick winners that are 5-1 or 6-1, and if you can run a few of those together, then you're in position to do something."

"Do something" like win $500,000, in Doyle's case.

I came across a great quote from Michael Beychok (whom I interviewed separately for this book) from an interview he did with *DRF*'s Jay Privman in the immediate aftermath of winning $1 million at the NHC in 2012.

Michael Beychok: "I can't really describe what it meant to win. The money's not real yet. I haven't deposited the check yet. I'm beginning to get my head around the drama of it all. Horse racing is decided a lot of times by inches, like Blame and Zenyatta in the Breeders' Cup Classic [in 2010]. To inject yourself into a small portion of horse racing—I don't want to call it history, but into the current events, and so dramatically—is pretty cool. It's memorable to people. It's a lifetime of work. I'm almost even."

Beychok used his big win to help a worthy cause.

Michael Beychok: "For years, I was guilty of taking for granted what these horses do every day on the track. We derive so many gains from them, both financial and recreational. They get oats, carrots, and if they're lucky, get treated as pets. We owe them more than that. From a horseplayer perspective, we don't pay them enough attention. When Glorious Dancer, an $8,000 claimer, won the NHC for me by a nose, I started thinking about the cheap claimer, and what could happen.

"She was a few races away from being off the track. I bought her—first as a sporting gesture, like, 'Hey, wouldn't it be fun to own the horse that won me $1 million?' We ran her; she won; and we had fun. Then I thought, 'Why am I running her? She changed my life.' Then a lightbulb clicked: she had nothing more to do on the track. I know you can't save them all, but for starters, I personally wanted to save this one. So I brought her to Louisiana, retired her, and thought about breeding her, but I donated her to a Louisiana rescue instead. She lives the life. Then, in my speech at the Eclipse Awards, I offered to contribute a percentage of my [NHC] winnings to horse rescue. Every time I do an interview, I try to talk about horse rescue."

John Conte: "In all honesty, in my psyche, I never tried to beat the game. I really just didn't want to work! I thought this would be an easier way to grind out, even if it just meant $100 a day—that would still be better than being cooped up in an office all day. Like anything else, in order to be good at something, you must put in a lot of hours. And at this point, being as old as I am and having started reading the *Daily Racing Form* at age 15, learning to dope it out, I've had plenty of hours. If it ain't broke, you don't fix it. But if it is broke, you adapt. Just like in business."

Now I know as well as you do that the worst interview question in the world is: "How did you feel?" But when I spoke with John Conte the day after his 2009 win, his enthusiasm was such that I could not resist.

John Conte: "This was my dream my whole life. My goal my whole life was to get to the top of the mountain, which is where I'm at right now. I'm not going to bet anymore. Why would I bother betting $20 when I'm sitting with a half-a-million? I'm almost 70 years old. I have enough money to take care of my family, to do what I want and have fun. I keep telling my friends, 'I'm done. I don't need the fix.'

"After the hell that I've been through in my life as a gambler, with all the ups and downs, I'm done. My wife's a great woman and it's not easy to live with a gambler, and she's put up with me all these years. And she's called 'Saint Arlene,' that's her nickname. Not from me but from people who knew her previously. And they warned me, 'You better be good to her.' And my license plate reads 'Saint A' for her. We've been married 21 years, and she's a wonderful woman. I'm looking forward to taking care of her because she's really helped me along through some tough times."

But my favorite family story, and the one that brings it all back home for me, came from the year Steve Wolfson, Jr., won the biggest prize in horseplaying. I interviewed the father-son Wolfson duo together, and this is what they had to say about Steve Jr.'s NHC win.

Steve Wolfson, Sr.: "It's been wonderful to watch my son grow and to love the same thing as I do. We look at each other often and are so glad to be a part of something that we have in common, forever. In the NHC in 2003, I was leading after the first day, and Caton Bredar interviewed me at the end of the day at Bally's. My experience in conducting and playing in these tournaments is that whoever is in first place the first day, rarely if ever, is in the top five the second day. So I wasn't celebrating at all. As it turned out, I finished fourth. Steve Jr., won the tournament, and that was the first year they gave an Eclipse Award.

"I remember the Eclipse Awards more than the win itself. In his introduction, Steven Crist talked about how Steve Jr., came by all this naturally and about how his grandfather owned Affirmed and that his father was the creator, the architect, of what we are doing today. And then when Steve Jr., accepted the first Eclipse Award handed out to a horseplayer, he said something really beautiful."

Steve Wolfson, Jr.: "I said, 'I really want to thank my dad, from whom I have learned so much and still have so much to learn.'"

Steve Wolfson, Sr.: "I remember getting so emotional when he said that; it was a great line. That meant so much to me that those were his thoughts on that day. Hope you still feel that way."

Steve Wolfson, Jr.: "I absolutely do."

4 Getting Started

"All great deeds and all great thoughts have a ridiculous beginning."
— **Albert Camus**

Okay, so you've decided you want to play in a handicapping contest. What's the next step? The easiest thing to do might be to start out by playing online. There are several websites that offer a variety of options including *Daily Racing Form's* own properties, NHCQualify. com and BCQualify.com. One of the easiest and best contest sites as of this writing is Derby Wars. It offers a variety of low buy-in, one-day contests with clear rules and a continually updating scoreboard.

In addition to writing this book, I also write a blog for *Daily Racing Form* about the contest scene and have a personal racing blog, The Unbearable Lightnesss of Betting (www.unbearablebetting.com). I also am very active on Twitter @loomsboldly. Rather than try to hit a moving target by offering too many specific suggestions of where to start, I'm going to encourage you to follow me in those spaces.

But another website I want to mention is *DRF* Public Handicapper (www.publichandicapper.com). It's a great resource for anyone looking to get started either in contests or with handicapping in general. Public Handicapper is always running at least one free contest, where contestants make mythical win bets in at least four races over the course of a given weekend. As presently constituted, the contests range in duration from two months to six months, but new options will likely include a broader range, including daily contests.

Scott Carson: "The goal of our site is not just to make people better contest players; it's also to get people handicapping, playing the races once a week. Public Handicapper is the only contest site where all picks are visible, and you have the option to write an analysis. So if you want to be Dave Litfin, you can be Dave Litfin on our site."

Prizes on Public Handicapper include cash money, NHC seats, free *Daily Racing Form* products, and a cool trophy proclaiming the winner to be "America's Finest Handicapper." This is a site that you want to check out.

Online Contest Sites/ADWs Offering Contests

PublicHandicapper.com	HorsePlayersQualify.com
DRFBets.com	Horsetourneys.com
NHCQualify.com	Twinspires.com
BCQualify.com	Xpressbet.com
DerbyWars.com	

ADVICE FOR NEW PLAYERS

I asked many of the players I interviewed what advice they had for new players.

Dave Gutfreund: "Know the game that you're playing and the right strategy for that game, because tournaments aren't just about picking horses: they are about picking the horses that best fit the strategy you need to win that particular tournament."

What's the best way to do this?

Dave Gutfreund: "A lot of tournament results are left up online for a long time so you can basically keep the results yourself for what it takes to win in various formats—very much the way poker tournament players figure out what the best strategies are for their games."

In addition to knowing the rules, it's important for new players to research and prepare for any given tournament.

Mike Maloney: "Do some research. Look at charts. Collect old *Racing Forms*. And when you have time, handicap those races. I talked about this in my interview for *Six Secrets of Successful Bettors.* If you don't know the result, it doesn't matter if the race happened two months ago. Handicap it anyway. Then go through the charts and go through the process. If a favorite runs bad, can you see a reason why? If a longshot runs well, is there any pattern evident there? The more races you handicap, the more you build the file in your head, seeing what works and what doesn't work. And then you can start blending in other people's ideas and getting some other ideas from books.

"I still think any new player starting out should buy Andy Beyer's books. I think you're crazy if you don't start out reading those. They're really readable and you don't have to be totally immersed in handicapping to read and enjoy those books and get something out of them. There are plenty of characters in there to keep you interested. That's a great starting point."

I should add a mention of three other books I think any beginner or even expert looking for a primer on the fundamentals of handicapping should own: James Quinn's *The Complete Handicapper,* Brad Free's *Handicapping 101,* and *Betting Thoroughbreds* by Steve Davidowitz.

Don Marr: "I've used a lot of *DRF* products. I also like the data I get from Jim Mazur's Progressive Handicapping products, but for me *DRF* is the main thing. I've bought books from them; I use Formulator all the time. I love watching the videos online with Mike Beer and Dan Illman. You can learn a lot just listening to those guys talking about the races, getting that language instilled into you. And then I can go to the *Form* and see what I agree with and what I don't agree with and make my own decisions. I spent 11 years in the military, and I treat the process of learning about handicapping like a training regimen."

Matt Bernier: "Now I've met all these great people and gotten a lot of great advice. And I've also read a bunch of handicapping books. But when I started out, I started out on my own. I have a friend of mine, and he just started getting into golf by watching a lot of golf played by people who know what they're doing, and he tried to emulate that. For me, with racing, it was the same thing. I watched a lot of guys handicapping on TV—obviously, some are better than others, but I'd listen to them and figure out what they were talking about, and then try to find it in the *Racing Form.*

"If one of the guys on the television said, 'This horse is going to be loose on the lead,' I'd look at the paper to see what he meant and how he figured that out. That's how I started trying to piece things together. And then when I got more confident and comfortable, I started analyzing on my own. It started out as a paint-by-numbers thing, but then I wanted to go off and paint on my own."

We'll delve a lot deeper into these topics later on in Chapter 6 about Game Plan. One final thing I want to add before we leave the topic of "getting started" is that it's never been easier for a new player to become a serious threat in tournaments.

Steve Wolfson, Sr.: "One of the biggest changes is the multitude of people who are playing now. When we first started playing, 12 or 13 years ago, you'd see the same people all the time. The audience has definitely broadened.

"We used to go and look around and know everyone in the room, and we could tell who we feared in that particular tournament. And now at the end we might say, 'Who are these people in the top five?'"

Joe Scanio was cynical on this issue.

Joe Scanio: "When I see the leaderboard in the beginning, and I see these strange names, I don't worry about it because, believe me, the cream always rises to the top. The seasoned guys will always be around at the end, and these novices will not."

I happen to agree with Steve Wolfson, Sr., on this one—that it's a lot more common for new faces to do well now than in years past. Scanio isn't wrong, because it's not necessarily novices winning, but it's just that there are so many good players who are lower-profile. The tournament landscape is changing, and it's hard to keep track of all the good players. And it's never been easier, especially with online play, to get the experience you need to compete at the highest levels—even if you're new to the game. That's one of the reasons contests are such a great growth area for the sport.

Scoreboards

It's almost hard to imagine this now, but there was a time not long ago when the hottest debate on the contest scene was whether or not to have a scoreboard tracking play. When many tournaments didn't have scoreboards, the cap question was largely irrelevant because no one knew precisely what score was needed to win. Here's what the late, great Jeff Sotman had to say on this topic in Noel Michaels' *Handicapping Contest Handbook.*

Jeff Sotman: "Posting scores is a clear penalty against a contest's strongest players—the leaders. If the goal of a handicapping tournament is to reward the best player(s), giving everyone in the field a target score to shoot for clearly works against this goal and is a crime against the leader, who must pray something wacky doesn't happen to steal the win. Scoreboards don't increase strategy; they reduce it by making it perfectly clear what everyone behind the leader should do in order to win."

Noel Michaels: "Long ago, when there was a small number of tournaments, most of them in Nevada, the only scoreboard they ever had was at the end of every day. That was the only idea you had. Before you saw that, you didn't have an exact idea of where you fit in. When tournaments started expanding, and tote companies got involved, it became easy to have scores posted after every race was official. The majority of people playing contests now, that's all they've ever known. But 20 years ago, players only knew about tournaments without a scoreboard.

"There might be a few old-school people who played in Vegas their whole lives who still feel that having no scoreboard is the right thing— and some of those Vegas tournaments still don't have one. But for me, the scoreboard is part of what makes a tournament a tournament— especially in the mythical-money format. It's what most people want and what they expect."

The advent of the pick-and-pray/lockdown format (see Chapter 2) helped heal this rift to some degree. Players who don't want to play against people playing the scoreboard can stick to those, and those of us who love the competitive strategy and game theory aspect of contests can stick to the formats where there is a scoreboard.

That's the thing about contests: there is no perfect format. There are pros and cons to each. It's all about what suits each player and his/her personal style. And in the Game Selection chapter, I'll talk with our players about just that. But first let's take a look at the relationship between contests and playing the horses day in, day out.

HOW ARE TOURNAMENTS DIFFERENT THAN EVERYDAY PLAY?

Maury Wolff: "To me, the phrase 'handicapping tournament' is a bit of a misnomer. There are tournament horses and real-money horses, and they're not the same thing. The horses you bet in life are often not the horses you bet in tournaments. In a tournament, you can get cute. You're looking for any rationalization you can to get you a big-priced result. It's a reverse process.

"The normal handicapping process is, 'Who do I like?' The second level of the normal process, which is a little more sophisticated, is, 'Who do I like relative to the price on the board?' That's quite sufficient for playing this game. That's what you're trying to do. If you've got a horse you think should be 2-1, and he's 4-1, that's a bet. It doesn't matter that he's 4-1. That's real money. That's not tournament strategy at all.

"In a tournament, you start the process in reverse. You ask yourself, 'What price do I need?' And then you find the horses that fit the criteria. You're not first asking, 'Who do I like? You're asking, 'What price do I need?' And then you go forward from there. In tournament life, I'm not going to spend one-tenth of a second on a horse that is 4-1. Next page. That's what tournaments are."

Dave Gutfreund: "A tournament isn't real life. It's a game with numbers and you have to be aware of that at all times. Even a live-bankroll tournament is just a game with numbers. If you have a little bit of mental discipline and you're comfortable with what you're doing, adopting a contest player's mindset shouldn't be a problem at all. If you know that taking a 4-1 shot, even a 4-1 shot that should be 5-2, isn't going to improve your standing in the tournament, then you can't play that horse. It's better to take a 15-1 shot, even a 15-1 shot that should be a 30-1 shot, if that 15-1 shot can get you to where you want to go. What's the point of betting the 4-1 shot that you love?"

But does the fundamental approach change?

Dave Gutfreund: "For me, it's not too different. I'm always looking for bad favorites to bet against or horses that raced against the bias. You're looking for the same fundamental things. The only difference is I'm discounting the shorter-priced horses."

Mike Maloney: "The difference for me is just that a 2-1 shot that I love that I could maybe build my day around on a normal betting day is worthless to me in a contest. So is a 30-1 shot that I feel real good about maybe running third. He's worthless too. Day in, day out, those are both a part of my game, part of what I'm good at, and they become completely out of the question in tournament play. Also, all my betting skills get taken out of the equation. It's night and day for me.

"You're looking for a horse at a price, and you're basically taking shots. Sure, you're hoping you'll pick three winners in a row, but in my mind, you're taking shots. Value is important, but it's not like value in an everyday race day where you can find value in a lot of different situations. Most of those are eliminated for me in a win/place contest format."

Joe Scanio: "It's two totally different ways of playing. If you're playing in a contest, you'll play a horse that could be more of a value play; other times you may have to play a horse that you don't even really like that much depending on the situation. It's a totally different mindset."

Noel Michaels: "You have to differentiate between what you do when you go to the track and what you need to do to win the contest. You have to realize that this isn't a regular day at the track. If you're betting, the game comes down to cashing a winning ticket. In a tournament, you have to sell out that this is not betting. Guys who can't do that won't ever win.

"The people who have been successful have all sold out to that idea. You can't just handicap and play horses you like. You have to totally change the way you play and look past the horses you really like. You have to acknowledge all the horses that can win and hopefully pick the right one of those at the right price. You aren't always going to be able to play your top pick in the race; you are going to have to bet the best of the contenders you can based on the situation. There's no gray area here. You absolutely have to do that or else you can't win."

Matt Bernier: "The biggest difference for me is finally realizing how much different a tournament is than a day at the track, where they are two totally different ball games. Where maybe I have acceptable odds while I'm at the track on a horse that's 4-1 or 5-1, realistically I can't play that in a tournament and have a chance at winning—it's just too short a price with the amount of people and as good as everyone is."

Brent Sumja: "My favorite bets are Pick-4s and Pick-5s. I feel as though I excel at identifying false favorites. My goal in a Pick-4 sequence is to find two really bad false favorites. Then I'm in. I play a base 50-cent Pick-4 but still might have a $400 ticket. When I feel the 7-5 is not going to win this leg, and there are maybe five horses that are going to be between 6-1 and 15-1, I'm not good enough to tell you which one of those is going to win. I'm just going to put all five of them in and hope to catch a price in that leg. However, pinpointing which of those longshots to pick is the whole key to tournament play. You've got to be good enough to say which of those is the winner. You've got to be the one to say 'This is the horse' and it can be extremely difficult."

What other challenges do tournaments present?

Matt Bernier: "It's very hard in a tournament when you have a horse you like and the morning line is 10-1, and then a few minutes to post you look up and see that it's 7-2. It's hard to have the discipline to call an audible and scrap that plan to play that horse you liked in the first place. On a regular day you don't have to do that, but in a tournament sometimes you do."

Mike Labriola: "With real money day-to-day, you play closer to the vest. In a tournament, you are definitely playing with the bigger picture in mind: let's say a tournament is three days and 36 bets. So if six or eight bets go down, and you've got a goose egg, it doesn't matter to you. The money's really gone when you put it up at the beginning. But in the real world, if you lose eight bets in a row, it's hard not to think about the money. You're bound to be more cautious. And then when you hit a nice winner, maybe instead of having $150 on him, you only have $20 on him. In a contest, everything is uniform, and when you have that big winner, you get rewarded for it in an equitable way."

Of course, there are some similarities between day-to-day betting and contest play as well.

Mark McGuire: "Contests parallel normal racing days in a lot of ways. You're still looking for a high ROI. You have to get value for your picks, even in contests. I've always been more of a longshot player, so contests probably fall a little better into what I've always done maybe than for a guy who is used to playing the Pick-6 where you still include lots of favorites."

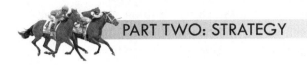
5 **Preparation**

"Failing to prepare is preparing to fail."

– John Wooden

We talked a little bit in the NHC chapter about how players prepare, and we've given some general advice to new players, but in this chapter we'll really examine both of these critical topics. From personal experience, I can tell you that I made a major leap in the proficiency of my contest play when I started focusing more on preparation and game plan, rather than just going from race to race and picking horses.

Paul Shurman: "The best advice I can give anybody is you have to be organized. The races come fast and you've got to know what's coming up and what you've got on each ticket. You've got to know how many races you have left. You see all the time where people don't even know what they have."

How does Shurman go about preparing?

Paul Shurman: "I make a checklist because I want to have all the most important information I use right where I can see it. I have a list of the three top speeds—whether they are real speeds or just fast out of the gate—notes on the pace scenario, including a list of the three best closers; track bias notes; pedigree notes; best speed figures; and a miscellaneous column. I look for things to match up. I used to forget to check things and now I have my checklist. I'm starting to think I might need a checklist for my checklist."

Kevin Cox: "When I'm betting at home, in online contests, I make charts: 'Ticket One,' 'Ticket Two,' bets one through ten, and then I put the track, and I physically write down the time for the race. You have to take into account sometimes that there could be three different time zones, so I make a column with the times. In a live contest you don't need that as much because you have all the TVs in front of you."

I love this idea, and I have started to do my own version of Shurman's checklists and Cox's charts—only in my case, it's a color-coded spreadsheet that contains a line for every playable race in the contest with fields for time, track, race number, what I think the general race outlook is (Is it likely to produce a favorite or a bomberoo?), field size, class level, logical paper picks, and interesting longshots, all with morning-line odds listed in parentheses. I code baby races and maidens with light (baby) blue and turf races in green. I bold my strongest opinions. I find it helps create a much clearer picture of what's coming up during the course of a contest. I still want my *Racing Form* printed out in front of me, but I want to have all the data organized in a way I can process it at a glance as well. I was curious to get some other players' thoughts on how they prepare.

Ricky Zimmer: "I show up at the contest with an idea in my head of what I want to do. I don't change too much on the fly. Obviously, value is important, so you have to adjust a little bit based on the odds, but any given contest day when I show up, I have a pretty good idea of which horses I'm going to play that day. If it's a ten-race contest, maybe I'll have a bucket of 20 races and I'll know my picks are coming from there. I don't do too much handicapping on the fly during contests. That's just too hard, and it's hard enough to keep track of everything that's going on, so I try to be as prepared as I can when the day starts."

John Doyle: "I try to assess who the favorite is going to be, then I'll look for other contenders that will be more mid-priced, and I also look for one or two horses that are maybe more of a stretch, live longshots. I'm a Pick-4 player; I approach the Pick-4 similar to how Steven Crist does it, breaking down the contenders into As, Bs, and Cs. Barry Meadow was the first guy to look at exotics betting that way, and I've been doing that for a long time. And for the contest, I used that approach as well. If I look at my notes and the tote and see that I have an A that is 10-1, then that's a play. Maybe I have a B that is 5-1, so I decide to skip that horse. I categorize all the horses, look at the tote board, and I make my decisions from there."

GOING BACKWARDS

Several of our players put forth what I thought was a fascinating idea for contests and one I've adopted myself: handicapping from back to front.

Paul Shurman: "You always want to handicap the card backwards, starting with the last races on the card and working your way to the front. That way, when you have that horse that you thought might be 8-1 and he's 3-1, well, you know if you have something else later on. If you do, you can pass that race; if you don't, then maybe you play him anyway. You always have to know what's coming up—it could be a bunch of six-horse fields and odds-on favorites. Most handicappers make the mistake of concentrating on the early races, and they don't really get to handicap the end races until they come up. In most cases, the end races are the most important part of all. You can't go in race-by-race."

Eric Moomey: "I start from the last race and work backwards. In the last race, you're either going to have to win, or you are so far ahead that the winner of the last race makes no difference in the final standings. If you think the logical horse in the last race is a favorite or short-priced horse, then you really don't want to be down in the tenth spot; you need to be in the top three going into the last race. If you think the last race is wide open and a 10-1 or greater is likely to win, then it's okay to be lower in the standings going into the last race. In that instance, you might pick a favorite two races out that you really liked beforehand to put yourself in position to win with the 10-1 shot you liked in the last race. In that instance, you don't necessarily shoot to be in the lead going into the last race.

"Look at the 2012 Breeders' Cup Betting Challenge. A former NHC champion explained to me, 'I wasn't impressed with him [winner Patrick McGoey] picking Fort Larned at 9-1 in the Classic; what I was impressed with was that prior to the last race, he wagered his entire bankroll on Wise Dan, a 9-5 favorite, to put him into winning position for the final race.' He made a double move, which was very smart. Most people don't think that way. They would have tried two longer shots and got nothing."

Moomey's idea of working backwards isn't just limited to his prep work.

Eric Moomey: "I do the same thing when I'm looking at an individual race. I start with the longest prices and work my way down to the favorite. It makes it a lot easier to find longshots. If you start looking at a race by studying the favorite, it's going to be harder to find a horse that looks better than the favorite does normally. If you look at the same information that everyone else does, you're going to come to the same conclusion. You have to look at it differently."

We'll expand on the benefits of being different shortly, but first Kevin Cox offers another reason to start at the end rather than at the beginning.

Kevin Cox: "Let's say I'm playing in a contest or doping out a Pick-6. I always try to handicap backwards, because you're more likely to get tired going into the last race, and you're not going to concentrate as hard, whereas if you handicap backwards, your mind is more fresh on the horses that other people make the least effort paying attention to."

Preparation can mean different things to different players. I'd describe Eric Moomey as one of the most prepared guys out there, but in terms of making his actual selections, he is rather loosey-goosey.

Eric Moomey: "I don't do too much work until the live odds come out. I start with an odds range I think the race is likely to produce. About five minutes before the race goes off, I look to see which contenders fall within that odds range. It takes me about a minute to make my decision and I might change my decision five times before the race goes off based on watching the odds. I will usually select the horse with the highest price in the odds range I'm look-ing to play. If I'm looking for a 10-1 horse and he drops to 5-1, then I'll cross him off and go to the next logical horse. Once I select a horse to play, I immediately identify which horse I'll replace him with if the odds drop below my target. Below 10-1 odds, the pub-lic does a pretty good job making an accurate assessment of the odds, so you can just trust their judgment. Above that price, not so much, and you will need additional tricks up your sleeve to find those longshot contenders."

Cara Yarusso: "I am not one of those players that is back in my room studying the *Racing Form* until the wee hours of the night before a contest. However, I know a lot of my competition is doing just that! I tend to handicap better during the day, so I prefer to do my studying while the contest is underway. It does require me to look ahead, though, so that I don't miss a great play by not being prepared.

"Additionally, with the wonderful group of friends I have made over the years playing tournaments, the evenings after the races are a great opportunity to socialize and reconnect over dinner. I wouldn't trade those opportunities to reconnect with friends across the country for anything. The preparatory handicapping can begin in the morning."

The approach that Moomey and Yarusso use contrasts sharply with what I heard from most of the other players, and that's probably a good thing for them and possibly part of their edge. Perhaps by not being up all night studying, they can be more nimble during the con-test itself. As we'll explore in our next section, in contests and in gam-bling in general, you can have no greater weapon than being different.

BEING DIFFERENT

Brent Sumja: "It's not very important if everybody sees it. In sports handicapping on the day of the game, you'll hear people say, 'Oh, it's raining and muddy out. It's going to be an under.' I think to myself, 'Do you not realize that the people who are setting this line have played this game on a computer a billion times and they know it's going to be raining too?' I try to ignore anything obvious unless I'm trying to bet against it. The days of a horse being three-for-eight on the Del Mar turf and no one knowing that are long gone. Now it's right there in the *Form*. So you can't pay too much attention to that. There are only a few things you can do on your own to get an edge and it takes a lot of work."

We'll get deeper into Sumja's methods in Part 3 of this book when we take an in-depth look at how contest players handicap, but for now, let's stick with the importance of being different. I asked Mike Labriola about his general approach, and he made a salient point on this topic.

Mike Labriola: "It used to be that I was a pronounced speed handi-capper, and I'd look for hidden speed. But hidden speed is harder to come by today. These days, I'm a better handicapper overall, but it's ironic because as I've gotten 'better,' I've become a little uniform and maybe lost a little of that wackiness that can separate me from the pack."

In the contest world it's okay—maybe even preferable sometimes—to specialize, as long as you gain proficiency. If you want to use Sheets, you better put in the time to learn to read them as well as anyone. If you want to use looks, you better keep the best looks database out there. If you want to study trips, you better watch every replay on your circuits carefully and come up with better stuff than the next player.

Eric Moomey: "Whatever system you use, whatever data you rely on, you want to make sure that you're really, really good, at processing that data or using that program or whatever it is—because you don't only have to beat all the players in the tournament, but you also have to beat all the players looking at the same things you're looking at."

Moomey also has another way of being different—by changing his pick methodology as the contest goes along.

Eric Moomey: "What I'll do is if I have a system of making picks that's working, I'll change it up mid-stream. Let's say I used the popular handicapping computer program HTR at the start of a tournament and five of us hit the same horse—that's not great for me, because while I'm in contention, I still have only a 20 percent chance of winning. So as soon as I hit that horse, I'll cross out the next HTR horse and start looking for another method to break away from the pack."

It may seem crazily contrarian to be so willing to abandon a plan that's working—but there are a couple of advantages to Moomey's plan. For one thing, as Moomey states above, he still has to beat all the other players who have landed on the same horses as him so far. Additionally, varying his play makes Moomey less predictable and harder to read in the endgame, a topic we'll cover thoroughly later on in the Endgame Theory chapter.

Another important point is that because of the nature of markets, what works today might not work tomorrow.

Mike Labriola: "Handicapping, like training, is a really dynamic thing that changes all the time. Just look at how people used to prepare horses for the Kentucky Derby, using the Derby Trial a week before the race. Seabiscuit ran 22 times as a two-year-old! Nowadays, if you tried that as a trainer, they'd lock you up. With handicapping, it's the same sort of thing. The same things aren't always going to work."

Michael Beychok: "There are a lot of good handicappers, and it's very rare that you win simply by trying to out-pick everybody. You need to think strategically. I like to look for horses that most people won't have. That will separate you. I like it when I have a horse that no one else in the contest has. When that happens, win or lose, then I know that was a good pick. And when you win in that situation, you move up alone. I don't know if there is a method to finding those horses, but that's what I'm trying to do. Maybe you can find one by coming up with a creative story."

Eric Moomey: "Select the horse that can separate you from the pack. If you can figure out what everybody else is likely to play next, that's a huge advantage. If there are ten horses in a race, they are not all played the same. There are some that 20 percent of the people will play and there are others that nobody will play. Look at the one that nobody will play. Can you make any case at all for that horse? If you can, play it. That's how I've won several tournaments, by being the only person to hit a certain winner. In my case, one was a first-time starter with nothing to recommend on paper. In another case it was an 0-for-43 maiden—but he was a front-runner, and that day he just kept running."

Ricky Zimmer is known on the contest scene for being a "lone wolf" who comes to the contests armed only with his *Daily Racing Form*. These days—with half the room sitting behind their computers—that's about as different as it gets. I asked him about this.

Ricky Zimmer: "I'm not a software guy. I prefer the old-school paper-and-pen handicapping."

I asked if he thought that might give him an edge in any way with so many contest players using technology and other specialized handicapping products.

Ricky Zimmer: "I think so, because a lot of players using Sheets or computer programs like HTR could wind up on the same horse. And I know they can use those tools differently, but I feel like, in general, they are all pointing in the same direction. So I feel like it could be an advantage for me, that by using just the *Racing Form*, I might wind up somewhere where they're not. That's really the way to separate yourself in the contest—you need to not only hit nice prices, but also hit them in places where other people aren't."

What other advice would Zimmer have for a player trying to separate himself or herself?

Ricky Zimmer: "The other big thing with contests is to be aggressive.

Because there are so many good players out there, and these contests usually have a ton of entries, you need to take chances—that's the best way to separate yourself from the pack. If you just try to go middle it along, you can't get away from the group. For mythical contests, don't dismiss anything—maybe go way over the cap—and for a live-money contest, maybe you want to go all-in early in the day. The key is to be aggressive."

GOING OVER CAP

The question of whether or not to play over the cap is another matter of much debate among contest players in general. Brian Troop agrees with the conventional wisdom on this one.

Brian Troop: "There's not really much sense in playing a horse over 20-1 unless you really like it, because there's a cap on it. If you get a $100 horse, you better like it quite a bit because you're only going to get $42 for it in tournament play."

One alternative strategy is to bet the over-cappers for cash.

Paul Shurman: "You'll see situations where you'll make more money by betting these way-over-cap horses to win than you will by finishing sixth or seventh in the tournament—especially if it's a lower cap like in the NYRA tournaments, it might make sense to bet that horse to win."

I tend to agree with this line of thinking, especially in a tournament with a small prize pool—one where you might be able to make as much money betting your over-capper for cash as you would in winning the tournament—or perhaps in a tournament where a super-high score wouldn't be needed to win. But there are several other instances where playing over cap makes a ton of sense. One is if you just happen to love the horse. If you think it should be 6-1 or 8-1 and it's 35-1, by all means play it. There are other situations where playing an over-capper makes a lot of sense as well, especially if you're trying to move up the leader board alone.

Kevin Cox: "A lot of people don't like to play a 25-1 or 30-1 in the contest, because in the gambler's mind, there's no value in that if the cap is 15-1. But that's only if you're looking to grind out a profit over the course of a year, where you're losing 25 percent of your value on a horse that's drifting up in odds. In a contest, what happens is certain people will ignore those because they are higher than the cap. But because of that, you're actually getting more value in the contest itself. So proportionally, you're actually doing better if you include those horses."

TOP-SHEETING

A very basic way any horseplayer needs to be different, regardless of whether we're talking cash play or contest play, is by delving deeper into the PPs than the average player is willing to do. Several players discussed this need to avoid what's known as top-sheeting.

Brent Sumja: "You know how people are when they see one bad race. Two or three races back? That's ancient history to them."

Mike Labriola: "I love intermittent bad events that can be explained away. Four back, this horse ran a good race at seven furlongs where he was there until the last call. Then three back, he broke from the 11 post, and the outside was playing terribly. Two back, it was sloppy, and he hates the slop. Last time was on the turf, and he's not a turf horse. Now today he's going six and a half furlongs, and he's two classes lower. If you look at that race four back, you see that wonderful hidden gem—and because people top-sheet and ask, 'What have you done for me lately?' they don't see it. You can get real nice prices that way."

Maury Wolff: "Never underestimate the power of the bad last race when you're looking for a price. And two bad races and you can be home. How many times do you see horses that would fit perfectly in the same spot three or four back, but they appear to have tailed off? Well, you know what? Maybe they have tailed off, but maybe they just ran a bad race or a couple of bad races. Horses run bad races all the time. And then today they come back at 20-1 and win. It happens all the time. Look at Palace Malice in the Belmont Stakes. That's a pretty good price for a horse that just had one bad race. He would have been a great contest horse."

12 Palace Malice
15-1
Own: Dogwood Stable
Green, Yellow Dots And Collar, Yellow
MITH M E (3 0 1 0 .00) 2013: (137 24 .18)

B. c. 3 (May) KEEAPR12 $200,000
Sire: Curlin (Smart Strike) $25,000
Dam: Palace Rumor (Royal Anthem)
Br: W S Farish (Ky)
Tr: Pletcher Todd A(56 9 10 9 .16) 2013:(350 87 .25)

Blinkers OFF
L 126

Life	**7**	**1**	**3**	**1**	**$271,135**	**93**
2013	**5**	**0**	**2**	**1**	**$209,135**	**93**
2012	**2**	**1**	**1**	**0**	**$62,000**	**88**
Bel	**1**	**0**	**1**	**0**	**$14,000**	**88**

D.Fst	**4**	**1**	**1**	**1**	**$112,000**	**93**
Wet(329)	**2**	**0**	**1**	**0**	**$9,135**	**89**
Synth	**1**	**0**	**1**	**0**	**$150,000**	**89**
Turf(316)	**0**	**0**	**0**	**0**	**$0**	**–**
Dst(310*)	**0**	**0**	**0**	**0**	**$0**	**–**

.Jun13 Bel fst 4f :47 2 B 3/46
May13 Bel fst 5f 1:00 1 B 7/28
May13 Bel gd 4f **tr.t** :47 2 B 2/35

May13-11CD sly S 1¼ :45 1 1:09 4 1:36 2:02 4 KyDerby-G1 **84** 9 1 hd 13½ 31 75¾ 1213½ Smith M E L126 b 23.70 81 – 15 **Orb**126 2½ **Golden Soul**126 1 **Revolutionary**126 hd 3 wide early, tired 19
***R-BIAS: –82 FLOW: 149 BL12: 29.6 CFR: 84**

Apr13 CD fst 4f :47 1 B 2/70

Apr13-10Kee fst 1⅛ ◈ :48 1:12 3 1:37 1 1:50 1 BlueGras-G1 **89** 5 5 5 4 3 3 2 2 1 2 nk Gomez G K L123 4.90 82 – 17 JavsWr123 nk PlceMlice123 nk ChrmingKitten123 1¼ Shifted out,led,denied 14
***R-BIAS: –14 FLOW: 93 BL12: 23.9 CFR: 79**

Mar13-9FG fst 1⅛ :46 1 1:11 4 1:37 3 1:50 1 LaDerby-G2 **81** 2 85¾ 67½ 41½ 84½ 77¼ Prado E S L122 3.60 80 – 10 **Revolutionary**122 nk Mylute122 3 *Departing*122 1½ Stymied 5/16 to 1/8 14
***R-BIAS: 12 FLOW: 187 BL12: 23.8 CFR: 98**

Mar13 PmMfst 5f 1:00 4 B 6/34
Mar13 PmMfst 5f 1:00 B 2/26

Feb13-10FG fst 1 1/16 :23 4 :48 1 1:12 3 1:44 2 RisenStr-G2 **93** 6 83¾ 9 3 5 3 2 1 3½ Napravnik R L116 5.40 90 – 11 IveStruckaNerve116 no CodeWest116½ PalceMlice116 no 2-3w,4w 1/4,rallied 12
***R-BIAS: 114 FLOW: 75 BL12: 16.6 CFR: 85**

Jan13-1GP sly S 7f :22 3 :45 3 1:09 3 1:22 2 OC 75k/N1X-N **89** 6 6 3 1 2 2 2 3 22¼ Castellano J J L118 *.80 88 – 12 MjesticHussr118 2¼ PlceMlice118 8 CityofWston120½ 5wd trn, clear second 8
***R-BIAS: –52 FLOW: –67 BL12: 0.0 CFR: 23**

Aug12-7Sar fst 6½f :21 4 :44 3 1:09 2 1:16 2 Md Sp Wt 80k **83** 7 2 31½ 1 hd 1 3 13½ Castellano J J L119 *.35 86 – 10 Palace Malice119 3½ Apex119 1 Hightail119 2¾ 3w bid 3/8, kept busy 7
***R-BIAS: –48 FLOW: 57 BL12: 1.5 CFR: 61**

Jly12-6Bel fst 5f :22 :44 3 :56 3 Md Sp Wt 70k **88** 4 4 4 2 3 1 2 1 2½ Castellano J J L118 2.20 97 – 05 CrriedInterest118½ *PlceMlice*118 6¾ Horsepower118 2¾ 3p 5/16,lite bump 1/4 8
***R-BIAS: . FLOW: . BL12: 0.2 CFR: .**

6 Game Plan

> *"The general who wins the battle makes many calculations in his temple before the battle is fought. The general who loses makes but few calculations beforehand."* – **Sun Tzu**

PLAYING TO A SCORE

Eric Moomey: "I pride myself on my proficiency at knowing how to play the game more than on my handicapping skills, which I consider to be on par with or even slightly below my competition. You need to recognize that each tournament is unique. For example, what are the odds caps, how many races, how large are the field sizes, how many competitors are playing, are they pros or amateurs, do you need to finish first or just in the top ten? I believe each contest has a most efficient way to reach your goal, so while other players spend their prep time focusing on handicapping horses, I am studying the uniqueness of each contest."

Part of successful preparation is coming with the game plan you'll need to win the contest you're playing in. There are many ways to go about this, but most of our players start the process by projecting the final score they'll need to make their goal—whether that's winning the tournament or, if the contest is a qualifier, getting a high enough score to move on to the next contest. Note that the quotes in this section all refer to coming up with the final score for mythical-money tournaments. Live-bankroll tournaments are a completely different animal, and they will be addressed in a later chapter.

John Conte: "When you've been in enough contests, you know within $20 or $30 what the final score is going to be. It depends on what the rules of the contest are, what the menu states. I've played in every contest format there is, so now as I'm going along, I know how my pace is compared to what I need to win. Will I be able to reach my goal of winning based on the number of winners I've picked so far and what they've paid?"

Once you know what contest you want to play, the next thing you need to do is figure out what score it's going to take to win. The answer might surprise you in that it's remarkably similar from tournament to tournament, if we're talking about mythical-money contests.

Paul Shurman: "The final score is usually 2 1/2 times the bankroll for a win/place tournament. So if it's ten races, $2 win and place, that means your starting bankroll is $40. Multiply that by 2 1/2 and you get 100—and that becomes your target score."

I first read about the 2 1/2 times benchmark in the *Handicapping Contest Handbook,* and I asked Noel Michaels if that number had changed since the book's publication in 2002.

Noel Michaels: "That mathematical formula still holds. It's the same today. If it's a win or win/place contest, you're basically looking at a final score that's 2 1/2 times your starting bankroll. That's the gold standard to me, always a good starting point."

Certain contest formats do tend to land around the same number.

Paul Shurman: "If you play in certain tournaments enough, like the NYRA tournaments, it can be a little more than that [2 1/2 times number]. There, you make ten bets each day, $20 to win, place, or show, with one of those bets being a double bet of $40. So your total bankroll there is $440. Two and a half times that is $1,100, but you know going in from experience that that's not going to be enough. There you'll need at least $1,200.

"There was a player a number of years ago at the Belmont contest who hit something like seven of ten win bets on the first day, with six in a row. If he had played a Pick-6 with those picks, he would have hit it on a $2 ticket. But then the next day, he didn't hit anything—he cashed for zero all day. So the joke was that on day one he was Stan the Man and on day two he was Stan Still. But the point is there are some contests where the final scores are incredibly predictable from tournament to tournament."

Noel Michaels: "I think the 2 1/2 will still get you pretty close in the NYRA contests. I know that going in, and I play to that number, right around $1,100. That's why you don't have to make rash decisions if a few longshots come in on the first day. You've got time. You know what the number is going to be. Focus on your races; play the horses you like."

There are a variety of factors that can increase the total final number.

Eric Moomey: "The final score depends on the races selected. How many races are in the contest in total? Are they large fields? Are they turf races or dirt? Is it a weekday or weekend? Are you playing against 30 players or 300? Are you allowed one ticket or multiple entries?"

Maury Wolff: "The number you're going to need is tied to the number of entrants, because the fewer entrants you have, the less you're going to need. The more entrants, the higher final score. Once you have an idea of what score you'll need, you need to try to figure out how many cap winners or at least longshots you're going to need to win."

Noel Michaels: "Another thing that makes the projected winning score higher is when you have tons of tracks. For example, in the Orleans contests, they have five or more tracks. And you know that with, say, seven tracks, over the course of two or three days, it's inevitable there are going to be prices."

The most important determining factor of all is the specific run of the races.

Mark McGuire: "I usually have a pretty good idea of what the final scores are going to be, but it all varies depending on what's coming in. If favorites come in, that drops. If longshots come in, that goes up. So you can have a general idea before a contest starts, but as you're playing, you have to pay attention to what's coming in. In a contest like the Wynn, where there isn't a leaderboard, you just have to play to a score."

This really comes into play when you're looking at a contest made up of all mandatory races.

Dave Gutfreund: "In a ten-race bullet contest, if there are a bunch of longshots that come in, it's going to take $125 to win. If there aren't a lot of longshots, maybe it'll only take $100. So you have to figure out what the run of the races is and what you need to do based on how the races are going. Obviously, the scores are based on the results of the races. If there are a bunch of short prices, the score is going to be lower; if it's a bunch of longshots, the scores are going to be much higher."

Noel Michaels: "In an online tournament with all mandatory races, you have to really pay attention to the scoreboard. Generally speaking, in an online contest where the races are picked for you, the scores will be lower. But on some days it can be the exact opposite. You're at the mercy of what happens in those ten races."

Why is there such a contrast?

Noel Michaels: "In a contest with a lot of tracks and a lot of different races, you have the luxury of just being able to play your own contest. You know basically what score it's going to take to win, and if you don't have a longshot to play in a given race, it's okay to just pass the race or even to play your pick if you know you've got some other races coming up down the line where you like some prices. You have the freedom to pass or play. Whereas online, if there are a couple of big prices early, so many people are going to have those horses simply because everyone has to make a pick. Now a lot of people have big scores and now you have to start looking at the other races thinking, 'How am I going to make up those points?' Now you can't take the 3-1 horse that you like. You can no longer be playing your own contest; you've got to start playing in relation to the other people and the scoreboard."

In other words, there are so many fewer races for the field to choose from online that you have less of a chance to make up the score. I was curious to know if Noel Michaels felt that the opposite held true. If an online bullet contest started out with all chalk, would he be tempted to start playing lower prices?

Noel Michaels: "That's totally dependent on the individual player and his style. I know players both online and off who will never take a horse below 10-1. And there are some other guys who will never really look at a horse that is below the cap; every race, all the time. Other people, myself included, are willing to look lower than that and take the lowest price we can based on the situation. If the scores aren't that high and you like a horse at 3-1, you should play it. You prefer to be in the spot where you can take the horse you like at any decent price and not have your hand forced into the horse that fits the tournament based on what the odds are."

In a contest that includes show bets along with win and place, the final scores will represent a lower multiple of the starting bankroll.

Noel Michaels: "If it's a win/place/show contest, because a third of your bets during that contest are going to be made to show, you're probably not going to need 2 1/2 times your starting bankroll. Maybe just two times will work there."

Not every tournament player treats projecting a final score as being of paramount importance.

Kevin Cox: "I don't go into a tournament looking to hit a certain score like a lot of guys do. They'll look at the average winning score over a number of years and play to that number. I play it by ear. You can't over-plan trying to get a certain number. On the first day, I just want to get a feel, pick a couple of winners. You don't want to lock yourself down too much or you'll go insane."

Mike Labriola: "I think that you can win tournaments without having an astronomical final score. In fact, not only can you win them, but also I think it's okay to go in with the idea that not every tournament is going to be won by a hellacious score. Sometimes you see them. Sometimes it'll take four times your initial bankroll to win. But sometimes two times your bankroll will do it.

"I've always told people, 'I hope the score doesn't get into the stratosphere,' because I'm a guy who if I see a 6-1 or 8-1 shot that I love, I'll play it. Obviously it's better to get off with a big-priced horse, but this idea that you have to go for bombs and hope they land isn't always right. I think if people look back at their play at the end of tournaments, they might see that they passed on four 6-1 winners, and had they played them, the outcome might have been different."

WHAT PRICES SHOULD YOU PLAY?

When playing to a specific score, how do our players decide what price horse they are looking for?

Dennis Decauwer: "In most tournaments, I know that I have to be able to scope out a minimum of one or two live horses that are going pay more than $20. And I know that if it's a ten-race tournament, several of my picks are going to have to be those types of horses if I want to catch at least two of them. You're not going to win most tournaments unless you find a bomb."

Eric Moomey: "I select whatever I think I can get out of a race. If it's totally wide-open, I will select nothing less than 10-1; if there is a logical 5-1, I might play it on all tickets. Typically, if I need to finish in the top ten percent to qualify for another contest, I look for a 5-1 or 10-1 shot; if I need to finish in the top 1 percent to win or qualify, I might only play 15-1 or higher, and I have played as high as 99-1.

"When I am in the lead and am vulnerable to a logical 5-1 contender, I will generally go for the block and hedge, using cash on any higher-priced horses that I also like. If I like both a 20-1 and a 50-1, I might play the 20-1 in the tournament and bet the 50-1 for cash, unless I am near the bottom of the standings and then I will play the reverse.

"A lot comes down to: what price do you need in the contest? I can tell you that if you need to finish in the top ten percent of the field to cash, the average value you'll need for a 10-race $2 win/ place contest is $64 or 1.6 times your initial bankroll. If you have to finish first out of 100 players to make your goal, there's a lot more variability as to what exact score you'll need, but it is much higher, likely around 2.5 times your initial bankroll. If you get a 20-1 shot and you only need $64 total, then maybe you only need to hit one and you're at your goal. But if you need $100 total, trying for two 20-1 shots is mathematically very hard to do, and you probably don't need that much to achieve your goal anyway. Maybe you can hit one 20-1 shot and back it up with a couple of 5-1 shots to get to $100, for example, or maybe you even mix a couple of favorites in there."

Maury Wolff: "You play for whatever you need. And if you've got a situation where there's no cap, then you start making cases for $60 or $80 horses. If there is a cap, you start making cases for horses around the cap. Maybe other people don't look at it this way, but you make the case for whatever you need."

Roger Cettina: "I'm looking for between 4-1 and 10-1 most of the time. If it's a big, full field, then those odds are going to go up a little more. I don't bet many 35-1 shots."

I mentioned to Dave Gutfreund that, like Roger Cettina, I feel pretty comfortable coming up with winners in the range of about 5-1 or 10-1 but have a lot more trouble finding cap horses that I like enough to bet.

Dave Gutfreund: "I hate to break it to you, but I've got the same problem as you do. Thankfully, over the years I've been pretty good in what you consider your sweet spot range. That's more my range. I'm amazed at some of these people who consistently come up with $50 horses. I'm not one of those people. One of the reasons I like the NYRA contest is that the cap is 15-1 as opposed to 20-1 or 25-1. I probably shouldn't give away this trade secret, but I'm not the longshot bomber that people think I am. You have to take some shots, it absolutely helps, but once you get above 4-1, you're fine at most contests until you get to the end, unless you're not in it."

Noel Michaels: "I come up with a lot of horses in the range of 5-1 to 10-1. I think the low cap is part of why I do well in the NYRA contests. You have to play horses in the odds cap range throughout the tournament if you're going to win. But you don't have to make every play in that range."

Ken Massa is happiest playing proper longshots, but he sees some merit in mixing in some mid-priced horses, especially early on.

Ken Massa: "It may be more important to gain momentum and confidence than it is to hit the bomb right away. I've found it a good strategy to try to get any kind of winner at a reasonable price—let's say 6-1 and up—and get it going. The most important thing that can happen to you in a tournament is to gain momentum and self-confidence right away."

Paul Shurman takes this idea and goes a bit further.

Paul Shurman: "From the start of a tournament, I'm not so much necessarily looking for long prices as I am looking for horses I like. It's okay to try to pick some winners. How many tournaments do you get to the end and you needed a 7-2 shot and you would have won? It happens all the time. Well, why couldn't you have gotten the 7-2 at the beginning of the tournament, you know?"

This gets to the crux of the single most divisive issue among our players: the question of playing shorter prices in tournaments. When I learned contest play at Santa Anita from the likes of excellent longshot players Jeff Sotman and Tom Quigley, I was told that favorites were verboten. But my ideas have evolved over time.

Paul Shurman: "Playing 7-2 is okay, especially if it's early on and there haven't been any prices. You can even play shorter than that in some instances. There are a lot of players who only play 10-1 shots, 15-1 shots. Once in a while you can win doing that, but you can't be afraid to try to pick winners. You're not going to win play-ing a bunch of horses at 9-5 and 6-5, but I'll happily take 7-2 in a format like the NYRA contests."

Maury Wolff gave me a little history lesson on this topic.

Maury Wolff: "In the early days, people didn't know how to play tournaments. Half of them were just trying to pick winners regard-less of price, which is of course totally useless. Very few people were playing for the swoop outcomes. Over time, people learned how to play optimally. I felt more and more people were playing properly so the equity was diminishing, so I stopped playing. It just wasn't worth it to me anymore."

It was my own opinion that over time, things might balance out a bit more. If everyone is bombing, perhaps there might be more equity in playing a mix of favorites and longshots, if only to separate oneself from the other people playing prices. A couple of our players agree with this strategy.

Mike Labriola: "In the early days of tournaments, people didn't get it, and the only people who won were the ones who played long-shots. But now, people think that's the only way to win. There's been a paradigm shift. You're still going to need to have longshots sprinkled in, but I'm not as quick to toss a reasonably priced horse as most tournament players are."

Paul Shurman: "I've come full circle in my approach to what prices to play. Everybody starts out focusing on picking winners. Then I went to seeking out 8-1 shots and above almost exclusively, really focusing on cap horses. Now, if I see a horse I really like and he's 4-1, I'll take it. You don't want to lose by a few dollars and know you passed a horse you loved that would have gotten you there. I still want to play longer prices, but if I love something shorter, I'll play it."

Maury Wolff wasn't convinced.

Maury Wolff: "It doesn't balance itself out because big prices are always going to be what it takes to win the biggest tournaments. Except in extremely unusual circumstances, you're not going to have a situation where you get that many short-priced horses in a row that will be sufficient to get that strategy home. It's the bunt versus the three-run home run. It's the Earl Weaver line: play for one run, lose by one run. That's what betting short-priced horses in a tournament is like: bunting when you should be trying to hit a home run."

Steve Wolfson, Sr.: "Unless it's late in the contest, I will never bet a horse under 5-1. Even if there is a strong favorite, I would much rather try to hunt out that 15-1 that I think will run second. If I really like a 3-1, and I know most people I play with will go ahead and bet that horse, I never feel bad if I miss that horse. At least I took a shot with a horse running second that probably would have paid more to place than the winner did to win and place."

I totally see where Wolff and Wolfson Sr. are coming from, but it's undeniable that there's a new breed of contest players who are ready, willing, and able to mix in more favorites, Kevin Cox chief among them, as you'll read in the Applications section about his experience at the Belmont contest in the spring of 2013.

Now that there are 50 guys trying to win by hitting three cap horses over the course of a tournament, how are you going to beat them? Maybe you're not afraid to find the chalky race and pick up some points with a favorite even though that strategy didn't always make sense.

Kevin Cox: "That's right. The illogical is the new logical."

A lot of it really depends on the specifics of what tournament you're in and what your strengths and weaknesses are as a player. I've had the pleasure of competing against Brent Sumja both online and in brick-and-mortars, and I've noticed that in the right contest where the scores won't be astronomical, he has no problem playing shorter-type horses. But in a format like the NHC, he adjusts.

Brent Sumja: "If a new player starting out really wants to cash tickets in a lot of races, a tournament like the NHC is probably not for him. When I first started in tournaments, I loved playing logical horses between 3-1 and 5-1, but you can't really play those horses in a tournament like the NHC. The mathematics just doesn't work out. If you're playing less than 8-1 or 10-1 in a contest like the NHC, you're kidding yourself. It's hard to take the 15-1 shots that you only kind of like, but what happens is, if you don't try to take them early on, later in the tournament you're forced into taking ones that you really don't like and you're just playing a number at that point. If you like anything at all about a 15-1 shot early on in the NHC, you better take it."

The endgame, which we'll cover more fully in the Endgame Theory chapter, is where the favorites typically have the most utility.

Michael Beychok: "I'll take a 7-2 shot if I think it can get me to my target number in a tournament, especially if I think it might get me in the hunt with three or so races to go."

Mike Labriola: "I have won tournaments by getting down to the end and just needing a 5-2 place horse for $25,000 or $30,000. That's a beautiful position to be in, and I think most players would do that. If it gets down to the end and I have bets left—contest players are sort of like squirrels, hoarding nuts in the winter—I'll even play a 7-2 shot if that's what I like in the race. Not only does it give you a lift psychologically going into the last few races, but you also don't know, maybe those 90 points are going to make a difference in the end. If my tournament brothers were here, some of them would scoff at that, but I've had a lot of success using that strategy."

Paul Shurman: "Depending on the situation and where you are exactly, sometimes it even makes sense to play the 9-5, especially late in the contest. That's what happened to me when I finished second in the Belmont contest a while ago. The money I got from the 9-5 shot late on the second day is what allowed me to finish second. You pick out who you like, and as you go along, the plan changes according to how your picks are going."

For me, Eric Moomey summed up this topic perfectly.

Eric Moomey: "There are plenty of good situations to play favorites, but you don't want to play them too often. And when you're playing them, you really want to have a strategic reason to play them. Avoid situations where you're playing a favorite just to get points and then a 15-1 shot wins instead. Then you're pretty much out of a lot of tournaments. If you are going to play a favorite, you have to be really sure about it. I think playing horses at too short prices near the beginning of contests is a big mistake a lot of newer players make."

I agree fully with Moomey on this point. Favorites can be used, but they must be used judiciously. Any time I see that a significant portion of the people I'm playing against are picking the favorite in the first race of a contest, I know that I'm not competing against the strongest field.

Once you have an idea of what score you need and some clue as to what prices you're looking to play, what happens next? You have to tailor your play to the contest you're in. Some players can get pretty specific about this.

Michael Beychok: "You have to look at the races in the contest in total. Say it's a ten-race contest with all mandatory races. In three of the races, the 6-5 or 7-5 horse looks legit, and I don't like anybody else to beat it. Now I am looking at a seven-race card. How do I take these seven races and come up with a plan to get to $100? Can I take those favorites and make it with one other horse? Or am I going to need more?"

Matt Bernier: "Going into a tournament, I have a target score in mind. Take the Saratoga contest. I went in there thinking it might take $1,300 to win over the two days. So then I want to figure out how I can get there. I'm looking at hitting three of my plays in the range of the cap as a realistic number, and hopefully I'll hit one of my $40 bets. So that will give me right around the amount I need to win [a $20 bet on a 15-1 in the NYRA contest yields $320; a $40 bet yields $640]. We look at the trainers' percentages and the jockeys' percentages. I'm kind of looking at the same thing for us, where if I'm hitting three out of twenty races, or 15 percent, in the right price range, then I'm going to have a chance of getting where I need to be."

Duke Matties told me that for the Orleans contests, he looks over a number of races and looks for 8-1 to 20-1 shots he thinks can win. He went on to describe a specific game plan.

Duke Matties: "Hopefully I can pick out 12 horses on each of the three days, and I just hope I can hit five of the 36 for the weekend. Basically that's what it comes down to. If I get five, I'm going to cash, and if I get six or more, I've got a chance to win."

As you probably can figure out for yourself, even the best game plans require tweaking along the way. I asked our players for advice about how to do this.

John Conte: "Money management is very important in all contests. Of course, you have to pick the winners. But at the same time, you have to know what price horse you need when you're trying to pick a winner based on where you are."

Eric Moomey: "Always know where you are on the leaderboard and where you need to get to. You have to plan ahead. You don't want to get to the last race needing a 12-1 shot, only to find that the highest price on the board is 10-1. You should have known that before you got there. At the same time, if you know you really like a 10-1 shot running in the last race, you probably don't have to worry about being in first going into that race. Maybe being in the top five is all you need."

Brent Sumja: "You better be willing to adjust. Making adjustments as the day goes on is something that I never would have figured out when I was younger. After a few races, you have to be willing to change your mind. You can't be too determined. If the speed is rolling, you better take that into consideration. You can't be stubborn. I'm a Sheets player, but some days the bias is more important than the Sheets."

John Conte: "With horse racing, it's very hard to predict. One day it's speed that wins. The next day, maybe all the winners come from behind. Maybe one day it rains and you need to find a horse that loves the slop, or maybe you noticed a horse a while back that had a bad trip, and maybe today he'll have better racing luck. It's a case of there are a hundred ways to lose and only one way to win."

Paul Shurman: "You can't make an exact road map. What you do is you have horses you plan to bet, but then, as you go along, based on how you've done so far, you vary it. Maybe that 4-1 in the fifth race you liked on paper isn't a big enough price because you've missed your first few bets, so now you have to reach for a longer price."

Do things ever go exactly according to plan?

Paul Shurman: "Sometimes—not often—things can go exactly according to plan, at least for a while. When I was fifth in the NHC the year after winning the NHC Tour, I had all my horses I wanted to play picked out ahead of time. I was very well-prepared, and they all ran. Now, at the end of the tournament, the horse I liked wouldn't have gotten me the number I needed to win, so my plan changed and I landed elsewhere."

Some players play the same way no matter where they are, but I don't think that's the right way to play. I love hearing the players talk about these complicated strategic issues—and I also love the fact that they don't all agree and that one can even find contradictions within one player's quotes. Sometimes it's "stick to the plan," other times it's "you have to adjust." It just goes to show what a complicated, contradictory game handicapping contests can be—a topic we'll tackle further in our very next chapter.

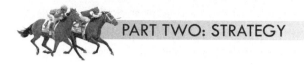

7 Picking Winners

"Do I contradict myself? Very well, then I contradict myself,
I am large, I contain multitudes."
– Walt Whitman

Mark McGuire: "This game is not about picking winners. This game is about making money, and a lot of people just can't get beyond that. People will brag about having five winners. I'll ask, 'How much money did you make?' 'Oh, I lost $20.' I hate to deflate your ego, but you don't know what you're doing."

In a way, contests change two things that are fundamental about playing the horses: the risk-reward structure and the fundamental meaning of what value is. The risk-reward structure gets turned on its head. Sometimes late in a contest, a 2-1 will pay like a 200-1, like the example Mike Labriola gives back in Chapter 6. Other times a 100-1 will pay more like a 10-1, as in the case of Frisk Me Now discussed on pg. 40. This is closely related to value. In everyday play, any overlay can be valuable at any time. A 3-1 that should be 2-1 could be your play of the day. In most contest situations, that horse is likely to be mildly helpful at best, useless at worst.

In a contest, even a 15-1 shot that should be 6-1 could still be an underlay. If you know that several other players in the contest are likely to play it, its contest value goes away even if its tote value is super strong. Value is still everything in contests; it just means something different. This is because instead of competing against all the people playing in the pari-mutuel pool, you're competing primarily against the other people in the contest and secondarily all the people in the pari-mutuel pool, since they're the ones setting the prices. The easiest way to combat this craziness is to become more selection-oriented, i.e., simply pick horses you like. Another way to look at it is that you should pick races you like—ones that should produce a price—and then find the value within those.

> **Kevin Cox:** "I try to figure out what races I want to play and then narrow ten-horse fields down to three or four, and then maybe I'll key in on one of those. And if it's a mandatory race and I have it down to six horses, and if I have multiple tickets, then I'll just play the horses with the longest odds. I don't have a style of con-test handicapping where I focus on picking one horse I like that's a standout winner to me. My style's not 'This horse can't lose'; it's 'Try to find the races where I like the fewest amount of horses' and go from there."

Earlier on, Paul Shurman referred to having certain picks going into the tournament. I figured that meant that his process was maybe more geared towards making selections and not so much towards finding value. He wised me up.

> **Paul Shurman:** "No, it's both. But it's absolutely value-oriented. My friends and I are very good at finding bad morning lines. I make my selections feeling that they will be value, 6-1, 15-1, 30-1. We go by feel. Sometimes we're wrong; then, if the price is too low, we just pass. If we all land on the same horses, then we know it's a bad morning line. You always want to pick out extra horses so you have other plays to make."

How does that work exactly?

> **Paul Shurman:** "In any race, I'll circle the horse I like and put lit-tle check marks next to ones I also like a little bit. I have my main horse and then the other possibilities. It's a selection-oriented approach that factors in value and helps you make allowances for where you are in the tournament."

Other players are even more selection-oriented.

Steve Wolfson, Sr.: "Steve Jr. is a great asset to me. He will ask how I am doing in the standings; I'll tell him I am doing well. Then he'll say I can get away with betting the 5-2 shot that is very strong because that's not how the other players bet. Strategically, Steve Jr. is very strong, whereas I just like to pick horses, pick winners. That's how I like to play: pick winners. And that's what it's about, picking winners."

Mike Labriola: "When I started betting, if I wasn't at the track, I was betting with the neighborhood bookie, and a lot of people bet in the neighborhood that I grew up in. It was almost a macho thing, more about picking horses than winning money. I think that's why I'm a better handicapper than I am a bettor. I'm cognizant of value. If you can figure out where a horse belongs in a race in terms of the odds, and you think you're going to be on the fifth choice in the race, and your horse ends up the favorite, then obviously you pass. That being said, I'm definitely more selection-oriented, and if I think I have a good chance, I'll play a horse even if the math doesn't necessarily add up."

I asked Shurman what happens if a horse he originally liked is actually a longer price than what he needs to make his target score later on in a tournament.

Paul Shurman: "It depends. For me to like a horse in the first place, that means I think it has a great chance to win. Most people get conservative if they have a big lead, but I'd prefer to play the horses I picked initially and try to put it away. But sometimes you get in a position where you don't have to play offensively, you have to play defensively, where you might have to play a 3-1 or 5-1 to block the people behind you. I like to play my own picks because there's a reason I liked them in the first place. God forbid I play the shorter price trying to block people behind me and my original long-priced pick comes in. Really what to do in that situation comes down to where you are, how many picks you have left, and what's happening behind you. But my default would be to play my original pick."

I also asked Ricky Zimmer about when he might make adjustments.

Ricky Zimmer: "I try to stay the course until very, very late in the day. I don't think you can start playing the board until you get really close to the end. If you're in front, the horses that can really hurt you are the longer-priced ones, so if those are the ones you have circled, keep going after those. And if it gets to the last race or two in a mythical, then you can start looking at the board or maybe trying to figure out what the people around you are doing and what play might make the most sense given the situation."

Mark McGuire: "The great thing in a contest is that when you're in the lead, you get to pick the horse you like. When you're not in the lead, you pretty much have to pick the horse that has a chance and is the best price. A lot of times guys are comfortable picking longshots until they get to the lead and then all of a sudden, where did the longshots go? They'll start chalking out. Sometimes it'll work for them."

I discussed this idea with Eric Moomey, and he was receptive to it.

Eric Moomey: "I know from my research that I can play favorites in every race in a fixed-bankroll contest and expect to lose about 15 percent of my remaining bankroll. At Keeneland recently, I had three entries and picked a different longshot on all three tickets very early on. I had a big lead. So had I taken one of my three tickets and just picked favorites in every race from there—I had $55 worth of bankroll left on each ticket—I would have made about $47 more or less. That would have got me to around $102, just over my goal of $100. Why didn't I bet logical favorites and then at the end, if I needed to, go for price horses again? That was a failure on my part. I was so far ahead of everyone else at the beginning that I should have played it differently. You have to know how to adjust. And most people are creatures of habit and don't know how to adjust. That can become your advantage."

Where does Moomey get his data from?

Eric Moomey: "I have my own database where I've collected data over time and found trends and analysis. I can't always tell you in which race a 20-1 shot is going to win, but I can tell you that from my research, I have a pretty good idea of what a 20-1 winner looks like, which types of races to focus on. If a 20-1 shot wins, I have a good chance of having it. Say there are five 20-1 shots in a race. I have a knack of identifying which one has the best chance. What I've found is patterns, things that are repetitive: certain conditions where the 20-1 has a 5 percent chance instead of a 1 percent chance. It doesn't always work, of course. Sometimes the 20-1 with a 1 percent chance still wins. And it's not like a 5 percent chance of winning even with the better 20-1 shot is all that great, but over the course of a day in a ten-race sequence, your chances add up.

"In a large field, over ten races, I tested this in more than 200 online contests, and a cap horse hit 42 percent of the time in at least one race. If you don't know how to pick a 20-1 horse 42 percent of the time, you can't win. I also did an experiment where I selected the favorite every single race. In more than 200 contests using that strategy, how many times do you think you'd finish first? Not even once, zero. How many times did the pick-all-favorites plan finish in the top ten? Once in 200 tries—whereas there are other strategies that can finish first 5 percent of the time or in the top ten percent far more than ten percent of the time."

THE IMPORTANCE OF STAYING THE COURSE

So what if you're not one of the players who has a longshot early on in the contest? Is all hope lost?

Dave Gutfreund: "In general terms, the later part of the tournament comes up much later than most people think. You'll see at a tournament like the Orleans, after somebody puts a monster score on day one of a three-day contest, people's jaws will drop and they'll think they have to change what they went there to do. There's no reason to change your strategy 33 percent of the way through a tournament no matter what the leader has."

Ken Massa: "If I'm not doing well, it doesn't really bother me very much; I try to keep to the same plan anyway, kind of like a baseball manager reminding his team that you've got to play nine innings. You have to keep swinging the bat and get something started."

Paul Shurman: "A lot of people tend to panic if a big-priced horse comes in. But if you just stay the course and go with your original plan—which you can do if you're well-prepared and you know what's coming up and you have options down the road—then what's happened so far in the tournament doesn't matter. You've got to have a plan going in. I'll have looked at every race in the tournament and know what's coming up at the beginning, middle, and end."

Michael Beychok: "The first half of a contest you can pick and pray. You don't need to focus on the scoreboard after race four in a ten-race contest. Some people do. When a bomber comes in, you can feel that people are freaking out. There are people who feel that if they don't hit a cap horse by their third pick, they can't win. But that's not the goal. The goal is to get to your target score. Just trying to beat the guy who is ahead right now isn't a plan; it's a recipe for disaster."

John Conte: "A lot of people get very excited early on, on the first day when somebody suddenly hits a limit horse. Maybe a guy who hasn't had a winner yet will start to panic. Instead of pecking away and getting a couple of logical $10 horses, he starts chasing. That's the wrong idea. Those $10 horses you hit on the first day might make you the winner if you have a good day on the second day. Don't start to take stabs.

"A contest handicapper sits there all day and prays for favorites until he can hit that one bomb he's looking for. Because when you hit the bomb, it's like being in a fight and hitting a guy with a right cross that takes the heart out of him. I don't let it bother me, but it does bother most handicappers. The guy next to you will look worried and say, 'The guy over there just had that limit horse.'

"But if you know what the score is going to be in the end, plus or minus $20, you don't panic; you don't let it bother you. Nine times out of ten, that guy who hit the limit horse is going to come back to the pack and the winner will finish with the amount I've predicted he will. It's amazing. To get there, you'll need a capper each day or something close to a capper, or maybe an abundance of middle prices. But you can't just start firing at everything. Chances in a contest are known as bullets. You have 30 bullets in your holster. You don't want to waste those bullets. You have to make every one count.

"And that's why a contest handicapper is happy when a favorite wins a race he didn't play, because somebody else just lost a bullet trying to hit a price horse. And if your opponent hits some 8-5 shot, who cares?"

Tournament player Peter Rotondo, Jr., jokes that when he's watching a race and he knows his horse isn't going to win, he gets in his "bomb shelter"—that is, he just prays for one of the favorites to win and roots like crazy against the longshots. I asked John Conte to spell out why the chalk winning is no big deal.

John Conte: "You'd have to hit ten of them each day to win the contest, and nobody picks ten winners in a day. So once again, don't panic when someone hits a big price; stay even-keeled and stick to your game plan, especially on the first day. I'm telling you all these tricks; you'll come back and beat me now."

Other players do tend to get off the bridle a little bit if they sense other people are hitting price horses.

Cara Yarusso: "A mistake that I still make is to 'chase the leaderboard.' If some prices run early in a contest, it's easy to quickly shift your approach to playing longshots to catch up. However, when there are still a lot of races left, it's best to stay the course and crank out your winners, even if they seem too low given where the top people stand. Ultimately, the required point total at the end of the contest remains fairly predictable. It shifts up a little and it shifts down a little based on the number of longshots or chalk. However, the goal remains roughly the same. It's best to stay the course and continue to claw your way up rather than bomb out and end up with zero.

"Tom Noone, one of the best tournament players I know (and without a doubt the best friend I've made through tournaments), was given the nickname 'The Pitbull' by Tom Quigley because of his ability to continue to fight on no matter where he is in the standings. Many times I've watched him claw his way up from the bottom to pass the early leaders because of his determination to stay the course with picking who he thinks will win. You can never count him out in a tournament."

DIFFERENT PRICES FAVOR DIFFERENT PLAYERS

Brent Sumja: "If the bombs come early on, I'm pretty much in trouble. I'll spend hours handicapping for a 12-race tournament, and if after two races the leader has $78, well, those next ten races that I spent hours on, I can't use most of the horses I've come up with. A 5-1? No good. A 3-1? Forget it. I know the races at least, but now the strategy is completely different. If the bombs don't come in and I can get by picking more in the 5-1 to 10-1 range, I'm going to be really tough in those contests. What I have to learn is how to prepare and play the one in three times when the winning score is going to be a lot higher than usual. I usually stick with my style and change on the fly when the bombs come."

Brian Troop: "If the favorites are winning all day, I'm in trouble. I played 30 horses when I won the NHC and only a few of them were less than 10-1. I'm basically looking for horses between 7-1 and 15-1. If horses are coming in between 7-1 and 15-1, there's a good chance I might have them. I'm not apt to have a lot of cap horses, and I didn't have any when I won the NHC. In my daily play, too, I'm looking for horses between 7-1 and 15-1."

You definitely don't want to give up on your strategy too early.

Eric Moomey: "I have finished first being in 38th place with only one race to go. That means 37 other people could have won but didn't; I have also finished second from 108th place with two races to go. You're never really out of it."

Here's a final real-world example of the importance of staying the course.

Ken Massa: "You can come from behind; you can win at any time. Most experienced tournament players understand that you tend to win in clusters anyway. When I finished second in the NHC, I was in 157th place with two hours to go in the whole tournament!"

8 Game Selection

"You can only fall in love six times in your life. Choose wisely."
– Douglas Coupland

Picture this: It is the middle of the poker boom. A freelance writer/ horseplayer experiences success playing online poker. He then goes to Atlantic City, racks up a few hundred bucks each time playing low stakes, hardly even putting in any effort, just not playing like a total idiot. His time spent playing horses decreases in favor of more poker. He plays in a home game where there are a couple of sharpies he avoids tangling with and a few bad players he exploits. He begins to think he is good at poker.

Fast forward three years. The online game in the USA is on its last legs. The poker space in Atlantic City has contracted. Now when he goes there, the other people at the tables seem to know what they're doing. He still makes a couple of bucks, but it is work. He wishes he'd flown out to see Lava Man in the Big `Cap instead.

Around that same time, he plays in that home game again. The same sharpies are there, plus a few new ones he doesn't know. The dead money is gone. I realized I was nothing special at poker and ran to the nearest newsstand to buy a *Racing Form*.

In the example above, it quickly became obvious to me that game selection was the key to my success—I had no special aptitude for poker. There is a similar example about how my luck with women improved markedly when I became one of the few straight men in publishing in the mid-'90s, but I'll save that one for the memoir. Horse-racing contests are a great example of game selection as well. These days, you aren't likely to find a field full of dopes to play against you in a handicapping contest. But there was a funny story that came up along these lines when I was doing the research for this book.

Maury Wolff ran second in the very first NHC in 2000. I had heard a rumor that a few of his friends on the contest scene had given him a hard time about the way he'd qualified, in a small tournament at the Bettor Racing OTB in Sioux Falls, South Dakota. The gist was that it maybe wasn't the toughest field that Wolff beat to qualify for his first NHC seat.

Maury Wolff: "People gave me a really hard time about that."

So what are we talking about here? The guy to your right was dozing off and the woman on your left was wearing a tin-foil hat?

Maury Wolff: "There were some formidable competitors there. Several of the players had *Racing Forms*."

Wolff has since proved many times over that his second-place finish in the NHC wasn't a fluke, but his qualifying experience underscores the point that good game selection is half the battle. In this day and age, you can certainly try to find a weaker field maybe by searching for the right type of online contest, or perhaps travelling far afield, but I wouldn't count on this strategy working necessarily. When I used to play in the Santa Anita low-roller contest, I was still butting heads with the likes of excellent contest players Dennis Decauwer and Tom Quigley every week—the farthest thing from easy pickings.

These days, the real utility of game selection is just to put yourself in the best possible position to win. This can be a very simple equation. If you're looking for an NHC seat, how many seats are being given away divided by how many people are playing in the contest? To oversimplify for the purposes of this example, you're obviously a lot better off playing for one seat in a field of ten than for three seats in a field of 500. The same logic holds true with tournaments with cash prizes. As we discussed back on page 43, with a little math and a knowledge of the structure of the tournament, you can choose to play the ones that offer that best chance of cashing with the least takeout.

Ricky Zimmer: "I look for contests with good value, and it's pretty obvious which ones those are: ones that pay out as much money as gets put in. I'm not looking to get on a plane to go to a contest that has takeout, because you're just going to bleed yourself dry so quickly. When I was playing online, it was the same thing. I tried not to play contests that were qualifiers for qualifiers. I tried to look for something that paid out at the end of the day right there. That's where I've evolved over time."

The financial structure of the tournament doesn't have to be the be-all, end-all, however. There are other factors to consider.

Mike Labriola: "There are people who won't play tournaments if there's a rake. They say, 'If someone is taking out 30 percent, I won't play.' But to me, if I've had success at a certain place, I'll play there because in a certain sense, if you're making money, then the takeout becomes irrelevant. Who wants to play in a place where there's no rake but they never win? Handicappers can be horses for courses, and I think tournament players can be horses for courses."

Mike Maloney: "For me to do my best, I need to see the horses on the track before I make my play. And it's almost impossible for me in some contest formats to see that happen, process the information, get to the window, make every bet that I want to make to cover my opinion in that race, and not risk getting shut out in the contest. That's the cardinal rule in a lot of contests: you can get disqualified if you don't make all the required bets."

Field size is another variable. There are online contests where you can play against one other person or against hundreds of other people. In smaller fields, you'll typically be playing for less money, and, generally speaking, fewer of your opponents might have the longest of longshots. Against a larger field, the prize might be greater, but you can bet that every horse under 50-1 will be covered by somebody. Which one is better? Neither. It all depends on what you are looking for.

Another part of game selection has to do with knowing your own strengths and weaknesses as a player and putting yourself in the contests where those are best rewarded. For example, are you a mad bomber who is particularly good at coming up with crazy longshots? Seek out contests with a high cap or even no cap. Are you more of a sweet spot player who will even—gasp!—mix in the occasional 3-1 shot? Well, the NYRA contest with its 15-1 cap might be a better place for you. Does part of your edge come from quickly identifying races that are likely to produce longshots? Look for a tournament with lots of tracks. Would you prefer to just focus intensely on handicapping just one track? There are plenty of tournaments where that's an option. Are you a vertical exotics player who is comfortable treating a few dimes like funny money? You need to get involved in live-bankroll tournaments ASAP. It all depends on what suits your needs.

Our players fall into several different camps on this topic.

Mark McGuire: "My favorite contest format is the old reliable mythical win/place mandatory races. Because it takes me so long to handicap a race, when you put seven tracks out there, there are so many races that I just don't have the time to get them all done. I'm at a big disadvantage. In that situation, I've got to cut it down to three tracks and just play my favorite types of races and pray that it's not longshot bonanza day at one of the tracks I'm not playing."

Cara Yarusso: "My favorite format is with all-mandatory races in a standard win/place format. These test your ability to truly handicap—to find both the long- and the short-priced horses on the card. They test your consistency as well as your ability to find higher priced horses."

Garett Skiba: "If I had more time, I would prefer the additional choices in a contest with a lot of optional races, but as primarily a weekend warrior, the issue for me is time. Looking at five potential tracks and nine to ten races at each track takes a lot of time and effort. You end up having to handicap both the horses and the races. Therefore, for me, I prefer contests with all mandatories. But I see the case for optional races. In terms of identifying handicapping ability, the increased choices do tend to mitigate the luck that will always be a factor in handicapping contests and the sport in general."

Judy Wagner: "A lot of longtime horseplayers love their exotics; they love the 'all' button. I felt I had an advantage in the early days of tournaments because I wasn't into all that and was more interested in just finding the best value horse to bet win and place."

Mike Labriola: "I like any format where you don't have to use real money. It comes down to the idea that I think I'm a better handicapper than I am a bettor. I have won real-money contests and have gotten better at them, but I like putting up the cash and having it just become mythical.

"I've done very well at the Wynn tournament. I think John Avello, who runs the Wynn tournament, is one of the more player-friendly race-book managers out there. I like how big the Wynn daily prizes are. I like the fact that only Wynn and NYRA have the double-bet rule where you can double-up on your play of the day. That's a very good rule because you should get rewarded if your best bet wins."

Noel Michaels: "From playing over the years, I have an idea of the kind of format I do the best in. Anyone can do well in any given format on any given day. But I know I shouldn't enter as many real-money tournaments because there are other people who are better than me at those. Some people excel at tournaments like the Orleans, which offer seven or eight different racetracks. They excel there because they're good at finding the right races to play when there are so many different choices—that's a skill in itself. Me, I don't like to handicap seven tracks in one day, so I don't play a lot of those types of contests. I focus in on brick-and-mortar contests with optional races, mythical money, limited tracks. That's where I've had the most success because that's what I'm good at, like the NYRA contests."

Others are looking for more choices.

Duke Matties: "For me, the Orleans contests are my favorites. I like them because I get to meet up with family and we can sit there from 9 to 5 betting horses, betting horses for the contest and betting horses with our real money. But I also love it because there are so many tracks, and I can pick my own races. There are no mandatories. And I'd rather pick my own races than have somebody else pick them for me."

I told Duke Matties that, like Noel Michaels, I found that format a little intimidating, having so many races to choose from. How does he choose what races to play?

Duke Matties: "In my regular handicapping, I'll probably look at anywhere from 40 to 60 races a day, and I'll bet like ten of them. I'm looking for races where a decent-priced horse looks good to me, anywhere from 4-1 and up. And I look to key that horse in my own betting, or I might just make a big win bet on him. But on a contest day, what I do is look for horses between 8-1 and 20-1 that I think have a chance to win, and that's basically my strategy."

Different types of contests attract different types of players.

Eric Moomey: "Brick-and-mortar contests have locals and they have outsiders, the people who go to all of them. When there's a contest at, say, Monmouth Park, and you have to make all your bets on some specified number of races at Monmouth, I have found it extremely hard to win that contest because there are experts at the track who have knowledge that is far superior to any knowledge that I have. But what if it's four tracks around the country and they pick the tracks and the races for you? Well, now I'm at an advantage because the local experts' advantage goes away.

"The same logic applies if there's a lot of choice in the contest. Maybe a guy is an expert at turf races or maiden races. He's going to do better than me in those races. But if the races are being picked by someone else, those might not be the races he's familiar with. So once again, the specialist's advantage goes away."

As Moomey pointed out above, the specific racetracks being featured can be an important part of game selection. Mike Maloney, for example, is synonymous with horseplaying in Kentucky.

Mike Maloney: "I played in the Del Mar live-bankroll tournament for a few years and it wasn't that I did poorly, it was just that those guys who play in that are so good, and they play Southern Cal so well, that they were just better than I was. I was having fun being in Del Mar on vacation, but I was probably fooling myself to think that contest was some great opportunity for me.

"I feel like the Keeneland live-bankroll contest is my best opportunity. If I can't do well in that, then it's my own fault. I know the track and I consistently do well at Keeneland. And I've done well in that contest. I have a great chance to qualify for the NHC there, and if I can't, well, then I'll wait 'til next year."

Another factor is what specific types of races you like to play. Spring-summer contests are likely to have a lot of races where you'll see horses doing things for the first time. If you're into pedigree, you should be right at home.

Judy Wagner: "I thrive playing in contests in the summertime: big fields, lots of turf races, first-time starters, or second-time starters that had trouble first out. When mythical win/place tournaments pop up in July and August, that's my strength."

In the fall, if you love the Breeders' Cup, you'll have several options to play in a contest focusing on just those races. A mid-winter contest is likely to be of interest to a player who has an edge in races where the horses have run against each other a few times. And here's a new wrinkle I learned from former NHC champ Michael Beychok:

Michael Beychok: "There is a period of time between November and January when I do the best every year."

Why is that?

Michael Beychok: "I work in politics, so for me the start of November is like Tax Day for an accountant. Leading up to that, you cram in everything you can from the previous two or three months, working 18-hour days. But once that's done, you're relieved; you have money in the bank, and that frees your mind and you have no worries. You feel stoked. I'm thinking, 'I'm pumped up; I made some money; let's tackle something else. Let's win some races.'"

Beychok will look to play in as many contests as he can during that time frame because that's when he does his best work. And that's what this chapter was really all about—knowing your own strengths and weaknesses and putting yourself in the best situation to succeed. So remember, you might not be as good—or as bad—as you think. A lot of what happens in life comes down to a simple matter of game selection.

9 **Playing Online**

> *"Gambling is the future on the Internet.*
> *You can only look at so many dirty pictures."*
> **– Bookmaker Simon Noble**

Michael Beychok: "Experience matters. The more you play and get yourself familiar with all the various situations that come up during a tournament, the better off you will be."

One major aspect of good game selection is knowing where to play: on-site or online or both? For me, and others, the chief benefit of online games is that they allow you to gain a wealth of experience in a condensed amount of time.

Noel Michaels: "In poker, you have all these young guys who come into these tournaments and they're able to outplay guys who've been doing it their entire lives. Why is the new generation better? They're better because they're going online and playing as many hands of poker in two years as the older guy played in 20 years. You can play an obscene number of hands online, and you can learn all about the mathematics behind the game. For people who are getting into horse tournaments, the same logic applies.

"The best way for new players to catch up real fast to the people who've been doing this a long time is to play an obscene number of online contests. And it's great now because if that's what you're into, you can find three low-money buy-in tournaments a day. Play as many as you can and you're going to get indoctrinated very quickly. You can still walk into a brick-and-mortar contest, and it's the first time you've ever played, and win. It's been proven time and time again that the novice can have success. But playing online is the best way not only to learn but also to catch up on experience."

Joe Scanio wasn't talking specifically about online tournaments in the following quote, but the message still applies.

Joe Scanio: "The more you do play, the better you'll be. If you think you're going to come in here, because you think you're a good handicapper, and you're going to kick ass, you're in for a rude awakening. You've got a number of stages to get through in this game. In this type of competition, your handicapping is just one aspect of it, and unless you play often, you're never going to get good; you're never going to get qualified."

What makes online play different fundamentally?

Noel Michaels: "The switch to having more contests online definitely changes your preparation because in most of the contests you'll see online, you've got to play the same 10 or 12 races as everybody else. They are narrowing the focus for you. Usually in an on-track contest, you find the horses or the races that you like throughout the card, and those are what you focus your play on. It's a completely different approach. In online you have to play a lot of horses and/or races that you don't necessarily like because you have to make the best of it. But to be fair, that's what everyone has to do, so it's still a level playing field."

There are exceptions to this, like the *DRF* Bets online contests, but the point is well taken. Even if you're experienced in online play, there may be a learning curve. But even if not, the live experience is one worth having.

Cara Yarusso: "For people who are new to tournaments or who have only tried online tournaments, I encourage them to get out and experience at least one live event. Perhaps pick one of the big tournaments in Vegas—like at the Orleans or something. You'll see a room full of strangers when you walk in, but strike up a small conversation at your table. You'll make some new friends who love the same thing as you. With time, you'll meet their friends and you'll meet new friends at new tournaments. Along the way, you'll find that you're meeting some of the most amazing people. Almost everyone is really friendly, and at the heart of it, we all love racing. And this is what makes tournament play so incredibly amazing."

Brent Sumja: "Brick-and-mortars are a little more fun than online because of the social aspect: you're there in person interacting with this great group of people. In terms of strategy and the actual handicapping, I see no difference at all between onlines and live. The onlines can be fun as well because it's so easy to play from your house."

Others—and I must count myself among this group—agree with this last point the most: there's no place like home.

Michael Beychok: "When you are online, you are in your total comfort zone. The first time I went to Vegas, I didn't even bring my computer and that was one of the biggest mistakes. From there on, I began to create the environment I'm comfortable in. Once you take someone out of their comfort zone, whether it's tracks they never bet, online, sports book, live tournaments, they are a duck out of water."

Another interesting difference in an online tournament is you're allowed the flexibility of more easily changing your bet as post time nears.

Steve Wolfson, Sr.: "One thing I do when playing online is I look around a little bit more and make last-minute changes that I wouldn't ordinarily do at a brick-and-mortar. It's a lot easier to push a button than it is to walk to a window, wait in line, going through the rigmarole of trying to change a bet."

Steve Wolfson, Jr.: "Online you have a better sense of where things are in the standings. You have much less excuse, unless there is a bad Internet connection, for getting shut out. Online you are able to gather information up until the last second, which is a big advantage."

To me, big believer in Murphy's Law that I am, this changing picks sounded like it could be a tricky business.

Steve Wolfson, Sr.: "I don't like to go through ad-libbing. I like to make up my mind, have an opinion, and go with it. Steve Jr., is famous for making a change and being right, whereas whenever I make a late change, I end up kicking myself."

Many online contests allow you to see your opponents' picks. This can be a powerful learning tool for new players.

Eric Moomey: "The first thing I wanted to do when I started playing in tournaments was to understand my competition, because what I've noticed is that there are a handful of people who go to the top most every time. And you can identify who they are just by looking at various leaderboards.

"The beauty of online tournaments is that in a lot of cases, you can see what selections the other players are making. That's very different than at the track, where you have no idea if the guy next to you is winning or losing. There is just not a lot of information available about everybody else at live tournaments. But with online tournaments, all the information is available at your fingertips. You can see what people play and how they did, this week, last week, whenever. So for a player starting out, the first thing I would encourage them to do is identify who some of the top players are and then look to see what they do. And that will give you a starting point. What kinds of horses are they picking? Are there any patterns?"

How exactly did Moomey go about doing this?

Eric Moomey: "I studied the moves of the best, most consistent players. How did I do that? First, I identified them on an annual leaderboard. I charted five people for maybe 100 of their last contests.

What did they do early in contests? Were they playing favorites or longshots? If they were playing multiple entries, were they playing the same horses on each ticket or different horses? And when I did that analysis, I found that there was a lot of commonality between those top players, and there are people I play against who I can tell you with a greater than 50 percent chance of success what their next selection will be.

"That's a good way to start learning, but you can't just mimic what they do because you'd just end up being an inferior version of them. They're going to beat you one-on-one near the end. So after you spend some time learning about your competition, the second thing you have to do is learn to be different."

We talked earlier about being different in Chapter 5, but you can't be different if you don't know what to expect from your opponents. Michael Beychok is another player who learned a lot by looking at other players' selections.

Michael Beychok: "When the online contests started coming in, I was pretty pathetic. So I started analyzing how the winners did it. I realized they didn't win all the races; they had two, maybe three winners. I reassessed my approach."

Many online tournaments are qualifiers, and while they provide a great opportunity to gain entry into major opportunities like the NHC and the Breeders' Cup Betting Challenge, they don't offer any cash prize money. Another possible drawback of online play is that there are so many different online tournaments available that fatigue and/or distraction can set in.

Ricky Zimmer: "The first two years of the NHC Tour, I was up near the top both years. By the end of the year, every week I was traveling to different places to play, playing online multiple times; I was just really worn out by the end of that second year. And I don't even know so much that I prefer brick-and-mortar contests, but I just want to limit the number of contests that I play in. Now I've pretty much given up playing online altogether, and I just use the brick-and-mortar events sort of as a way to set my schedule. I try to pick my spots a little better, rather than trying to play everything."

I believe it's best to create a contest schedule for yourself with a mix of onlines and in-person contests, where you keep your commitments manageable. Both onlines and brick-and-mortar contests have something valuable and different to offer. Before we move on here, I want to mention that there's a new trend among tournament players borrowed from the world of poker: multi-tabling. It's not for me, but it's a concept that belongs in the book.

Dennis Decauwer: "Some of these players today are much more talented than I am in that they can split their focus into three different directions. I love to just focus on one tournament when I'm playing, but I know some players who were playing multiple entries in the tournaments I was playing, and they were playing one or two other tournaments at the same time online, with multiple entries in those. Brent Sumja is amazing in this regard."

Brent Sumja: "I am the most impatient person in the world. However, when I trained horses, I had the most patience a person could have for the animal. I think in doing that, I lost patience for the rest of my life. Back in the early 2000s, before the Internet gambling ban, I wagered a lot on baseball. I have a room in my house with nine televisions in it, and I had multiple games on every night and I was playing all of them. After you've been doing that every night of baseball season for a few years, watching just one game is like watching paint dry. It's like going back into coach after flying first class. I feel the same way about tournaments: I don't want to play just one. I don't have the patience for it."

Is there any edge in it?

Brent Sumja: "What I think it enables me to do is make better decisions in the moment because I don't have any down time. When I am down to one tournament and there are 30 minutes in between races, it drives me crazy. I'll try to do things around the house; I'll take my bike out in the driveway; I'll do whatever I can to only give myself eight minutes to look at the race. I don't want to look at it for 30 minutes—because you know what happens when you look at it for 30 minutes, you'll change your mind seven times.

I prefer to not give myself the opportunity to do that. I'm just going through and going with what comes in my head, and sometimes it's real good and sometimes it's real bad."

Eric Moomey: "I'm still trying to figure out if playing more than one contest at once is profitable for me. There are two ways of doing it. One is to play the same horses in all contests and the other is to hedge by playing different horses in the different tournaments. I don't mind doing it when I'm playing in three contests that all require different strategies. Maybe in one contest you have to finish first out of 70; another contest where you have to finish in the top 10 out of 100; and the other is a head-to-head. There, it's easy. I'll look for a longshot for the first contest; a mid-price for the second; and a favorite for the head-to-head and I might win two out of three."

It occurred to me that multi-tabling makes sense on another level as well. If you've done the work on a series of races, why not play them in more than one tournament? Because at least as the handicapping is concerned, there's no extra heavy-lifting; it's already done. With this concept in mind, some online contests will even deliberately offer contests on the same set of races as other sites in an effort to get players to participate in both.

A FEW OTHER BITS OF ADVICE

When playing online, it's always a good idea to put in default picks at the start of a contest. There is no reason to feel beholden to these picks as the contest goes on, and they are easily changed. The idea is to have something in there just in case life gets crazy or race post times encroach upon one another. During the early days of writing this book, I had one instance where the baby was crying and I thought I had put in my bet in a head-to-head at Belmont on a Christophe Clement first-time starter. Turns out I never put in the play. But my opponent sure did. Another time I was so busy crowing in a chat about a nice hit at Saratoga that I didn't realize the next race at Del Mar had already closed. I didn't even get the post-time favorite because I hadn't put in a default pick, and at most sites, it's no pick, no play.

You also never want to get shut out. Some contest sites, like Derby Wars, freeze picks with approximately one minute to post—so make sure you get your bets in on time or at least have your default picks selected in case you lose track of time.

Some sites also offer you the chance to put in alternate picks in case of scratches—and it's a very good idea to take them up on this. Why do you want to get stuck with a post-time favorite when you can at least try to make sure you get in on a horse you like? Also, as the day goes on and you have more of a sense of what price you need for your goal, you can change your alternates accordingly as well as your main selections. If you're in a position where you need a longshot, make sure your backup is a longshot too. If you're just jockeying for position late, maybe your alternate can be on the shorter side. It doesn't come up often, but the extra edge you can gain by being mentally prepared for these unlikely scenarios might pay big dividends down the line.

One thing I can't help you with, however, is those frustrating days when your main selections go down the tubes and four of your alternates win. You'll want to be mentally prepared for those as well—but, hey, that's why there is a tote, so you can always bet cash on those alternate selections.

10 Optional Races and Mandatory Races

"You'll always miss 100 percent of the shots you don't take."
— **Wayne Gretzky**

When it comes to winning one of the big Vegas tournaments, there is no more important skill than being able to choose the right races to play—it's absolutely as vital as picking winners and understanding value. This may come as a shock to many online players because in that world the races are almost always picked out for you, but it's a shock online players must get over if they want to win the biggest prizes.

There have been several references from our players in the book about choosing optional races. Now that we've established many of the key ideas about handicapping contest strategy, I want to go a little deeper on this issue. One of the big questions I asked everyone I interviewed was: how do you pick what races you want to play?

Dave Gutfreund: "Once I have my strategy established, the next thing I'm trying to do is figure out which races in the tournament I am not going to be interested in so I can cut down on my work and focus on what I need to be focusing on. If it's a tournament where you're going to need mostly big prices, you can cut out short fields almost immediately. There are certain types of tournaments where you can bet in short fields, but normally win, place, and show bets in short fields are horrible tournament bets in the long term."

Paul Shurman: "In a tournament like the NHC, where there are 60 races a day to look at, you can probably take an initial glance at the races and eliminate ten of them. I'm talking about short fields or legitimate 1-5 shots or two short-priced horses you don't think can lose. That will help you time-wise. But you pretty much have to look at everything."

Ricky Zimmer: "In a tournament with a lot of tracks and optional races, I'll usually just focus on three or four tracks. I know that puts me at a disadvantage because the prices on that day could be coming from one of the tracks I've left out, but I just can't wrap my head around that many races in one night, especially in a multi-day tournament. I'll go there prepared for the first day, maybe part of the second—you know you have to go back after a long day and have to handicap again that night for the next day; it gets to be a little too much."

Steve Wolfson, Sr.: "You want to get a sense of the races generally enough to know what you like. Can you beat the favorite? In the summer with bigger fields, young horses, unproven form, there are good opportunities for double-digit odds. I'll spend a lot of time looking around for those."

Paul Shurman: "Some guys are turf specialists and they'll just pick out all of the turf races. Breeding experts will pick all the maiden races and focus on those. Some people will do it that way."

For John Conte and others, the grass is greener.

John Conte: "For the non-mandatory races, you look to pick something that you specialize in. I'm known for being a grass handicapper, so I'll reach for those. Grass races have big fields, and bigger fields usually mean bigger prices. And, like a doctor who is a shoulder specialist, I'm not a general practitioner; I'm a grass specialist."

Steve Wolfson, Jr.: "Handicapping turf races is more consistent and there are closer finishes; it's a really good combination for a lot of players. A lot of tournament players appreciate turf races. Absent any breeding information, there are other factors that lead to value. Then you add breeding, and you can make a better case for a good-priced horse; turf is where it's at."

Another fertile ground for optional races are maidens.

Eric Moomey: "I like first-time starters because they tend to be overlooked at the windows and offer great value. Also, since most people don't really have a clue what their true chances are, they feel uncomfortable and just won't play them in the contest. Of the horses that have run, you know who the most likely winner is most of the time. You don't really know about the firsters. They might have the best chance to be the logical winner, but we don't know that going in."

Cara Yarusso: "My edge tends to come from my ability to pick maiden races. These races often produce nice payouts, which is great in a tournament. When a tournament allows for optional plays, I'll concentrate more on the maiden races. Unless I think the favorites look strong, I'll typically jump in with one of my hopeful longshots. I think the key is knowing what type of race you are best at—turf races, maiden races, etc.—then leveraging this to narrow the field of races when faced with 80+ optional races in some formats."

Like so many other elements of the contest world, it all comes down to the ability to handicap yourself and do what works for you.

Dennis Decauwer: "I've spent a lot of time analyzing my statistics and looking at how I do overall, understanding what types of races I'm best at and what types of races I think I'm weakest at. And if I get an opportunity, whether it's just gambling on a given day or playing in a contest, I certainly want to look to my strengths first."

And what are those?

Dennis Decauwer: "I know that my best races are sprints, whether on the main track or on turf, and then my next best races are other turf races. My least favorite races, by far, are distance races on the main track. I believe that distance races on the main track yield the highest percentage of favorites. I believe that on the dirt track in a distance race, trouble is going to mean less than on any other surface—the longer distance gives the best horse a chance to overcome trouble. Therefore, if you assume the best horse is usually one of the betting favorites—not always but usually—then I'm going to choose those races last as my favorites to play."

How about the logistics of exactly how to choose the specific horses you want to play?

Brian Troop: "Let's say there's a tournament with six tracks where you have to play ten optional races. I go through the *Form*, and I'll probably make marks next to somewhere between 15 and 30 horses. I'm looking for horses that will be in my range of odds I want to play, and if they're not in my range, I'll forget about them. If they are, I'll play them."

Troop also looks for overlays on the morning line to identify possible plays.

Brian Troop: "The first thing I do, when the opening odds come out before a race, I write them down and compare them to what the morning line is to see if there's anything that's out of whack. Then I go through the horses I have marks next to and go from there. I find that you have to do that because sometimes, even at a track that you're not paying much attention to, you'll find something. You might see a horse that is 20-1 on the morning line and he opens at 9-5."

I asked him for a practical example of how this can help.

Brian Troop: "One day I was writing down the odds at Louisiana Downs, and a horse I'd marked down as a speed horse was 20-1, and he opened at 9-5. He kept taking money, then he gradually drifted up to 10-1. I played him and he did as advertised. He went to the front and never looked back."

SHORT FIELD, LONG PRICE

As you've read in this section, conventional contest wisdom says that you want to choose races with big fields, and this makes sense—in aggregate, large fields produce more market inefficiencies and therefore longer prices. Plus, if you're making win/place bets, you're going to obviously get much better place payoffs in a large field. However, there is a contrarian line of thought. I remember the first time I heard it, succinctly described by a gloating Jeff Sotman after he tabbed a 12-1 shot in a six-horse field on a Friday at Santa Anita circa 2008: "Short field, long price!" Mark McGuire expands on the power of Sotman's maxim.

Mark McGuire: "There are a lot of theories about which races to choose. A lot of people like maiden races, but those aren't a strength of mine. If I'm playing a race with first-time starters in a contest, I might as well be rolling dice and praying. Everybody likes to play turf races and full fields in general. But I've started to branch off a little bit. Another strategy is to focus on completely different races to try to play horses that other people aren't going to be playing. So I've started looking for big longshots in short fields on some tickets—especially if I'm playing with a partner or have multiple entries—just to try to pick up horses that nobody else has."

BEATING FAVORITES

Another common, effective method for choosing an optional race is to find vulnerable favorites. The number one thing a player can do to tilt the odds in his or her favor is to find a weak favorite to play against. The idea is simple: favorites win 33 percent of the time, which means that they lose 67 percent of the time. Contests are typically won by playing longshots or stringing together mid-priced winners, so you want to be playing as much as possible in the 67 percent of races where the chalk isn't going to win.

Ricky Zimmer: "I'll look at whether I think the favorite—or maybe the first two or three favorites in that race—is vulnerable or not. If I feel like the top few choices are vulnerable, then that's a race that I want to pay close attention to during a contest. That's the main thing for me: to decide whether a race is going to be playable for contest purposes."

Brian Troop: "I'm looking for mistakes. It's a lot like the stock market. In the stock market, you're looking for a mispriced asset. In horse racing, you're looking for a mispriced horse, and it happens every day. You know as well as I do that people over-bet the favorites."

Roger Cettina: "My first instinct in every race I look at is, 'How do I beat this favorite?' I don't want to like him. Give me any reason to throw him out: horses coming off perfect trips; horses that have gotten easy leads; horses beating weak fields are just some examples."

Maury Wolff: "Look for races where there are odds-on horses that you can make good cases against. What does that look like? How about this for an easy one: a horse just won for $10K, and now he's in for $7,500. Yes, a lot of times those horses are stealing, but a lot of times they didn't come back too well. These are the kinds of races I would gravitate to in a contest."

Dave Gutfreund: "You're looking for horses that aren't as good as they look on paper. Maybe a horse broke his maiden against a crap five-horse field. And maybe he was on the lead on a day when speed was good, and now he's back first-time against winners and there are three other speed horses in the race. But because he earned a glossy 95 Beyer, he's 3-5. But the scenario today is completely different. The circumstances that allowed him to run the 95 first time out are not in effect today."

Brent Sumja: "Another way to find a false favorite would be to look for a horse that had a perfect setup in his previous race. There were five speed horses and he was the only closer, or the opposite—he was a lone front-runner. Today might not be such a fortunate setup."

The idea is that you have to have a healthy skepticism of the obvious. Go beyond the first blush. Look for the opposite of what happened last time. Dave Gutfreund cited a prime example of that from the 2013 Triple Crown trail.

5 Orb
Own: Janney III Stuart S and Phipps Stable
3-1 White, Cherry Hoop, Cherry Sleeves
ROSARIO J (133 22 24 23 .17) 2013: (672 156 .23)

B. c. 3 (Feb)
Sire: Malibu Moon (A.P. Indy) $70,000
Dam: Lady Liberty (Unbridled)
Br: Stuart S Janney III LLC & Phipps Stable (Ky)
Tr: McGaughey III Claude R(23 4 5 3 .17) 2013:(102 22 .22)

L 126

Life	9	5	0	1	$2,395,850	104	**D.Fst**	8 4 0 1		$981,050	97
2013	5	4	0	0	$2,340,900	104	**Wet(407)**	1 1 0 0		$1,414,800	104
2012	4	1	0	1	$54,950	78	**Synth**	0 0 0 0		$0	-
Bel	1	0	0	0	$3,650	51	**Turf(283)**	0 0 0 0		$0	-
							Dst(296)	0 0 0 0		$0	-

18May13-12Pim	fst	1 3/16	:483 1:131 1:38 1:572	Preaknes-G1		**92**	1 66½ 55¾ 75¼ 69 49	Rosario J	L126	*.70	81-16	**Oxbow**1261¾ Itsmyluckyday126½ Mylute1266¾	Bid btw 5/8,rail 5/16	9
13May13 Bel	fst	4f	:47	B	5/98									
4May13-11CD	slyS	1¼	:451 1:094 1:36 2:024	KyDerby-G1		**104**	15 16101618 54½ 2hd 12½	Rosario J	L126	*5.40	95-15	Orb1262½ **Golden Soul**1261 **Revolutionary**126hd	Awkwd st, bold 6w move	19
												***R-BIAS: -82 FLOW: 149 BL12: 29.6 CFR: 84**		
29Apr13 CD	fst	4f	:474	B	5/43									
21Apr13 Pay	fst	5f	1:02	B	3/5									
14Apr13 Pay	fst	4f	:48	B	2/8									
30Mar13-12GP	fst	1⅛	:482 1:124 1:373 1:504	FlaDerby-G1		**97**	6 52½ 54 51½ 31 12¾	Velazquez J R	L122	2.90	83-13	*Orb*1222¾ Itsmyluckyday1222¼ Merit Man1225	4 wide, drew clear	10
												***R-BIAS: 6 FLOW: -72 BL12: 6.7 CFR: 26**		
25Mar13 Pay	fst	4f	:481	B	3/7									
23Feb13-11GP	fst	1 1/16	:23 :452 1:084 1:421	FntnOYth-G2		**97**	1 78 68 55½ 21½ 1½	Velazquez J R	L116	5.40	100-04	*Orb*116½ Violence1226¾ Speak Logistics1172	Circled 4 wd, up late	9
												***R-BIAS: -25 FLOW: 89 BL12: 16.0 CFR: 78**		
6Jan13-5GP	fst	1⅛	:49 1:132 1:373 1:51	OC 75k/N1x-N		**83**	3 75 62¼ 3½ 11½ 11	Rosario J	L118	2.40	82-08	*Orb*1181 Duke of the City1182¾ Indy's Illusion1182¾	Tight 1st, bid, clear	7
												***R-BIAS: 73 FLOW: -120 BL12: 7.6 CFR: 18**		
4Nov12-2Aqu	fst	1	:231 :47 1:121 1:383	Md Sp Wt 67k		**76**	4 75¾ 65 23 21½ 12	Rosario J	120	4.50	76-12	*Orb*1202 **Freedom Child**1202¼ ***Revolutionary***120hd	4w run turn, driving	7
												***R-BIAS: 78 FLOW: 32 BL12: 11.1 CFR: 74**		
0Nov12-4Aqu	fst	6½f	:224 :453 1:09 1:152	Md Sp Wt 62k		**76**	6 9 95 85¼ 55¼ 45½	Rosario J	120	3.70	95-04	***Vyjack***1201¾ *Clawback*120no Retreive1203¾	Driven 4w into stretch	10
												***R-BIAS: -13 FLOW: -184 BL12: 0.7 CFR: 3**		
8Sep12-1Bel	fst	1	:231 :464 1:122 1:381	Md Sp Wt 71k		**51**	1 55 55 57½ 513 422½	Rosario J	120	*.70	50-27	Tizracer12010½ New Line1203½ Royal Art1208½	Acted up gate,off slow	5
												***R-BIAS: 154 FLOW: 70 BL12: 0.0 CFR: 92**		
8Aug12-4Sar	fst	7f	:222 :45 1:093 1:224	Md Sp Wt 80k		**78**	1 8 814 810 44½ 31¼	Rosario J	119	29.25	89-08	*Violence*119nk *Titletown Five*1191 Orb1192	Off very slow,6w 1/4	8
												***R-BIAS: -98 FLOW: 64 BL12: 3.0 CFR: 50**		

Dave Gutfreund: "At the risk of doing some serious red-boarding, look at the whole Orb-mania thing in the two weeks after the 2013 Derby and how he was such a ridiculously short price in the Preakness. It was beyond belief. Orb had run two seconds slower than a filly in his prep for the Derby, and now he's the second coming of Secretariat because he got a good setup and took full advantage of it? He was the best closer in a race filled with speed. How his being 3-5 versus 7-5 changes how he runs, I don't know. It doesn't. But that's a classic favorite to bet against."

Several players cited trainers as a major factor in horses they are looking to bet against.

Brian Troop: "In football, people over-bet the Dallas Cowboys. It's the same in horse racing; they over-bet certain trainers. And if they're over-betting something, that means you're getting a price on something else."

Kevin Cox: "Certain trainers are always over-bet. I'll just see them in the *Form* and go, 'Next!' Like Pletcher and Baffert with first-time starters."

Cox also mentioned a good example of another type of "bet-against."

Kevin Cox: "Certain running styles are over-bet: closers in sprint races that are now stretching out. No, thank you. You're better off with the opposite: horses that have been tiring in sprint races and are now going farther. Maybe they can set a slower pace and carry their speed longer, especially if they're bred for it."

One of Harvey Pack's "Laws of the Track" applies here.

Maury Wolff: "Any time you're asking horses to do something for the first time, you have the potential for over-bet favorites. That great line of Harvey Pack's: never bet a horse as the favorite doing something he's never done before."

Another key point is that the favorite you want to beat doesn't necessarily have to be "bad" per se; he just has to be over-bet, thus creating good value on the other contenders in the race.

Maury Wolff: "To find longshots, you don't only have to beat bad favorites; you just have to beat horses that are strongly bet. You see 3-5 shots all the time that go down in flames even though it looked like they couldn't lose on paper. Just because Justin Verlander is on the mound doesn't mean the Tigers have to hang up a W. Maybe he doesn't have his stuff or maybe he pitches great and they lose 2-1. We don't think anything of a 1-2 shot losing in baseball. We accept it as part of the game. But in racing some-times we think, 'This horse can't lose.' Well, of course he can lose. You can get lucky and beat him because someone else runs an A race or you can get lucky and beat him because he runs a B race. You do have to be careful betting against 3-5 shots in short fields because even if they lose, the winner is still probably only going to be a $12 horse. But if the 3-5 shot blows in a ten-horse race, then you're on to something."

As with everything else in the contest world, there is of course another way of looking at the matter.

Mark McGuire: "I'm not that great at finding bad favorites just because I'm always trying to beat the favorite."

Scott Carson: "I don't really look to take down favorites; I look for horses that have upside potential that are overlays. So if I see a horse that's 15-1, I'm going to look to make sure he can deliver. So I'll look in the *Racing Form* to make sure the trainer is competent and that the horse's running style won't be compromised."

Finding over-bet favorites is one of the keys to selecting optional races, and when it comes to mandatory races, evaluating the favorite is critical as well. The difference, as we'll learn in our next section, is that in a mandatory race, playing the favorite can sometimes be a good idea.

PLAYING MANDATORY RACES

As I've stated earlier, much of the online world is centered around mandatory races. For some players, this is a huge advantage because no time is required on the tricky business of race selection, and that means there is more time for the actual nuts and bolts of handicapping. The biggest difference between optional races and mandatory races is that with the latter, it's no longer such a bad thing to play favorites, at least according to most of our players.

Dave Gutfreund: "You can play any price at all in the mandatories. Obviously, a mandatory means you have to play the race. The gun is pointed at your head. You have to do the best you can. You're better off making an average bet than a bad bet if the opportunity to make a great bet doesn't exist."

This may change late in a contest when things get desperate. Then you still might be better off making the "bad" bet if the good or great value play is certain not to help you anyway, but I think it's generally dead-on advice because you never know when even a few points will help you in the standings.

Paul Shurman: "In an early mandatory race, if you play an 8-5 and it wins, that $9 sure looks good on your scorecard after the race. I'll even play 4-5 in that spot sometimes if I think the horse can't lose; I just want to get the points."

Cara Yarusso: "In the mandatory races, I will play whoever I think is going to win, no matter what the odds are. While a cap horse winning without you having it can be devastating, you can't afford to let the obvious winners pass you by if you think they will win. If I start lagging behind in the totals, then I stretch what I'll play in the mandatories."

Steve Wolfson, Sr.: "It's much different in online contests with all mandatory races. You have to figure out the difference between the races where you can really fire that gun and other spots where you have to take shorter prices in spots where the favorite can't be beaten."

Brian Troop: "I don't play chalk too often. Sometimes in mandatory races, you can take a shorter price if you really think a horse is going to win. When I won the NHC, I played a favorite in a mandatory race on Friday. I'd read about the horse [Andina], and I knew the connections thought she was a stakes horse. I was getting 3-1, and I really thought she would win, and she won by five lengths or so, as easy as you could. That was a free one."

Ken Massa represents the other line of thought on this issue.

Ken Massa: "I just can't believe some of the low-priced horses people are willing to play, even in the mandatory races. I don't see any sense in it, but they're still doing it. They think they're taking what the race gives them; that's usually the attitude. But that's a bad attitude to have in tournaments, believe me. Because every time you think, 'This chalk is a sure thing,' you're going to get snake-bit on that."

So is there a case where Massa would play the favorite?

Ken Massa: "I wouldn't put in the favorite under any circumstances, because it won't hurt you if it wins. There's no point in it. I've never gotten anywhere by having the chalk, even accidentally—you know like when you scratch and they give you the chalk or something? It's never helped me. I'd say let the favorite beat you and go with something else. There must be a 4-1 shot in that race that has some chance to beat him. And since 6-5 isn't going to hurt you, why not take a shot with the other one, in case the favorite stumbles or something?"

11 Strategy for Different Formats

> *"One of the worst things that can happen to you in life is*
> *to win a bet on a horse at an early age."*
> **– Danny McGoorty, from** *McGoorty:*
> *A Billiard Hustler's Life*

Now that we have established the basics of contest strategy, let's take a look at some of our players' specific advice about strategy in various contest formats.

PICK-AND-PRAYS/LOCKDOWNS

As mentioned earlier, pick-and-prays or lockdowns are contests where one puts in all bets ahead of time and can't make any changes based on what happens along the way.

Brent Sumja: "For me, pick-and-pray contests are true handicapping challenges. you put in your 12 picks and it's over. There's no throwing darts and using strategy depending on what's come in so far or any of that. I believe I have a big chance in those. When it comes to just straight up picking horses, I feel like I'm better than the next guy. When it comes to regular tournament play, I'm definitely not better than the next guy because I still have so much to learn."

I asked Patrick McGoey about why he liked tournaments in general, but his answer applies to pick-and-prays in particular.

Patrick McGoey: "I like tournaments because I fit them into my schedule. I can put in my picks in the morning and still go to my kid's soccer game. If I have time to sit in front of the computer, I will. It's a fun hobby that I can work into my real life."

Don Marr agrees with both McGoey and Sumja.

Don Marr: "I work during the day, so it's nice for someone like me who can do the handicapping at nighttime and put in my picks and not be at a disadvantage against someone who is sitting there, watching all the races, adjusting his plays as the day goes on depending on what prices are needed. I also like them because they force everybody to actually handicap and not just play the board."

It's true. There is no just playing to catch the leader in a pick-and-pray—once your picks are in, that's it.

Don Marr: "I call that 'chasing the bubble.' Like in the days of the old single-prop airplanes before computers where a pilot would use his instruments almost like a level and try to land the plane that way. They would overcompensate one way, then the other—a dangerous way to fly. Some people do that in contests; they don't think about what the best play is, they just play whatever the number is they need to be in the lead. That doesn't seem like skill to me, and that won't help you in a lockdown where all the picks need to be in beforehand. You need to have solid handicapping skills."

What specific advice does Marr have for pick-and-prays?

Don Marr: "I don't play morning-line favorites at all in a lockdown. I've seen people play plenty of morning-line favorites and have that work for them, but that's not for me. I'm looking for under-the-radar horses. I think that's what most of us are doing. A lot of my winners in lockdowns are in between the favorites and the monster longshots. But I'm not too hung up on the price range other than not wanting the morning-line favorite.

"I'm not necessarily looking for the most likely winners, just one of the likely contenders where there might be some value. Instead of the A horse, maybe it's a good B or C horse. Depending on what I think of the card, I might play a lot of second choices or I might go longer. But at the end, over those last two races, I'm looking for 5-1 and above. I'm looking for a separator at that point."

Eric Moomey looks at pick-and-prays from a different perspective.

Eric Moomey: "There's one website that offers two tournaments on the same set of races. In both, you need to finish in the top ten percent. In one, it's pick-and-pray where you don't get to change your picks. In the other, you get to change your picks. Here's a question for you: which one, time and time again, has the higher final score?"

I guessed that the regular format would yield higher scores because people push each other to pick more longshots because you can change your picks as you go.

Eric Moomey: "That's right. The normal contest format is way higher most times. There are two reasons. If I hit a longshot early, why do I need more longshots? Why can't I just play favorites at that point? And if I'm not doing well, I can adjust and pick higher prices near the end. And if a bunch of people hit longshots early, I know I need to adjust in that direction. You have to constantly think and adjust and change your tactics. I like the pick-and-pray because most people tend to pick logical horses. So maybe I want to be the guy picking longshots in the pick-and-pray, especially near the end when they always seem to come in."

Ken Massa gets more specific on this last point.

Ken Massa: "One piece of advice that I would give people playing pick-and-prays is that you should always play a high-priced horse in the last leg. The idea is that if you're in contention anyway, or if you're in the lead, you want to protect yourself. And if you're not, then you need to come from behind anyhow, so you need a bomb in the final race, so no matter what, you want a bomb in the last leg. I mean, I can't tell you how many times I've won or gotten in the money in those pick-and-prays because I put a bomb in the last race and passed everybody up at the end."

I thought of a third reason to play a bomb in the last leg. A lot of people play pick-and-prays precisely because they want to avoid losing in the last leg to a longshot, so maybe there's an edge to be gained by trying to do exactly that! Kevin Cox shared a recent practical example (see also the benefits of playing over-cap horses in general on page 75).

Kevin Cox: "My wife had two entries in an NHC qualifier pick-and-pray on horsetourneys.com. She was in fourth place on one ticket going into the last but was drawing dead on the good ticket, as two of the three ahead of her had the same horse. However, on her other ticket, she picked a horse she knew would be over the cap. It ended up winning and paying $111! Only one of 40 people ahead of her had it, so she finished second and qualified."

SURVIVORS

The survivor format was first developed a number of years ago as an online racetrack promotion that went under various names, like "Showvivor." The idea was that people would sign up online and choose one horse in one race a day that would have to at least show for the player to advance. Thus "Survivor/Showvivor" was born. The format has evolved over time to where you can now play under these rules daily in a bullet format—you must pick one horse to show over a designated series of races; if you miss a race, you're out, and if you survive the longest, you win the contest. If there is a tie at the end, that is, if more than one person survives, the prize money is typically split equally, but in some instances, higher combined mutuels can provide a tie-breaker. As always, make sure you know the rules going in.

Matt Shifman: "I find survivor tournaments a great way to have action. Don't tell my boss, but I can play a one-day survivor while I'm at work. I can handicap the races during lunch and then take a minute or two here and there to check the progress of the tournament and make any needed adjustments. I also like that there is very little financial risk when playing survivor tournaments, as they either have a very small entry fee or are free to enter."

Michael P. Ryan: "I like that winning or losing is completely up to the player. No one can beat you with a 30-1 in the last race. Unlike any other wagering or contest, the odds don't matter for scoring. Pick the horse you like to show, regardless of price. I also think it's a great game to get people involved in contests."

What special strategies do you use?

Matt Shifman: "These tournaments are aptly named; it is essential to remember that you are trying to survive. It does not matter if your horse wins; your pick needs to just finish third. It sounds easy, but in reality, easy is the last word I would use to describe survivor tournaments. I get knocked out of plenty of these in the first leg, but I also win my fair share. I have been playing with the same initial deposit in my tournament account for a couple of years now and even have a profit. That is not something I can say about my ADW account."

Michael P. Ryan: "Having multiple entries is a huge advantage in a survivor tournament. Having three entries allows you to spread in open races. I'll put all my entries on a strong contender and then use multiple picks for when there's a more open race. If the first race on the card is open, it's important to spread there. I see a lot of people will put all their entries on the same horse for the first two or three races, thinking they need to have them later in the contest. That's a strategy that makes sense. The game is all about being alive for the next race, so make sure you are."

Matt Shifman had a different take on multiple entries in these contests.

Matt Shifman: "Some players deal with bullet survivors by buying more than one entry into the tournament. Online sites allow players to buy up to three entries. Sounds like a good idea, but I find it a bit disconcerting, feeling like I am playing against myself. You need to skillfully identify when you are spreading your entries on different horses or putting them on one horse. I will play two entries from time to time, when the races are extremely difficult to handicap and I really feel like I need two tries to survive."

What are the biggest mistakes you see people making in the survivor format?

Michael P. Ryan: "People tend to look at the win odds to find the 'best' horse. That may not be the most logical horse to finish in the top three. A horse in good form who's 1-for-10 with several seconds and thirds can be great in these games."

Matt Shifman: "I agree. People focus on the odds in the win pool, and we survivor players are looking for a horse to show. It is important to avoid letting the win odds influence your picks. A great example is the perpetual maiden, you know the one that has run 18 times and has very little chance of winning but has finished second or third 75 percent of the time by always passing tired horses. That horse is a big favorite to survive but not to win."

What horses do you want to avoid?

Matt Shifman: "There are two kinds of horses that I avoid playing. First are the front-runners that have a tendency to fade going down the stretch. Second are the deep closers that get very far behind at the start of the race. The front-runners are at risk of getting passed at the end of the race, and the deep closers require a perfect trip, because even a little trouble means they might not have time to get there.

"When either of those running styles shows up as the favorite, that creates an opportunity in a survivor tournament that you want to take advantage of."

Michael P. Ryan: "If you identify the favorite as a horse that looks like the class of the field but you suspect he'll win or not show up, that's a horse to avoid. In most contest formats, the odds-on favorite is one to avoid. In a survivor, it could be the most logical choice."

What betting situations are you looking for?

Michael P. Ryan: "Races that have a strong favorite that looks like the winner and a strong second-choice and then a weaker field are nice races for survivor. When you see that, I tend to play the second choice. Most all end up on the favorite, and if one of these doesn't show, you're out or you've eliminated most of the field."

Matt Shifman: "I look for races where there is a bad favorite, and by that I mean a favorite that is vulnerable and could finish out of the money. I have played in survivor events where one of those favorites runs out and takes 75 percent of the tournament field with him."

What price do you want to play?

Matt Shifman: "For the most part, I do not concern myself with the odds of the horses because it is hard enough to find the right horse to survive, and ultimately that is the key to success."

Michael P. Ryan: "Unlike every other contest, finding longshots doesn't really help you. In a recent contest, one participant went with a 22-1 that won the race, but it didn't really matter since most everyone else advanced anyway by playing more obvious horses. Survivors are all about getting to the next race. If you think the 22-1 is the best horse, put a few bucks down, but I will say that in a wide-open race, it's better to be a longer price than a shorter price simply because most will be on the shorter-priced horses."

How does a bullet survivor format compare to a "Showvivor" format where you're only looking for one horse to show per day? How does that change the strategy?

Matt Shifman: "Every year, Santa Anita, Portland Meadows, and Monmouth Park offer what they call 'SHOWvivor' tournaments that are free to play. In these you have to pick one horse to show from any race you choose from the entire card in order to advance to the next day. These events typically draw thousands of players, and the track puts up the prizes.

"In these you have to look through the entire card to find your show horse. I like to look for fields where a significant number of horses have no chance at all. You have to grind it out in these tournaments day after day, but typically they don't last the entire meeting. One year at Santa Anita, it ended fairly quickly and the track started up another.

"The bullet survivor tournaments take place in a given number of races usually in one card, but sometimes over a weekend covering stakes races. Often these tournaments find a survivor before the allotted races have been completed. If more than one person goes the distance, then the prize pool is chopped up between all the winners.

"In the one-day survivors, you can end up having to handicap some very tough, evenly matched, full fields of veteran runners or a field of unraced two-year-olds. In the one-show-horse-a-day tournaments, I would never choose to play one of these races."

Michael P. Ryan: "The longer show contests are really battles of attrition, and they last so long you really have to remember to get in your picks. Read the rules carefully. In some of these contests, the tie-breaker comes down to bankroll, so I know some are looking for the price horses more than they would in a one-day survivor."

In terms of getting great action and invaluable learning experience for your dollar, survivors might just be the best place of all for new players to get their feet wet in contests—though you might want to read the next section before you leap to that conclusion.

HEAD-TO-HEADS

Head-to-head formats are exactly what they sound like. It's just you and one other player, so that changes the tournament dynamic quite a bit: in a head-to-head, you can typically win with a score that's just a little over your starting bankroll and sometimes way less than that. Head-to-head expert Garett Skiba had a lot to share on this unique tournament format.

Garett Skiba: "I find head-to-head matches one of the most enjoyable types of tournaments out there. Everyone knows that betting every race on a card is a sure path to consistent losing. Playing a head-to-head match is a great way to have a vested interest in each race on an entire card without having to put your bankroll at risk in positions where you know you lack historical success."

Are there any special strategies you use?

Garett Skiba: "The key to the head-to-head match is grabbing a lead. The power of a lead is extremely important in the later races when game theory especially enters into the equation. Taking a lead into the last race is powerful, as it allows you not only to eliminate the horses that, were they to win, would still allow you to win, but it also allows you to block one of your opponent's 'live' shots. There is nothing better than to see that you both have the same horse once that last race closes and realize that, no matter what, you have won."

Do you really try to put yourself in your opponent's mind right from the beginning of a head-to-head or do you just play your own contest until the last race?

Garett Skiba: "I think that becomes important only later in the contest. Early on, I think as a player you are best to focus on just picking winners and not so much worry about what your opponent is attempting to do. However, undoubtedly, scoreboard-watching is part of the game."

Do you track other players' tendencies at all in head-to-head games?

Garett Skiba: "I have played about 240 head-to-head games against 50 different opponents. While there are players who I consistently see online, I would say that playing the race is still more important than playing the player. The only time when you may want to play the player would be late in contests."

FREE ONLINE NHC QUALIFIERS

One of the most popular tournaments of all is the free online qualifier held up to four times a year by the NTRA on www.ntra.com. It typically attracts around 1,500 competitors, and, as you might imagine, it's really, really hard to win.

Eric Moomey: "I qualified through the free qualifier in 2012.

There were eight contest races, and I picked seven of the winners, including a 40-1 shot, and didn't even finish first."

Dave Gutfreund: "In a tournament like the NTRA online contest that can qualify you for the NHC, where there are thousands of people playing and the top five get in, you basically need to have your miracle day. You need to concentrate on the races in the contest and hope you run like God. If a big price comes in, and you don't have it and somebody else does, that's the end."

My first instinct was that maybe you really need to bomb away to have a chance.

Paul Shurman: "No, it's the opposite actually. Price doesn't matter as much because to win that you basically have to pick all the winners."

12 Live Bankroll

"If you're going to try, go all the way. There is no other feeling like that. You will be alone with the gods, and the nights will flame with fire. You will ride life straight to perfect laughter. It's the only good fight there is."
— **Charles Bukowski,** *Factotum*

In an earlier section, we discussed what final bankroll you'll need to shoot for in mythical-money tournaments. With live-bankroll contests, where you can play exotics and also reinvest your winnings, the wicket gets stickier.

Noel Michaels: "With real-money contests, it's tough, especially when you put exotics into it. You can have one or two obnoxiously giant scores that are going to skew the range and make it unpredictable. It's easy to get blown out of the water."

Maury Wolff: "It's a dynamic process, especially with live-bankroll. If somebody hits big early, that changes what everybody else is playing for. In those situations you have to add or subtract to the projected final total depending on the type of results."

What happens to the old 2 1/2 rule of thumb?

Duke Matties: "The final score will vary a lot with live-bankroll, but it's always going to be more than 2 1/2 times your bankroll.

Two and a half times your bankroll won't get you close. I've played in some live-bankroll contests where it took 12 or 13 times the bankroll one year, and the year before that, it took six times the starting bankroll. But you're going to need to shoot for a minimum of five times your bankroll, and even that might not be enough."

Paul Shurman: "The final bankroll you'll need depends on the specifics of the real-money tournament. There are real-money tournaments and there are real real-money tournaments. At Monmouth, where there's a small initial bankroll, there I'm looking for a final score of around ten times my initial bankroll. So if you start with $200, the winner might have $2,000.

"But if you're starting with $5,000, that's really *real* money there. I'll look for $20,000 to $30,000, maybe four to six times the initial bankroll. Sometimes the prize money isn't that great relative to the bankroll. That will keep scores lower as well. Let's say there's a tournament where I have a $5,000 bankroll going into the last race and only $10,000 to the winner. Why would I go all-in and risk $5,000 to only make an extra $10,000?"

And then there's the big daddy of real-money tournaments, the Breeders' Cup Betting Challenge.

Paul Shurman: "The Breeders' Cup Betting Challenge is another animal. There the prize pool is really good. People are more willing to blow their whole $7,500 bankroll. There you have to shoot for ten times your bankroll again. If I have five or six grand still going into the last race, it's all going in. It doesn't make sense to go home with a couple thousand when you can win so much. Pick a straight trifecta and pray. It's a once-in-a-lifetime opportunity to win $250,000 between the live bankroll and the prize money."

STRATEGY FOR LIVE BANKROLL

As you might imagine from the wide variation in both the rules and the expected scores, the overall strategy changes considerably in live-bankroll tournaments as opposed to fixed-bankroll tournaments. Live-bankroll tournaments are much closer to everyday life but still contain their own game-within-the-game aspect. I remember Cary

Fotias telling me that he loved the Breeders' Cup Betting Challenge because it wasn't just for, ahem, "contest dorks"; people had to be willing to really risk their money. Another pro player, Duke Matties, shares this perspective.

Duke Matties: "Not all contest formats are too appealing to me, like the ones where there are ten races, everybody bets the same races, and whoever hits the longshots wins. I prefer tournaments where we actually wager, you know? Where you actually have to do some work and manage money a little bit. If you're betting your money and not just picking longshots, that's a much better way to determine who the better handicapper is. If I hit an exacta that pays $35, but I bet it for a hundred, I think that's much more of an accomplishment than these guys picking a 15-1 shot just because he's 15-1."

In live-bankroll contests, the money may be real, but it might not be the best strategy to treat it as such.

Maury Wolff: "One of the rules I consider sacrosanct in live-bankroll tournaments is that if you're not willing to go broke, you shouldn't play in them. An exception is if you're doing it for other reasons, such as you want to go to the Breeders' Cup and bet the races, and it's a better value to play the tournament. But live-bankroll tournaments are heavily biased towards people who are willing to go broke. If you're not willing to go broke, you're basically playing with one hand tied behind your back. There's a simple way to do it: treat the bankroll in the live-bankroll tournament exactly as if it were mythical tournament money. You're not trying to break even here. That's not going to win the tournament."

Noel Michaels: "The right strategy is to treat your whole bankroll like the entry fee. If you're really trying to give yourself the best chance to win, you need to have the attitude that if you lose, all your money is gone.

"That's an advantage that a lot of big-bankroll players have. Guys who are happy day in, day out betting $500 or $1,000 in a race are going to have a much easier time doing that than the guy betting $5 and $10. If that smaller-bankroll guy is sitting on a real bankroll of $1,500 at the end, he might get a little tight. But the only way he has any realistic chance to win the tournament is to go all-in. When you play in a real-money tournament and you're not a big-bankroll player, you've got to learn to turn into one real fast."

One thing you can't do in live-bankroll formats is be too passive—that's like a poker player who calls and checks more than he raises and he folds.

Ricky Zimmer: "In live-bankroll contests at Monmouth or Delaware, where the whole bankroll is only $100, sometimes I'll see people betting 5-2 shots to win for $20, not even close to their whole bankroll. What are you even accomplishing? You're not really doing anything but just sort of hanging around."

It's not just not caring about the money: many successful live-bankroll players pretty much treat live-bankroll tournaments the same as mythical ones when it comes to strategy as well.

Maury Wolff: "My strategy doesn't change much from a mythical-bankroll tournament to a real-money one. For most people, it's a radical change. If the money that you're paying for the entry fee doesn't matter to you, there's not a lot of difference between how you would play a fake-money tournament and a real-money tournament. If the money does matter to you, you're going to play much more conservatively.

"Let's say you reach the last race, you've got $400 left, and your only shot is to bet a preposterous longshot, a horse you wouldn't bet with counterfeit money. In a fake-money tournament, everyone will bet that horse without hesitation—it's the only chance to win. It's a lot harder to bet that horse when there's real money involved."

As a result, those longshots that win so many mythical-money tournaments might be easier to move up alone on in live-bankroll formats.

Dennis Decauwer: "When you're playing in a $2 win/place format, people tend to be looking more for big price plays, and if the field is large enough, somebody's going to have just about every one of them.

When you're playing in the typical live-bankroll format, with a bigger bankroll that you can reinvest, it's more like a typical day at the track, where people might be doing more regular exotic bets, like exactas and trifectas. There, people are looking more to 'How can I make a good score?' So it's more likely that a big longshot will hit and no one will have it. I'm not opposed to an exacta or a trifecta, but in a live-bankroll contest, I try to look for the one or two horses that I really like and bet them to win."

Roger Cettina: "Even in a live-bankroll contest, I always bet to win and place. Then one night I played in a live-bankroll contest at the Meadowlands and I won it. And I looked back at the end of the night and I had two winners and four seconds. I had the winner of the last race, and I won the contest. But if I'd only been betting to win all night to that point, my bankroll would have been a lot lower, and I wouldn't have had enough to bet on the winner in the last to win the whole contest.. That made me say, 'You know what? I'm going to stick with what worked and bet to win and place.'"

Maury Wolff: "At this point, most everyone in a tournament knows how to play decent strategy. Then the important thing becomes learning the rules and understanding how to make the rules work for you as opposed to against you. If the rules are that you don't have to make any bets until the last race, then unless you love a horse before the last race, I wouldn't be making any bets before the last race. I thought what Patrick McGoey did in his two wins in the Breeders' Cup contest, as I understand it, was brilliant. He bet nearly his entire bankroll on a longshot in the Breeders' Cup Classic. Unless I found something early on that I absolutely loved, that's what I'd do, because unless you had a really strong opinion early, why not try to win it when you have the most information?"

The problem with waiting until the end these days is that you're sure to have company, because in most instances, live-bankroll tournaments are won in the last race.

Noel Michaels: "Everybody waits till the end in pretty much all of them.

The overriding strategy in those types of contests ... some of them make you bet a certain amount in every race, but in others, you just start off with a bankroll and whoever has the biggest bankroll at the end wins. In those contests, people are playing one of two strategies. Most of the people are trying to tread water through most of it and shorten it down to a two-race contest. They'll pick two races at the end of the contest and know they have to bet what they have left on the first one, win that, and then take all that money and play it back in a giant bet at the end. More than half the field will be doing that.

"The other strategy is that a lot of people try to get something big early to set a score; then they know they have their money, so they look to tread water until the last race, and then maybe they let it rip again at the end to close out the tournament. The thing those two strategies have in common is their common approach at the end of the contest—they're letting it rip with whatever they have."

Duke Matties: "What I do is I try to hit something early on to create some kind of bankroll, because you need more money to bet with. I think that is a real key. I know there are a lot of guys who like treading water until the end, to see what score they'll need, but I go the opposite way. I try to hit stuff at the beginning, and you'll see that my name is always on top at the beginning, because that's what I try to do. Now I can manage maybe double what everybody's got, and I just keep betting from there. I don't worry about still holding the lead; I want to increase my lead, because I know the way the other guys play: they tread water and then they go all-in. Whether it's the last race or the race before it, or the race before that, at some point they go all-in.

"You don't want to just set that target, then they know what they have to get. That's why I don't stop betting. I don't reach a limit and say, 'Okay, now I'm going to tread water at $4,000.' I want to get my bankroll as high as I can make it, basically. The last few live-bankroll contests I've been in have come down to the last race, and I don't like it that way. You know, some guy hits some bomb in the last race and passes you, or he hits the tri for $25,000, you know, or something like that. They go right on by you. Of course, it happens both ways; I've gone by guys at the end too, so it does equal out, if you play enough of them."

Ricky Zimmer: "I think you just want to cut down as much as you can the number of bets that you make. I feel like the less you can expose yourself to the takeout, the better. I'm always looking for a way just to try and bet it all on one thing. If there's nothing I feel that strongly about, maybe I'll break it up a little bit, but I don't like making small bets in a live-bankroll format, because I feel like you'll just grind down your bankroll over the course of the day. At Monmouth, where you had to make a minimum of ten wagers, by three or four o'clock, hopefully, I'll have bet eight favorites to show, hit maybe seven of them, and have my original bankroll— and then I just find something to go all-in on."

Roger Cettina seconds that strategy.

Roger Cettina: "If the rules allow you the option of only making ten bets, then you should only be making ten bets. The reality is, the more bets you make a day, the less chance you have to win. It's harder to pick winners the more races you bet. It pays to be selective. I think the issue is focus. You have to zero in on the races you like, and then when it comes time to bet a horse, you really have to bet it. You can't nickel and dime 'em.

"If you have a contest where you have $100 and you have to bet ten races, by about the sixth race I'll have bet my hundred, and if I didn't hit up till then, I'll be done, so be it. A lot of guys would go bet show for four hours. If I'm going to do that, I might as well stay home. Don't get me wrong: people bet that way and they win. That's just not me. To me, if it's live-bankroll or if it's not live-bankroll, I'm going to bet it the same way, and the biggest contests, you have no chance to win if you're playing conservatively and betting chalk. Maybe that gives me a little advantage because so many people are just grinding away. To me, betting favorites or betting to show is like betting with scared money."

Later on in the Endgame chapter, Duke Matties tells us that he always goes for the win in tournaments. I assumed that meant he always would be willing to bet his whole bank in the last race of a live-bankroll tournament.

Duke Matties: "Not necessarily. I'll just give you a for-instance. In the last contest I played, I had about $3,300 and I risked about half of it, and I took half of it. That way I was going home with a profit regardless of what I did. That's usually what I do. I don't like to give it all back—though I know there are a lot of guys who do always bet it all. But if I have a chance to take a profit and still have a chance to win the contest, I'll do that. I just feel bad when I blow it all on a race I might not even have wagered on to begin with."

I mentioned Maury Wolff's idea to Matties, how not going all-in in the last race is like fighting with one hand tied behind your back. But for Matties, given the overall picture of his wagering life, maybe going all-in just isn't worth the aggravation.

Duke Matties: "Well, yeah, because I do this every day. And most people probably bet like this once a year or a few times a year. But if I'm close to the lead in a big contest, like the Breeders' Cup Betting Challenge, where all the money's on top and maybe I can win an extra hundred thousand, I might bet it all there. If it's a race I like anyway, then I might bet it all. But in just a normal live-bankroll betting contest, there's not necessarily enough incentive to do that every time."

Matties makes a great point, but still, he'd be the first to tell you that more often than not, a certain aggressiveness is going to pay off.

Ricky Zimmer: "It can pay to be aggressive. If you hit something really huge early, you can break the field over your knee, and they'll start looking at second and third. So it's okay to go all-in early and put that number up there and get people thinking. If you are targeting the minimum amount you think might win it, and you put up that number early, that's okay, too. It might not hold, but that's okay, because at least you'll be in a position where you can try to climb back up to the lead later in the day. There are many benefits to being aggressive early. Obviously, you might knock yourself out and end your day early, but if everybody is doing the same thing, sitting and waiting for the end, you want to try to do something to separate yourself from them."

I asked Zimmer if it was true that live-bankroll contests always come down to the last race.

Ricky Zimmer: "Live-bankroll contests usually come down to the last race. It's all about getting yourself in that position to make that last play to win, because invariably this stuff comes down to that last race. I also feel like a disproportionate number of longshots come in in the last race—it just seems that suddenly crazy things happen, but maybe that's just the ones I'm remembering."

Maybe there's a bit of a memory bias there, but you also have to remember that the last race is often chosen to be the last race because it's chaotic—especially in California where they have a Super High-5 wager and they live for Pick-6 carryovers, so that might account for some of the late craziness. It's another good reason to save a bullet for the end.

While aggressiveness can be a key to victory, there is also such a thing as being too aggressive.

Mike Maloney: "One mistake I was making in the beginning with those live-bankroll contests is I was just too aggressive. The first time I saw an opportunity where I really had an opinion, I was ready to win the contest right there. I've found out over the years that I don't have to do that. I have to tone down that aggressiveness that I might use on a day-to-day basis. Why would one be different than the other? Well, the difference is that it's easier for me to hedge on the regular days. Usually I'm using a lot of different pools to build a scenario that mirrors my opinion of that race and where the value is in that race, and I'm building in lots of little hedges and different possibilities. In live-bankroll contests, I shorten things up and try to just play the upper 30 to 40 percent of my bets on a range—the most likely results. And then I hope I don't get burned."

Maury Wolff: "I remember one year in the Cal-Neva contest, which was a live-bankroll tournament, where a guy ran up a score on the first day that would have been good enough to win most years. He was betting aggressively, and he came out on the second day playing the same way and he ran down his bankroll enough that he lost. There is no excuse for that. Once he'd gotten to the number he needed, he should have played ten show bets and hoped to hit eight of them. He still would've won. You're supposed to make them beat you; you don't beat yourself."

As you might have guessed from reading through these quotes, live-bankroll formats aren't for everybody.

Paul Shurman: "My problem with live-bankroll contests in general is that the buy-ins are really high, and there are people, including me, who will bet all their money, and unless you get lucky early, that's what you have to do. You have to go for broke and be willing to lose it all. It always comes down to the last race, and to me, it's too much. And except for the Breeders' Cup Betting Challenge, those tournaments don't pay out a lot of money. It's a much better situation when you win your way in through a qualifier. That makes it much easier to blow that ten grand."

Cara Yarussso: "I am not very strong at live-bankroll tournaments. In these, you need to not only handicap well but also develop winning wagering strategies. While I've always been comfortable with both handicapping and wagering, as a small player, I find myself up against less risk-averse players who are willing to go all-in with their bankroll in one race. Nonetheless, I am excited to dig deeper into live-bankroll contests and work to improve my skills there. It's just another challenge and each comes with its own twist."

Eric Moomey: "The format I have the hardest time with is live-bankroll. I'm the first to admit that I haven't figured it out yet. This isn't mythical money. Now you've got to bet $200 on a race. I played in the Players Challenge in South Dakota in 2012, where I was supposed to bet $2,500 over a certain number of races. I had three entries, and the first race had a field of six horses. So what I did on the very first race of the day is I picked three different horses and bet $2,500 on each of them. Then I took my own money and bet on horses 4, 5, and 6 in the correct proportions. There wasn't much money in the pool when I made these bets, so the odds went way down until I made all my bets and then the odds normalized. No matter what happened, I wasn't going to go home a loser after one race. Either one of my three contest plays would win and I'd be in good shape in the contest, or one of my cash bets would win and at least I'd get my money back.

"I practiced this strategy at home 100 times, and I won 83 times, meaning that if I found a race with three logical horses, I would bet all three and survive more than four times out of five. I had no expectation of losing. The idea was to turn my $2,500 starting bankroll into $10,000. That's the number I thought it would take to win that contest. I was hoping people would change their tactics after that and be forced outside their comfort zone early in the contest. I didn't want to wait too long, but I didn't really want to use this strategy on the first race of the day either, but I was so nervous that I just wanted to get it over with. As it turned out, that was my only play of the contest. The longest shot on the board crossed the line first and I won $8,400 cash on the race, but I was out of the tournament completely so it didn't feel like I'd won. Going into the contest, there were six possible races I had considered for using this strategy. The other five races I could have chosen I would have won."

Paul Shurman: "Eric's problem was that he got a little greedy—he was trying not to lose the takeout. If he had spread his contest money around all the horses in the race in the right proportion, it would have worked. For a new guy on the scene to think of a strategy like that, consolidating three tickets into one, however, it was clear to me that he was a force to be reckoned with."

Eric Moomey: "I'm okay with people thinking I'm greedy. I take big shots and they either work out or they don't. That was a way different strategy than what a lot of people had seen. I had people coming up to me after saying, 'Wait. What did you do?' And after I explained, a lot of them said, 'Yeah, that's a really good strategy.'

"Paul Shurman came up to me after and said, 'Why didn't you just spread your contest money around and bet all the horses in the race?' I had to admit that in retrospect, that sounded like a much better idea. For me, once again, it was all about trying to be different."

This strategy of Moomcy's wasn't a new thing. It's something that's been an issue in live-money tournaments since their inception—the idea of several people attempting to turn two or three or however many entries into one monster entry.

Ricky Zimmer: "There are always certain groups, whether it's a husband and wife, brothers, fathers and sons, or whole families, and I think particularly in a live-bankroll contest, I feel like you could really use that to your advantage. Let's say your group has four entries in a $500 dollar live-bankroll contest, you could decide to get all those dollars onto one ticket, you know? You might lose the takeout, but you could probably get it pretty close to four times that $500, just by spreading out bets and covering everything in a race. I don't think it's a bad thing because the more entries help the prize pool, but particularly in the live-money contests, it can be a real advantage."

Is it an unfair advantage?

Ricky Zimmer: "No, because you know it going in that that's a possibility. There's nothing in the rules against it, and it's impossible to enforce: there's really no way to legislate against it, so I don't think it's unfair."

Duke Matties: "I don't like it because they're just trying to monopolize the contest, where it's not a true contest. They get such a huge advantage because they can afford to lose three or four of their entries, and then they've got a huge lead."

Kevin Cox: "At Del Mar, in 2013, I was second halfway into day two, and then a guy had $500 to win on a 20-1 shot—which you're only going to do if you're part of a syndicate. I know they're out there, especially in California. I found out later that there's a group of three that finished first and third, and the other guy bet his whole bankroll on one horse on the first day. He didn't care because he was part of that syndicate.

"So the new leader got back $14,000 in one race; he went up to $22,000. I was in second place with $8,000. I wasn't going to blow my wad to try to catch $14,000. The money means too much to me. So the syndicate got it."

I asked Cox if he felt robbed.

Kevin Cox: "I have no problems with the syndicates. With multiple tickets, you become a syndicate of your own. But you can't buy contests no matter how many partners you have. They'll strike out too, eventually. You can't worry about what others are doing."

I was a little worried that players attempting a consolidation strategy might taint a contest like the Breeders' Cup Betting Challenge. Paul Shurman put my mind at ease.

Paul Shurman: "From my viewpoint, if someone or some group wants to spend $50,000 and put $12,500 into the prize pool to try to consolidate those multiple tickets into one entry in the Breeders' Cup contest, let them try. It would be very difficult to consolidate tickets on Breeders' Cup days. Fields are too large and too evenly matched. What you really need is a crappy five- or six-horse field at Aqueduct to have a chance at somewhat pulling it off. Even if you consolidate or play the five tickets as one, you can only win or come in the money once. So if you don't hit plays after the consolidation, you are not going to collect anything. And say you do spend $50,000, win the tournament and collect $200,000. That is a 4-1 payoff. That is not why you are there."

These types of team tactics can be an issue in mythical-money tournaments as well. Beware of spies!

Kevin Cox: "Be careful leaving your written picks down on the table, or talking to people who you don't trust. There are people who play in syndicates; you think there's just one ticket, but they come in packs like wolves—three, four people."

Duke Matties: "The idea is they'll find a race where they think a longshot will win, and then each of them will cover a different horse, so if a longshot comes in, they'll definitely have it. Then that becomes their main ticket; they'll put a little more focus and energy on that one and then still have the other tickets to cover the other possibilities."

Even if there isn't out-and-out collusion going on at a tournament, it's not always easy to know when it's OK to share one's opinion.

Steve Wolfson, Sr.: "I have a problem still, when we are in a group, on how forthcoming to be, because it's such a competitive thing. If Pete, who I just met, asks me who I like in a race and I say I've narrowed it down to these three and he says 'Me, too,' and I say something about one of them maybe pointing out something that you haven't seen, and then you beat me in a huge tournament. . . It's one of those things. It's a real tough call."

I think it's the type of thing where you have to trust your own judgment but my default attitude would be this: trust no one but your mother, and even she might be trying to put one over on you.

BREEDERS' CUP BETTING CHALLENGE

The Breeders' Cup is synonymous with great racing, but for horse-players, it's also synonymous with great wagering opportunities: big, full fields; super-talented runners; and monstrous payouts. For the last several years, the Breeders' Cup Betting Challenge has given horseplayers another major opportunity to make a big score: by parlaying a $100 online qualifier on BCQualify.com into hundreds of thousands of dollars.

I asked two-time winner Patrick McGoey about his win in the 2011 tournament.

Patrick McGoey: "I bet $7,000 to win on Drosselmeyer in the last race, the Classic. It paid a little more than $110,000, and that took me to first place in the contest, which got me $160,000 in prize money on top of that. The way I look at it, I thought the horse should have been around 10-1, and his odds were 15-1, so I thought there was a good chance that if I hit it, I would win, and it would pay 40-1 for me.

"There were 114 other players, and it was posted that first place would win $160,000 of the prize pool, and that the prize pool would pay out to the top-10 finishers, and that first place was going to need to be between $55,000 and $60,000. I had only $8,500 going into the last. I wasn't in the mix. I had to decide if I wanted to just go back home with the money I had or if I wanted to take a shot.

"Interestingly enough, guys were talking about the champion from the prior year who had put all his money on Blame and wound up catapulting ahead of everybody and winning the tournament. It had been several races since I picked a winner, and I just said, 'This kind of opportunity doesn't come around every day, so I'm going to take a shot.'"

What was it like watching the race itself?

Patrick McGoey: "I'm usually nervous if I make a $100 bet, but once I made the Drosselmeyer bet, I was really calm. When they were going into the gate, we were standing outside, and I told my brother, 'If we win this, don't go crazy—act like we've done this before.'

"We watched Drosselmeyer go around the track the whole race. I couldn't tell you who was on the lead or who was in second. All I watched was Drosselmeyer. When they got to the top of the stretch, my brother yelled, 'We've got outside! He's got outside! He's coming!'

"I had lost the two previous races by noses, with Turallure and Union Rags, so as Drosselmeyer was coming, I said to myself, 'I've seen this play out before. I don't know that we're going to get there.' But 50 yards before the line, my brother started going crazy, and I was just really calm. It was really weird."

Part of McGoey's willingness to go all-in had to do with how he ended up in the event in the first place.

Patrick McGoey: "The 2011 Breeders' Cup Betting Challenge was the first contest that I had ever done at a track. I qualified through a $100 qualifier at BCQualify.com. The fact that I didn't have to put up $10,000 of my own money to buy in absolutely affected my decision to go for it at the end."

Maury Wolff: "The Breeders' Cup Betting Challenge is a great opportunity, especially for weekend-type players. You take your bankroll, you bet it inside the tournament, and you're really increasing your equity. From what I understand, the amenities are very nice. Strategically, I absolutely love it."

There's another added benefit to playing in contests that consist of true top-level racing like the Breeders' Cup.

Maury Wolff: "Another great thing about the Breeders' Cup is that over those two days, there are many times when you look at your *Racing Form* and say, 'That's pretty darn good paper for a 15-1 shot.' That certainly makes those races a little easier to play in a contest."

For a lot of contest players, it's just another world in that room.

Joe Scanio: "I played in it and I couldn't believe the way some of the players were betting: $1,000 exactas, $400 triples. The guy I was sitting next to, so help me God, at the end of the first day, he had $60,000. At the end of the second day, he had zero. I couldn't believe it. But the people in that contest, maybe they won a buy-in somewhere and it was like found money, and they were shooting for six figures. Me? I said, 'I'm going to set a $2,000 limit. If I lose that $2,000, then I'm going to walk out of here up $5,500, because that $5,500 is a nice payday.' I lost what I was willing to lose, went up to the window, cashed out, told the teller, 'Thank you very much,' and got on the next plane back to New York."

Scanio understandably just couldn't get behind the win-or-go-home mentality when dealing with a bankroll like the Breeders' Cup Betting Challenge. I mentioned this to Maury Wolff, ever the voice of reason.

Maury Wolff: "There is another way to look at it; it's just not how I look at the world. The other way is to just play the Breeders' Cup like you would have anyway with the added benefit that you are playing for the contest prize money if you happen to do well.

That's one way to effectively reduce the takeout. Then you throw in the amenities and maybe it's a break-even game."

To some, the Breeders' Cup Betting Challenge is the single most important contest of the year because of its tie-in to racing's richest day, great atmosphere, and excellent prize money. If you're interested, I definitely suggest spending some time at BCQualify.com where you'll find many opportunities to win a ticket to the big dance.

13 Should You Play Cash During Contest Play?

"For most men (till by losing render'd sager)
Will back their own opinions with a wager."
– Lord Byron, "Beppo"

One of the most discussed topics on the handicapping contest scene concerns multitasking. Should a player abandon his or her normal play when playing in a contest? The consensus answer of the old-school tournament player is this: absolutely.

John Conte: "If I'm in a contest, I never, ever, ever make a bet at the window. Let's say you like a 2-1 shot, and if you weren't in the contest, maybe you'd bet that 2-1 shot, but you know that you can't play that 2-1 shot in the contest. You're not going to win the contest playing a short price like that. Maybe in the morning you'd made a list of three horses you might use in that race according to what the odds are. So now you're going to play your second choice whose odds are 7-1. So why would you bet the 2-1 at all? Your main priority here is the contest. If you're doing all that other stuff, it just gets too confusing."

Joe Scanio: "Another one of my rules—and I'm not so good at this one myself, it's more like 'Do as I say, not as I do'—is if you're gonna play in a contest, do not gamble at the same time. It's a distraction and it will cost you. If you like some horse you don't want to play in the contest for whatever reason and you want to throw a $20 bill on him, that's fine, but you don't want to get caught up in all these other bets, exactas, trifectas, Pick-3s. There just isn't time to do them in a professional manner."

I can recall one of the first contests I ever played in, a low-roller Friday contest on-track at Santa Anita several years back. Frank Scatoni and I were playing as partners and ended up running second—a frequent and frustrating theme for us in that contest. Throughout the day we had various other bets going on, and I recall our friend Jeff Sotman explaining, "When you're doing this, you don't want to be doing that. It's too distracting."

On some level it seemed silly to me, the idea that a $40 contest should supersede a normal day's action. But as I played in that contest more and more, I came to realize that Sotman's point was right in a lot of ways. As we've already discussed, a distinctly different mentality is required for contests versus real-money play. And while many players are capable of the mental jujitsu to switch between the two in seconds, it turns out that I am not one of them.

Easy Money

"I want the easy, easy money
Easy money, I could get lucky"
– Billy Joel, "Easy Money"

Speaking of live betting during contest play, the phrase "easy money" is only ever uttered at the track with heavy irony, lest the speaker be hit by lightning on the way out of the track. It's quite simple: there is no such thing, and anyone who tells you differently is selling something. That said, I've become fond of a little shorthand expression from a Rodney Dangerfield vehicle that I will bust out from time to time. After a particularly facile cash bet win, during a contest or just on a regular day, I will occasionally text a betting partner, "Cue Billy Joel."

Noel Michaels: "It's probably 50-50. I hate doing it. Some people do it because, and I'm not meaning this term negatively, they are degenerates. They can't wait a half an hour for the next contest race. I'm sure there are a lot of people who are successful doing that. But to me, especially at a live contest, it takes away too much of my attention and focus. I think you're bound to miss things and end up hitting yourself in the head saying, 'If only I had been focused on the contest, I would have seen this horse at Delaware, but instead I was playing the third race at Philly.' When I'm at a tournament, I'm there for the tournament."

Some people feel badly if they really love a horse and they have him in the tournament but don't bet him for real. So it can go both ways. I think it just comes down to the individual player.

Brent Sumja: "All I know is that if you fall in love with a 7-2 at a tournament where that price is not going to help you, you should go to the window and bet the horse with cash so at least you're not kicking yourself if it wins."

Ricky Zimmer: "I very rarely play on the side when I'm playing in a contest. I just try to keep things as simple and focused as possible. I see it a lot with people in a mythical tournament: they'll be playing the contest, and they're trying to decide on a horse, and they'll say, 'I don't know whether to play this in the contest or play it on the side.' They make the cash bet and the horse will hit, and they won't even be happy; they'll just regret that they didn't play it in the contest. I'd rather just avoid all the extra mental aggravation and just focus on the contest when I'm playing a contest."

Paul Shurman: "When I'm playing a tournament, I usually don't bet a penny. I find it too distracting. Are you betting on yourself? Are you betting against yourself? In one tournament, between my two entries, which had one play each, I hit the first four races at Churchill. The Pick-4 paid $64,000! It would have cost me $32 to play my picks. Not only did I not hit the Pick-4, but I didn't even have a win bet on any of those big-priced winners. And I didn't get mad at myself because I just don't play them."

When will Shurman play cash?

Paul Shurman: "Sometimes I will play cash because it's tough to use your bullets. You only have so many. I mentioned before that sometimes it's better to bet cash on way over-cap horses, especially if there's a lower cap. Sometimes it can backfire. Back in the NHC maybe five years ago, my brother was leading after day one. In the last race at Aqueduct, there was a horse we both loved named Letterman's Humor. It had been off for a while, and the price kept going up and up and up. We worried it wasn't ready, so we decided not to use it for the contest, but we had $10 each on it. The horse won, and that would have won him the tournament on day one. The $10 win bets weren't much consolation."

That brings up a good point: if you're going to hedge with cash, you want to bet enough where you'll still be making enough money to feel good about your decision if the horse wins. But there is definitely merit to the concept. Here's a similar example in reverse.

Steve Wolfson, Sr.: "As far as my personal betting, here's a story for you. At Bradley's Autotote, 10 or 12 years ago, I loved a horse going into the last race, a 7-2 named Albatross. Instead, in the contest I used Gary Stevens at 30-1. What I should've done was used the 7-2 in the tournament and bet the 30-1 cash. Fifty dollars on a 30-1 is better than most tournament finishes I will have. Instead, when the 7-2 won, I lost my cash bet, and I lost the tournament; I took fourth. Thankfully, back then the top four qualified for the NHC. Tom Quigley won that year. The fact that the name of the horse was Albatross has stuck with me for a long time. So now, if I like two horses—one a moderate price, say, 10-1 or 15-1, and the other a huge price like 40-1 or 50-1—I'll bet that longer-priced one with cash; I'll never bet that one in a tournament. But there are different schools of thought. Steve Jr., he'll play that 20-1, 30-1 in the tournament."

That harkens back to our conversation on page 75 about the benefits of playing above the cap.

Eric Moomey: "There are a lot of ways you can play it. You can bet the logical horse and then make a wager for cash on the longshot. Put $20 on the 50-1 you kind of like even a little bit, because even though you're not going to use him in the contest, you'll at least win $1,000. I love that scenario. Recently, I had a choice late in an online contest between a 10-1 shot and a 47-1 shot. I used the 10-1 in the contest, knowing that was the one everyone was going to pick. But the 47-1 shot was the horse I really loved. I bet the 10-1 in the contest to block everyone else, and I put $100 on the 47-1 shot.

"The 47-1 shot won, so I didn't win the contest because someone else had it, but I got $4,700 back, and I still finished third in the contest and got a couple of thousand for that. I was happy with that. You don't always have to win to be happy. If you're in first with one race to go, it's like being 5-for-5 in the Pick-6 singled to the favorite in the last race. Are you going to put any of your money on the price horses in that last leg? Of course you are. If you can throw out the favorite—because you're going to win with him anyway—you can make money. I've made plenty of money that way."

Mike Maloney, one of the biggest bettors in the country, has an interesting perspective on this topic.

Mike Maloney: "It doesn't help me in contests that I'm usually making my typical bets as well. But Keeneland is important enough to me, and I do well enough there, that I'll still bet two-thirds of what I normally bet in a day. I'll jump in a live-money line as soon as I get my contest bets on, and I'll get my normal bets down over there. When I'm betting live money, I'm making complicated bets, and by the end of the day, I'm mentally very tired. There are more decisions, and it's all very time-consuming. I'm looking for biases at the contest tracks, and the few minutes it takes me to make my live bets takes away from the time I am focusing on the contest races. People who aren't playing live money have more time and energy to focus on what they need to do well in the contest."

What about the NHC?

Mike Maloney: "I do the same thing at the NHC. I know it's not the best idea. But this last time at the NHC, I didn't do that well in the tournament, but I had good betting success and it ended up being a profitable trip for me. So it's a bit of a Catch-22. I'm just not wired to bet a fictional $2 win and place bet and leave it at that. If I have an opinion on a 2-1 I love or a 30-1 that I think will run third or fourth, I'm going to bet it. My friends who I sit with and who observe me tell me, 'You've got to stop that. You can't do well in a contest doing that. You're making it too hard.'"

For a player like Maloney, whose nearly every bet has a positive expected value (my words, not his), foregoing cash bets during a contest creates a massive opportunity cost that might outweigh the gains of focusing on the contest alone. But if he's playing for a seven-figure purse at the NHC, that might be a different story.

Mike Maloney: "When it comes to the NHC, I think it has to have an effect and it takes away some from my contest. At Keeneland, I'm confident enough where I can get away with it and still do well in the contest. In the NHC, it's probably crazy. I'm just another guy out there, and I've got all I can handle just trying to keep up with those guys. I would love to win the NHC, so logically I should quit betting live money there. But sometimes I see that number on the board and I can't help it. And because I've had some success betting the live money there, it just reinforces my behavior. Even as we're talking here today, I'm debating this in my head."

My general advice is that if that type of multitasking is within your skill set, by all means go for it. As we discussed earlier, multitasking is becoming the norm for some players, anyway. It's all about increasing your equity. Keep track of the plays you make during contests and make an objective assessment of how they're working out. Numbers alone won't tell the tale, though. You'll have to use a little feel to balance if the gains made at the windows are enough to offset any negative effect the cash play might have had on your contest play. Like in so many other areas in horse racing, you have to be able to handicap yourself.

14 Playing Partners

"I get by with a little help from my friends ..."
– John Lennon and Paul McCartney

I'm a big believer in playing with a partner in contests. I'm very lucky to have a playing partner, Frank Scatoni, who I play particularly well with.

Our styles match up well in that I'm a little more aggressive, and he's the voice of reason. I'm more impulsive; he's more patient. He's more studious and creative; I'm more ... actually, I have no idea why he plays with me.

One of the exercises we like to do is to go horse by horse through a card that we're going to play, ideally coming up with a 100 percent value line for each race. Obviously, this isn't possible for a big Vegas contest, but it works quite well in a bullet format or even the NYRA contests. I haven't heard of other players taking this approach, but we find it helps us be super-objective in our decision-making during the contest, and it helps us highlight the best opportunities on the card ahead of time. It's not something I'd have the patience to do alone, but being able to do it with somebody forces me to do the work and also makes it fun.

The kings of partner play are Dennis Decauwer and Don Beardsworth.

Dennis Decauwer: "My betting partner, Don, and I will typically play one entry each, and we play it as a team. We do our handicapping somewhat together, somewhat apart; we go over our notes together; we'll play an entry in each of our names, but we'll collaborate a lot on what we do."

How long have they been playing together?

Dennis Decauwer: "We've been friends for almost 50 years, since we were teenagers, and we respect each other's opinion enough that if somebody has a strong opinion on something, we will usually go with it. If we're not sure why the other person likes that horse, neither person is shy to say, 'What is it you like about that horse? What am I missing?' We'll talk about it. I would never talk him off playing a horse that was any kind of a price nor would he with me. We might be more apt to talk each other off a horse that was a shorter price. We will always go with the stronger opinion of the two, and the good thing about it is that neither one of us will ever blame the other for something if it doesn't go the right way. We've had quite a number of successes doing those things together. We've played in the NHC many times, and he was second in '08, and I was second in '09. So for all intents and purposes, we finished second two years in a row."

There are lots of ways to approach a partnership.

Paul Shurman: "For bigger contests, my brother and I will both try to qualify and play as partners, but if we don't do that or only get one entry, we might buy into a tournament like the Breeders' Cup Betting Challenge. But we don't like to do that because we don't always agree.

"In a lot of other tournaments, my brother and I don't play as partners per se; we have percentages of each other. I do know that there are people who will partner up, especially for a tournament like the Breeders' Cup Betting Challenge where maybe two people will each put in five grand. That's very hard to do, though, because no matter how similar you are to the other person, there will be a point where one person's pick goes, and that's very difficult.

When I play with my brother, the Wolfsons, or some other people, we always have 5 percent or 10 percent of each other, but then each person is in charge of his own ticket and they pick what they pick. I'd never tell anyone what to pick. I'd never try to talk anyone off anything. We just give each other advice and ask each other questions: Who looks good on the Sheets? Who looks good on HTR? Who has got the best breeding? People aren't going to play a horse just because somebody else tells them to; they're just going to feel better about their own opinion if somebody else agrees with them."

Having partners helped Steve Wolfson, Jr., win the contest world's most prestigious prize, the NHC.

Steve Wolfson, Jr.: "It is great to have that support. When I won the NHC, I was about to get shut out of a mandatory, and it was great to have the people around me, reminding me to get my bet in. You don't want to try to do everything by yourself—even if it's somebody you don't have a formal arrangement with."

Judy Wagner: "Some tournaments my husband and I start off playing separately, then if one ticket looks like it has a chance, we really start playing as partners. He got me into this, and at first I was intimidated. We each do our own handicapping, and then we talk about it in the end. If we each have a price horse, we'll split them up, and conversely, if we both like a 7-2, we might play it on both tickets. Other times we'll really be competing against each other, not in a mean-spirited way, because we are one another's biggest cheerleaders."

That type of arrangement makes sense for a husband and wife— who have 50 percent equity in each other, anyway—but it's a good idea to be a bit formal if matrimony isn't involved.

Steve Wolfson, Jr.: "It's usually best to have your arrangements clear going into the tournament. You don't want to have to decide after the first race, 'Are we partners or are we not partners?'"

It's important to be on the same page, but sometimes it works out okay even if you're not.

Patrick McGoey: "My brother wasn't doing well on Saturday, so with about three or four races to go, he said, 'I'm getting out of the contest.' In the Breeders' Cup Betting Challenge, if you bet a Pick-3 or Pick-4, it disqualifies you, so that's what he did—and he couldn't win the prize pool. Then when I told him I was going all-in on Drosselmeyer, he looked a little surprised to say the least."

It's also possible to share the risk and reward but not change any other aspect of the process. This is what's known in poker simply as "having a piece" of another player.

Mark McGuire: "In the past, when I've played with a partner, we've just played our own tickets and shared the wins or losses. That's the simplest form of playing partners. But there are groups of people who work together. One guy knows everything about Del Mar, so he does all those races. Another guy is a turf freak, so he does those. They sort it all out. That's the smartest way to do it."

That way makes a lot of sense to me, especially at a big Vegas contest with a lot of tracks: divide and conquer and maybe you can get an edge just by having more brain power concentrated over more contest races. Of course, some partners are particularly valuable.

Steve Wolfson, Sr.: "Paul Shurman has been the most successful in our group in the last five years. He is always very generous with his opinions and quick to say, 'Dinner is on me.' He's always been a great partner. If he asks me something, I feel comfortable answering—not because there's something in it for me, but because he is so appreciative of it."

I asked Steve Jr., more about the group of people he plays with.

Steve Wolfson, Jr.: "It's still an evolving arrangement, but it's great that you have that shared experience and we can help each other, point out certain things and share some percentage. If we play our own entries, of course that's straightforward and easy to do. I'm not averse to the idea that if we both really like this horse, then we should both play it. When it works, it's extra good; and when it doesn't, it can be very frustrating."

Other players eschew partners.

Ricky Zimmer: "I just feel comfortable making my own decisions. I don't know how well I'd do in a partnership structure. Handicapping is so personal to me. I couldn't see being part of a group decision on how to play something. I have to do it myself."

Joe Scanio: "I would never recommend playing partners. However, if you're playing with a partner, you must decide who's going to make the decisions prior to the start of the contest. This never works out because if you have a partner who knows anything about the game, he or she is going to have a mind of his or her own. So if he picks something and it doesn't win, and the horse you wanted wins, it's just a disaster. Have a little confidence in yourself. I mean, where's the advantage in having that other partner? I'm not a believer in partners at all."

I went out on a limb and told Scanio that it sounded to me like he'd had a negative experience playing partners.

Joe Scanio: "About three or four years ago in the NHC at Red Rock, it was the last race of the contest, and I was sitting about 12th or 13th. I was sitting next to a friend of mine, who is also my accountant. I liked the 10 horse, and I said to Bart, 'I really like this horse; he's 25-1; he'll put me right where I want to be.' He said, 'How can you bet this 10, Joe? I like the 1 more than him, and he's 70-1.' We got in this whole conversation, and he changed my mind.

"And, of course, the 10 won, and I would've finished third for about $75,000. I didn't sleep for three days. I didn't fire him as my accountant or my friend, and I did manage to get that year's taxes for free, but I learned that you should never volunteer opinions unless you're asked, and even then be very cautious."

This reminds me of a quote my friend and mentor William Murray was fond of: "One of the cardinal sins of the racetrack is tipping without solicitation."

Steve Wolfson, Sr.: "I know a lot of players share information about who they like in the race. I'm less likely to do that because I don't want to talk someone off of their selection. I'm reluctant to do that because I'd feel such guilt. I don't want them to talk me off my opinion, either. I recall standing with Andy Beyer, who I didn't know at the time, and three others, standing at the second floor of the clubhouse at Saratoga. We were talking about the race, sharing opinions. I liked this horse shipping from Monmouth, Mail Order. Andy looked at me and said, in his inimitable Andy Beyer way, 'No shot.'

"The fact that Mail Order won had nothing to do with anything except for the fact that this is such a wonderful game of opinions. It all turns over so quickly, you don't have to wait years and years to know if you are right or not."

I liked this Dennis Decauwer quote about the perils of joint decision-making. With a baby to care for as I was writing this book, it really hit home with me.

Dennis Decauwer: "When a husband and wife are raising children, a lot of decisions need to be made. What's the right decision? The right decision is what feels best at the time you make the decision. It doesn't only have to do with the outcome. And just because it was my final say this time, that doesn't mean we take your final say next time, because they might both be wrong!"

Then there's another type of partner who isn't really a partner. Call them shills, call them beards, call them what you will, but they've been a reality on the contest scene since day one.

Joe Scanio: "Years ago, you'd go to a contest and know there were certain individuals who had a million people there as shills. There was one guy; he took his grandmother, who was literally in a wheelchair and on oxygen, and here I hear him yelling at her, 'Grandma, go bet the two.' 'The three?' she asks. 'No, Grandma, the two! T-W-O!' I said, 'What is going on here?' At least most guys used people who at least knew something about horse racing. Here's the funniest part: can you picture if Grandma had won the NHC?"

Does Scanio feel like it's unfair to use shills?

Joe Scanio: "If they put up their money and they're good enough to qualify several times, then guess what? Good for them."

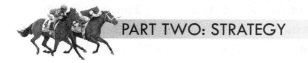

15 **Multiple Entries**

> "You get as many chances as you want; as many as you
> dare to make for yourself."
> — Edward Bloor, *Taken*

The whole "shill" concept described at the end of the last chapter developed as a way to work around the fact that until the 2013 season, the NHC allowed only one entry per person. The benefit of having shills was and is to get extra entries. Why were people willing to go to such lengths to ensure they had more than one entry? The answer should be obvious: it can be a powerful advantage.

Mark McGuire: "If the odds don't tell me who to play, that's when you want to have multiple entries."

Brent Sumja: "My theory about having multiple entries is that if I have three and you have one, it's a lot like poker. If I am starting with pocket aces and you're starting with pocket kings, you might win an individual hand, but over the long term I'm eventually going to win and you are going to lose."

Paul Shurman: "There are two main strategies and both of them are pretty simple. The one that most people use is that early on, you play two separate horses until one of them comes in. Then that becomes your good ticket, and then you play the horses you like on that ticket. Then on your other ticket, you play the longer-priced horses, and if you hit one on the longshot ticket, then that becomes your good ticket and your previous good ticket becomes your bad."

Mark McGuire: "The two common strategies are totally different. Some people will play the exact same horses on both tickets until the end, and that gives them quite a bit of power, because they can branch off at the end and have a better chance to win the tournament. I prefer the other way, where I'm picking different longshots I like on each ticket, trying to get into the lead. I play much better as a front-runner, since I've been so conditioned to finding longshots that I sometimes look for them too much—but when I'm on the lead, I'm able to take the horse that I like the best. I don't have to throw a horse away just because he's 4-1. If I'm in the lead and I think he's a winner, I can play him. By the same token, if I like a 16-1 shot, I'm going to play the 16-1 shot."

What happens from there?

Mark McGuire: "Once I make the lead with one ticket, I'll use the other ticket as a protection ticket. On that one, I'll play the most logical longshot. The strategy is going to change after each race. If you've done your homework, you should have studied the last two races already to see if you have viable longshots in those races."

Of course, having multiple entries doesn't make winning easy. In fact, it can add to your frustration.

Paul Shurman: "The biggest problem with multiple entries is that often times you'll split your tickets. You have $500 on one and $500 on the other, and $800 would have won it."

Dennis Decauwer: "If I'm playing solo in a tournament, 95 percent of the time I play one entry only, and the reason I play one entry only is that I'm unhappy later if I zigzag in the tournament. I think my focus is better if I play one entry and I'm not just hoping to catch a bomb—the last thing in the world you want is to play two entries and they come in 11th and 12th, or eighth and ninth. I see some people who are marvelous at doing it, but it's not for me."

Joe Scanio: "Sometimes I'll say, 'Okay, I'm going to play this one horse on the good card and then this longshot on the dead card.' And you don't know how many times it happens where the longshot wins. You'll always hear players say, including myself, 'I had him on the wrong card.'"

Of course, you almost must consider that some of those horses that gave you points on each ticket you simply wouldn't have had if you were playing only one entry. Memory bias comes into play here, as people tend to blame the multiple-ticket strategy for the times when they split tickets and are quick to credit themselves rather than the strategy for the times when they played multiple tickets and things worked out. I spoke to a quant who hypothesized that, over time, the optimal number of entries to have would correlate with the average number of starters in a horse race, in order to ensure maximum coverage. I balked a little, saying I thought that sounded like a recipe for splitting tickets. He told me, "It might feel that way, but mathematically, over time, that's probably the way to get the most equity." I am hoping he will run a study I can share on my blog at some point.

Ken Massa sums up why it's a good idea to have more than one entry.

Ken Massa: "When you are looking for longshots 8-1 or higher, it can be a little frustrating because even the ones that fire finish second or third twice as often as they win. It's just like throwing darts. When you play contests, you usually have that question to answer: 'Should I play more than one entry in the contest so that way I can throw more darts at these longshots?' To me, it makes sense to play maybe two in the middle ground, not three or more, because that becomes splitting up your ticket too much. Playing only one lessens your opportunity for longshots. So when you're dealing with live longshots, you need to find a compromise between being cost-effective versus not having enough ammo."

Joe Scanio has another interesting way of splitting tickets.

Joe Scanio: "In a contest with mandatory races and optional races, if I have multiple entries, I might play them the same for the mandatory races and split them up in the optional races. It gives me a chance to make more selections and maybe catch something."

This makes sense to me. What makes even more sense to me is not dividing so much by optionals and mandatories, but by which races look chaotic to you versus which ones look like they'll be won by logical horses. If the race figures to produce a logical winner, there will be less variance there, so play both entries the same. Races likely to produce longshot winners will necessarily be more chaotic, so that's where you want the additional coverage of two different selections.

Yet another way to go—maybe the best way of all—would be to let the strength of your opinion dictate: your strongest opinions, be they logicals or longshots, should get doubled up. Wherever you feel the most uncertainty, regardless of the prices you're torn between, split and cover. Steve Wolfson, Jr., agrees with this last idea.

Steve Wolfson, Jr.: "I'm more of the mind that if you play two entries, if you like a horse a lot, then you shouldn't mind playing it on both entries."

It's becoming an increasingly popular strategy to play two tickets the same until you get to a certain target number, then split them to maximize your options in the later, potentially more important races. Why are the later races possibly more important? Because at that point you know exactly what you need to make your goal.

Eric Moomey: "When I started out, I was more inclined to play different horses on each entry, but I did a little research on my own play and I'm changing that now. I noticed over time that top selections were outperforming my backup selections by a wide margin, and I realized I'm probably better off just sticking with those in the early part of a tournament at least."

Again, though, conceiving the strategy is one thing; sticking with it is quite another.

Joe Scanio: "It's easy to outsmart yourself in a contest; you could get too cute. Let's say there are multiple entries allowed: one of my strategies is if it's a two-day, like with the New York tournaments, I'll mirror-match my entries on day one so that two entries are actually one entry. Then the second day, I may split them up. Then what'll happen is somehow the devil gets in your system, and you weaken just when you thought you shouldn't be weakening. In this recent Saratoga contest, I mirror-matched the cards and I split them up in the last race on day one, and of course that's a race where one card won and one card lost. So now I got one card in sixth place and one card in God-knows-where, and if I'd stuck with my plan, I'd have been in sixth and seventh."

Root, Root, Root for the Home Team

A few years ago, in the Santa Anita low-roller contest, there was a run of dominance like the contest world has never seen. At the time, the track was running these little mini-contests every Friday, Saturday, and Sunday. The rules were simple: $40 buy-in (a $10 entry fee with a $30 fixed bankroll), $3 win/place, had to play any five Santa Anita races, no cap. Final scores varied pretty wildly, from as low as $50 to as high as $170 (the effect of short fields on the one hand and no cap on the other). There were cash prizes as well as an entry into a bigger tournament, which was limited to two entries per person. But that didn't seem to matter to a man named James Root. Root turned the contest into his personal ATM for a couple of seasons, piling up in-the-money finishes and wins—even when he'd already maxed out his entries into the bigger tourney. At some point, Tom Quigley jokingly texted a group of us the news of Root's latest win along with an all-caps one word note: "STOP!"

I never met Mr. Root in person, but over time, I noticed something: when the final scores swung towards the lower end of the spectrum, Root's name was everywhere. I'd hear the winner had $62, and without knowing who won, I'd say to Frank Scatoni, "Root again, huh?" However, when the scores were on the high end of the scale, Root's name was usually absent. Eventually, Root's name became part of our vernacular, especially when splitting tickets. We'd play one ticket trying to take advantage of the fact that there was no cap in the contest, playing some crazy longshots that would make Maury Wolff proud. We uncreatively called this "The Bomb Ticket." On the other ticket, we'd play short-priced logicals, especially when we thought it would be a chalky day. This was what became known as "The James Root Ticket," as in, "Okay, put the Moon Han firster on the bomb ticket and the Mandella stretch-out on the James Root ticket."

In a frustrating aside, I must say that our record of in-the-money finishes in that tournament in those years was second only to the great James Root. However, we never managed to win the damn thing, not even once. It's our white whale. Or perhaps, given the stakes involved, our white guppy.

This chapter has more on the perils of playing multiple entries than the benefits, probably because those are the more fun stories for our players to tell, but the benefits clearly outweigh the risks.

It's my strong belief that if playing multiple entries weren't such a good idea, then so many of the best players wouldn't all be in such a hurry to do it. Here's a unique story of using multiple entries that ends well.

Paul Shurman: "I have another strategy I sometimes use in the NYRA tournaments. That contest you have to do $20 to win, place, or show, and it's over the course of two days. The thing about the tournament is you can win it if you start day two with as little as $200 or $300, but you have close to no chance if you start day two with zero. So what I do is on one ticket I play chalk to show, just so I get a collection. I'll end up with maybe $220. Then I'll play my other ticket normally, so I know that on day two, I'll have one ticket with at least $200 on it. Then if I hit something on my non-show ticket, I change it up: I start playing by the good ticket/bad ticket theory.

"I've come in second in the NYRA tournaments four times, and three of them it was on the ticket that started as the show ticket. A couple of weeks ago at Belmont, it was very embarrassing, actually. The first race I bet the chalk to show and it paid $2.10. But nobody else had anything. So there I was up at the leaderboard at number one, with a $2.10 show bet! A friend of mine saw that and said to our group, 'What's Shurman doing? Has he lost his mind?' But I explained myself and he understood. There's nothing worse than going into day two with zero on both tickets, and it's certainly possible."

How important are multiple entries in the final analysis?

Mark McGuire: "In one way, multiple entries aren't as big a deal as some people think, and in another way, they are the biggest thing there is. Some people out there complain about other people playing multiple entries, saying that if they too were able to afford multiple entries, then they'd win. In fact, for a lot of people, it's not going to help a whole lot. It's like the lottery: if you have 100 tickets, it's not that different from having one because there are so many people in the contest. In the NHC, where there are 500 entries, I don't care if 40 people have two entries, it's not going to help that much. But if I'm in a contest with only 50 people and ten of them are multiple entries against my one, I'm getting hurt quite a bit."

Kevin Cox is intrigued by the rule change that allows two entries per person in the NHC.

Kevin Cox: "Of course it's a big deal to have two entries in the NHC, because your odds of winning $750,000 go from 460-1 to 230-1. If my wife qualifies as well, then the Cox household has about a 150-1 chance. But to me the big jump is that first one from 460-1 to 230-1."

All you can do in a contest is to put yourself in the best possible position to win, and playing multiple entries provides many players extra chances to do just that.

16 Endgame Theory

"To improve at chess you should in the first instance study the endgame."
– **Jose Capablanca, chess champion and author**

The endgame is the part of contest play that really separates itself from everyday play. You have a wider range of options of horses to consider because favorites really come back into play, and now you must play your opponents as well as the races themselves. In the endgame, one mistake or one brilliant decision can mean absolutely everything to the final outcome.

Ricky Zimmer: "When you're just playing the races on a normal day, it's all about handicapping and money management, but with contests, there's that third element where you have to think about what the people around you are doing."

It may no longer be enough to pick a winner in the last race of the contest; now you might well have to strategically pick a winner that no one above you will have. If you choose wrong, you might be drawing dead. Since you're competing against a select group of people, to really excel you need to get inside their minds. In this way, handicapping contests can be more like poker than a typical day at the track.

Granted, in a big tournament with 100 or more players, this stuff is less important, at least early on. Just to recap material we've covered so far in the book: first you need to sort out how many dollars/points it's going to take to win; then you need to build a plan to get to that number. Early on, you pretty much want to play your own contest and not worry so much about everybody else.

As a contest progresses, however, you need to be aware of what other people are likely to do, and you better be sure you know what's coming up next. What I really want going into the last race of a contest is to be "drawing live"—that is, having a horse that will win me the tournament. If I'm the guy in first, I want as many of my opponents as possible "drawing dead"—I want them to have no chance to pass me because I've blocked them by playing the same horse.

Let's say you like the favorite in the last race of the contest. This is an instance where you really want to do everything you can to be in the top position going into that last race. Shoot for the stars in the second- and third-to-last races, because maybe you can end up far enough in front so that even if the player in second plays the favorite, he or she can't catch you. This is ideal, because then you can play another horse in the race with the idea that you'll block someone under you, essentially giving you multiple bullets in the most important race of the contest—talk about having an advantage!

If you like a range of prices in the last race, suddenly the last few races before the finale become a little different. In that instance, instead of really wanting to be in the lead, you really just want to be jockeying for position. The idea is you want to be in a place to play the horse you like and not be blocked. Obviously, it still wouldn't be a bad thing to be in first, but it's a lot less important.

When it comes to perfecting endgame play, experience is the best teacher.

Eric Moomey: "Experience does pay. You try something, you get burned, and you learn, okay, that's why players don't do that. Look at the person in the lead with one race to go and write down what their last play was; record what the top-10 players did. You'll get really good insight, and you'll find that time and time again, people will do pretty much the same thing. Over time, you can figure out exactly what they're going to do. So let's say you're heading into the last race and you're 20 cents behind the leader and you know he's going to pick a longshot whether he's in the lead or at the back. Well, that opens up the possibility for you to play the favorite.

"Let's say you're at the end of a tournament and you're in second place. There's going to be a horse that can move you up to the next level. Sometimes it's going to be the favorite; other times it might be a 4-1, 6-1, 8-1, whatever. What is the percentage of time that the leader picks that first horse that can beat him? Over a sample of tournaments that I have recorded, it happens 48 percent of the time, less than 50 percent. I talked to one of the guys who I monitor very closely who always plays a longshot even when he's in that spot. I asked him, 'So when you're in the lead at the end, why don't you play the favorite?' He told me, 'Because the favorite still has to win.' I said, 'Yeah, but it's the last race, and that's the most logical horse to win.' And then he remembered, 'Hey, wait a minute; you actually beat me out one time doing that.'

"You have to pay attention to what individual people do in that spot. If they do the same thing most every time, which many people do because they are creatures of habit, then you have to use that knowledge. Some guys have a lot more than a 52 percent chance of not betting the favorite there, and that might mean you can bet the favorite.

"It also matters how many people there are below you who can catch you with the favorite. Is there one person, five people, or ten people? If there are ten people who can beat you with the favorite, then you probably need to select the favorite. But if there's only one person, you probably don't need to select the favorite, especially if you know what the person in second is likely to do."

I asked Moomey to walk me through a few endgame scenarios.

Eric Moomey: "If I'm in the lead going into the last race, I'm looking to play a logical contender but usually not the favorite, because the person behind you will rarely play the favorite. They assume that since you're in the lead, you're going to play the favorite. That's different if there are ten people who can beat you. Out of ten people, someone might play the favorite. Another reason to play the favorite in that spot is because maybe someone from the back will hit a longshot and finish ahead of the score you had going into the race, but maybe the favorite will run second and give you enough points to still beat him, the idea being that

179

people are shooting for your score, so even a few extra bucks can be critical. But if there are only one or two people who can beat you, don't worry about the favorite, and if they pick the favorite, let them beat you and be happy that they won. It's okay.

"Conversely, if you're in second and don't think the leader will play the favorite, go ahead and play the favorite. You can use it for you, and you can use it against you. But I can tell you that generally people in second through tenth place will not select the favorite. The favorite will often go un-bet by people in the top ten. So use that as a data point. If you're in second and you do select the favorite, and the guy in first blocks you, that's okay, too. It happened 48 percent of the time in the subset of contest races I studied in my database.

"I once played in a contest that was tight at the end, where I was in fifth place and won by playing the favorite. And he didn't even win; he came in second. It can happen."

Personally, I agree that this can be an effective strategy if there are one, maybe two, people who can nab you with the favorite. If five people can get you with the favorite, and you like the favorite, you better play the favorite—because for me, game theory is one thing, but the situation I never want to be in is losing to the horse I liked when playing him was an option. Roger Cettina was famously on the wrong end of an endgame situation, at the 2012 NHC.

Roger Cettina: "I was ahead by very little going into the last race. It was a few minutes to post at Santa Anita, and I just hate betting favorites. That's just me. I don't bet favorites. I decided to take a shot on a longshot that didn't run at all. The favorite didn't win either, but he ran second. Nobody who could have passed me with the winner had the winner, but the guy in second bet the favorite, and the place money was enough for him to beat me for $750,000 by $1.20. It was absolute torture. It's all game theory. I would have thought that he would have thought I was going to protect myself by betting the favorite. But obviously that wasn't the case."

What I've been pretty good at in my tournament play is putting myself in situations where I'm using game theory to draw live in the last race. I'll go through the players ahead of me and think, "What are they logically going to play?" If it's likely that three folks ahead of me will play the top three choices, then I'll start looking at the fourth choice. If the betting choices aren't clear, I'll do the same thing by looking at the odds. If the people ahead of me need 6-1 and lower, I'll be looking for 8-1 and higher.

Eric Moomey had some advice on this.

Eric Moomey: "Another good strategy is to overshoot to avoid being blocked. Say it's a contest where you need to finish in the top three: I don't try to beat the third-place guy. I'll try to beat the second-place guy or the first-place guy. That way, if someone above you is trying to block you, at least you still have a chance to finish in the money. Never go for just enough unless it's a horse you have confidence no one else will pick.

"If you notice, near the end, a lot of people play it safe. The player in the lead is worried about the people in second, third, and fourth. Well, what about players six through a hundred? They're shooting for you, too. That also means that if you're one of the people in the chasing pack, you never want to pass on a viable longshot that can put you in the lead."

THE IMPORTANCE OF MATH
"My advice to the unborn is, don't be born with a gambling instinct unless you have a good sense of probabilities."
– Jack Dreyfus, financial expert and owner of Hobeau Farm

Want to start a debate between contest players? Ask them how important math is to the game. Some will nod and offer up a non-committal response; some will unequivocally declare it irrelevant; and others will offer you thoughtful responses like these.

Mike Labriola: "Math is a pure and absolute science, and handicapping isn't. We know that. When you talk about the ingredients that go into being a good bettor, there's the scientific part—which is where math comes in—but there's also an intuitive part. And let's not forget the most important part, which is luck. You need to have all of those things, but you need to start with the math.

"For instance, if you look at a race, and let's say that today's race is six furlongs, and you look at the horse's last race, and see that he was there at seven furlongs until the last call, you can extrapolate from that information that within the right circumstances in terms of pace and class, six furlongs is probably going to be a good distance for this horse. You have to know fractionally how the race you're keying off of translates into today's race. That's one rudimentary example of how math is important."

Eric Moomey: "Contests are all math! Quick: you are $29 behind the leader in a $2 win/place tournament ... what odds do you need to win? You have 30 seconds to make your last selection. Answer: assuming no one blocks you: 9-1. You can divide the number of points you need by three to get a rough answer, but I've put together a spreadsheet that varies with the field size to give you a better estimate for the place money."

Implied probability is another area where math comes up a lot in horse racing. In horse racing terms, implied probability simply converts the odds of a horse winning into the percentage chance of the event happening. To be 100 percent accurate, we'd also need to account for the effect of takeout, but that's going down a math rabbit hole we can leave alone for now. For an example of how implied probability works in horse racing, if a horse is 2-1 on the board, the implied probability of it winning is 33 percent; a 4-1 has an implied probability of 20 percent; a 9-1, ten percent, and so on. The math is simple to do. The formula is: denominator/(denominator+numerator).

Let's say we want to know the implied probability of a 5-2 shot. Following the formula above, we take 2 and divide that by 7 (2+5). We get 0.286. Then we multiply that by 100 so it can be expressed as an implied probability percentage (28.6 percent).

Just in case you don't want to make all the calculations manually, here is a little table to help you out:

IMPLIED PROBABILITY CHART

Odds	Implied % Chance of Winning
1/10	91
1/5	83
2/5	71
1/2	67
3/5	62.5
4/5	56
EVENS	50
6/5	45.5
7/5	41.67
3/2	40
8/5	38.5
9/5	35.71
2/1	33.3
5/2	29
3/1	25
7/2	22
4/1	20
9/2	18
5/1	17
6/1	14
7/1	13
8/1	11
9/1	10
10/1	9
11/1	8
12/1	8
14/1	7
15/1	6
16/1	6
20/1	5
25/1	4
30/1	3
40/1	2.5
50/1	2
100/1	1

Eric Moomey: "What I have found, when you have horses that are 20-1, you'd think they have around a 4 percent chance of winning, but that's not the case. A lot of them have more like a 1 or 2 percent chance, but occasionally you can find a 20-1 that actually has a 4 or 5 percent chance of winning, or a 10-1 that actually has a 9 percent chance of winning, rather than a 4 percent chance of winning, which many 10-1 shots have in real life.

"Normally at the higher odds, the odds are either representative of the implied probability or they are not even close. Take the Kentucky Derby in 2009. Mine That Bird was 50-1 or whatever he was, but on the offshore books, he was like 300-1. The point is: that one way to find value, without knowing anything about the horse, is you look at what fixed-odds prices are being offered. Look at the Breeders' Cup where there are a lot of overseas shippers. Who knows better than the offshore books or the UK gambling sites how good an overseas horse is? They will tell you what the price should be and you can see if the tote price is good value or not."

We touched briefly on the idea of using the board to help you make your selections, but we haven't talked about the math behind it. When it comes down to the last few races, you better have a good idea of what your chances are of catching the right price or prices to put you in the lead. Here are the mathematics of trying to get to your target score from two races out.

Eric Moomey: "It's much easier to get one long-priced horse than to get two mid-priced horses back-to-back. A 10-1 is easier to find than two 5-1s."

In Noel Michaels' *Handicapping Contest Handbook*, player Joe Hinson, one of the most successful tournament players of his day, breaks down the math.

Joe Hinson: "Let's assume you have two bets left in a contest and need $18 or more to reach your goal. When you can play two horses at 8-1 odds or two horses at 7-2 odds, you should always plan on playing the two horses at 8-1. Your chance of hitting at least one of the 8-1 shots is approximately 18 percent (assuming a 15 percent takeout). If you try to make the same $18 with two 7-2 shots, the probability of doing so is only 3.6 percent! In this example, going for the higher-priced horses gives you almost five times the chance of reaching your goal."

I asked Maury Wolff to walk me through this example.

Maury Wolff: "For simplicity's sake, we're going to say that a 7-2 shot has a 20 percent chance of winning after takeout, which is a little high but makes it easier to write up. There are four possible outcomes; let's start with the 7-2 shots.

Both horses lose: .8 x .8 = .64
Horse A wins and B loses: .2 x .8 = .16
Horse B wins and A loses: .8 x .2 = .16
Horse A and B both win: .2 x .2 = .04

"Here are the probabilities for the 8-1 shots, again adjusted for takeout.

Both horses lose: .91 x .91 =.82
Horse A wins and B loses: .91 x .09 = .085
Horse A loses and B wins: .91 x .09 = .085
Both A and B win: .1 x .1= .01

"So you have an 18 percent chance of getting at least one horse home. What is probably confusing you is that the higher probability of one horse winning doesn't buy you anything. One $9 winner is the same as a 0 return because it doesn't get you to your goal. In real life, you bet one winner and one loser at 7-2, and you have won $7. But at the end of a tournament, because the additional $7 doesn't get you to your goal, it's an all-or-nothing proposition, so it is worth nothing because you don't pass the leader."

While this example holds definitely true at the end of a contest and it's a useful lesson in general, there are plenty of times you might want to go with the mid-prices in the middle of a tournament, depending on what your opinion is and what the scores are.

THE GOLDEN CHILD

There is another way to think about handicapping contests entirely, a way that makes them much more like poker. This speaks to the point Ricky Zimmer made elsewhere in this chapter and is very much related to what Dave Gutfreund, an excellent poker player himself, was getting at earlier in the book when he described contests as "a game with numbers."

There are players who can do OK in contests without even picking up a *Form* or booting up their laptop—all they need to do is study the toteboard and apply the proper game theory. One such player, a poker professional from California, was such a man. To this day, I don't know his name, only that everybody called him Golden and I could never figure out why—the guy is white as a ghost and his hair is darker than mine.

I remember a day when Frank and I, sick of finishing in the low money in that contest, decided we'd really put our best foot forward and attack the card with an NHC-like focus. So we spent hours handicapping, watched all the tape, scrawled Sheet numbers and value lines in the *Form*, and carefully examined every horse that walked by before analyzing, debating, and finally making our selections.

Golden had a beer and chatted casually with the gang at Quigley's Corner. Then he looked up at the tote board and went to bet. In the end, we managed third that day. The winner? You guessed it: Golden. He played horses in or just above the typical James Root odds range all day and then in the last played the 8-1 he needed to win. On the plus side, I had finally figured out why they called him Golden.

THE PROTECTION OF THE CHALK

Brian Troop's plays on the second day of his NHC victory are a great example of what Jeff Sotman called "The Protection of the Chalk." As mentioned earlier, Troop put up $187, the highest one-day score in NHC history on day one. On day two, he played a lot of longshots and only hit for $34.

Brian Troop: "A lot of people said to me on Saturday, 'All you have to do is play low-priced horses and cash and extend your lead.'

Well, no, because the low-priced horses weren't going to hurt me, anyway. I knew perfectly well if they were betting 3-1 and 4-1 shots that I was going to probably be okay. I knew they'd all be playing longshots, so in the races I played, I knew I might as well play the best longshot I could play myself. It might have looked like I was backing up to the field, but I hung on."

The "protection of the chalk" concept really comes into play in the very last race of a tournament.

Michael Beychok: "Blocking your competition becomes very important at the end. What horses am I trying to protect with? If the guy behind you is trailing you by $10, you already have the 6-5 favorite and the 2-1 second choice covered. You can't lose if either of those horses wins. So then you want to try to eliminate your opponent's selection. So you ask, what horse can he beat you with? At this point, it comes down to strict math. For example, if the 5-1 third choice is the first horse that can beat me, I'm taking that horse. Math is on my side. I've got the first favorite, the second favorite, and the third favorite. Over time, I'm going to come out a winner in that situation."

There is some disagreement over some of these endgame issues, of course.

Mark McGuire: "Even experienced players make mistakes all the time. There are subtle strategies all throughout any contest you're playing in that will vary depending on the specifics of the rules. You'll see people in the last race, even when they own the horse already, they'll pick him anyway. You see that all the time."

Eric Moomey already mentioned one contrarian idea that might account for this seeming blunder. There is a good reason you as the leader might play the favorite in the last race, even if you theoretically have the protection of the chalk. For this to work, you would really have to like the chalk's chances of either winning or running second. But assuming that's the case, here's what you have to consider. You know that all the players below you are gunning for your score going into the last, sometimes down to the penny. So if you play the favorite, even if it just runs second, the place price you get might leapfrog you over the person who just caught the winner. You win anyway. You are essentially trading one "out"—the opportunity to block whoever is chasing you—for a potentially better "out": the chance to have your horse run second and still get the money.

Is this the best strategy in all situations? Certainly not. But I can think of several scenarios where it would be a brilliant play, assuming you love the favorite and blocking your opponents isn't a feasible option because there are too many horses in the price range that can catch you. In any case, this is an example that should get your brain working along the right lines to play tournament endgames.

PLAYING THE OTHER PLAYERS

I was curious to get a few more ideas from our players about the importance of knowing one's competition, especially as it relates to endgame strategy.

Eric Moomey: "A lot of people in a brick-and-mortar tournament are flipping through the *Daily Racing Form* to do their handicapping. I don't even have a *Daily Racing Form* with me when I show up, and that's not just because I've already done my handicapping. It's because I'm not focused on the horses; I'm focused on the players in the competition. That's a big difference from most contest players, I think. If you talk to poker players, they don't care about the cards; they care about their opponents. It's the idea of playing the player, not the cards. If I know what the player is going to do, then I can beat him."

I asked Moomey for a practical application of what he was talking about.

Eric Moomey: "What if I'm in fifth place and I have a pretty good idea of what players one through four are going to do? Well, I can't play the same thing they are, because I'm not going to be able to beat them if I do that. So I know I have to do something different from what they're going to do, so at least I have a chance of getting past them."

Moomey isn't the only one who incorporates this aspect of game theory into his play.

Mike Labriola: "Every player has an individual style. I can usually make a pretty good guess as to which tournament players will have which winners based on things like the odds and running style of the winner. In order to win, you have to have the types of things that you do in your handicapping be applicable on that given day. Most days, the things we use aren't applicable—that's why it's an inexact science. But if your style fits the type of winners that are winning on that day, you're going to do well."

John Conte: "You have to think about what the other people are going to do. Quite often you're in contests with the same people, and the same people end up on top at the end. You have to chart—just like you chart the races—the other players' moves to see what type of horses they're betting. That's part of my theory."

Other players think this line of thinking goes a little too far from the name of the game.

Paul Shurman: "You can't get too hung up on who you are playing against. It's easy to outthink yourself. You have to play who you like."

THE MONEY IS AT THE TOP

Sometimes you get in situations at the end of the tournament where you have to decide between looking for a minor cash award or being more aggressive and going for the win.

Duke Matties: "I play every contest to win. Sometimes I'll give away the third place just to try to win it, because the first prize is always so much higher. The money's all at the top, as it should be. You've got to win or else it's just another day."

John Conte feels the same way, as you can see from his NHC endgame story.

John Conte: "I was in ninth place heading into the second day, and the thing about me is that I'm an all-in gambler. If I'm not going to win $90,000, I don't care if I win $10. I'm not sitting there for two days to grind out a profit. If I'm stuck in a spot where I'm going to

THE WINNING CONTEST PLAYER

win $50,000, I'll take the gamble and try to win $500,000, whereas most of the people, they'll say, 'I'm eighth or ninth; I don't want to lose my position.' They'll be happy going home with less because maybe that money means a lot to them. It doesn't mean a lot to me—and it's not that I couldn't use the money. But as a contest gambler, I only think of one thing—winning. I'll do anything I can to win. I don't care if by betting a longer price, I might drop ten positions. If I hit the race, I can go up ten positions."

How did this come into play the year of his NHC win?

John Conte: "I was in 11th place [heading into the final race], and I saw that I needed $50, and I could have easily picked a 3-1 or 4-1 shot and moved up or held position. But then I thought about it. The odds were if I picked a logical 3-1, 4-1, or 5-1, that these people ahead of me who just wanted to hold their positions were all going to have the same horse. I wouldn't make up any ground. But I didn't think they'd have the guts to pick a 22-1 shot, and the guys who are really in front, they don't need a 22-1 shot; they're just looking to hit an even-money shot to maintain their positions in first or second."

Eric Moomey: "Always play to win. That's rule number one. A lot of times it will come up at the end of a tournament that you can easily get into second or third place, and maybe with a longshot, you can get into first place. All you have to do is see one 15-1 shot win and that seventh-place guy shoot past everybody and win to realize that that should have been you. If you have a shot to win, you've got to take it—assuming there's a difference between first and third. If it's $10,000 to first; $5,000 for second; $2,000 for third, then you've got to go for first. You don't get into contention every time. So when you're in contention, you have got to go for the win. Go big or go home."

"Go big or go home" is usually good advice, but I wouldn't say it's always good advice. There are going to be times, as happened to me this summer, when it makes more sense to play for second. I was in about seventh place going into the last race. The leader was way in front, and there was a pack of about six of us all vying for the minor awards. Everybody in two through six pretty much needed a cap horse—and there were only four cap horses, none of whom were too appealing. Meanwhile, there was a very strong-looking even-money shot in the race who would give me enough points to sneak into second place and a $2,000 payday. If I went for the win, I estimated my chance at about 1 percent to win the $5,000 first prize.

First of all, I'd have to pick the right 20-1 shot, and because the five people ahead of me were also likely to play a 20-1 shot, I'd have to pray that I didn't get blocked, an extremely likely scenario. So what's better? A 1 percent shot at $5,000 (expected value $50) or a 45 percent shot at $2,000 (expected value $900)? It doesn't take Maury Wolff to know you want to choose what's behind Curtain B.

I went with the chalk, who won, and I got paid. I figured no one in front of me was going to play the chalk because they were all trying to win with an impossible horse. No matter which capper I'd picked, I would have been drawing stone-cold dead. I know that's an unusual scenario, but it just goes to show that the right answer when it comes to most of these contest strategy questions is, "It depends." Every tournament is unique, and every endgame scenario is different. You have to factor in all of the data before you make your final decision.

D-F-L

Another great piece of advice I got from many of our players concerned the importance of shedding your ego when it comes to your final score. I recently had an incredibly frustrating experience, the worst thing that can happen in a tournament. Did I zero out? No, that would have been fine. I ran ninth in a tournament that paid down to eighth. I'd far prefer to run DFL (Dead Flippin' Last).

Eric Moomey: "It's Okay to finish last. In fact, you will find most of the successful players in one of two places on the leaderboard, either right at the top or right at the bottom."

Ricky Zimmer: "I think early on in my contest play, I was more concerned about being on the board than being at the top of the board. And yeah, I feel like my play early on was a little bit passive, and that hurt me. If I could go back and give my younger self advice, I'd say, 'Just go for it; always go for it.'"

John Conte: "A lot of people play not to lose. They don't want to finish too far down the leaderboard. But sometimes you have to be willing to finish last if you want to try to win."

Ken Massa: "Experienced tournament players, we're not worried about the humility of getting a zero. That doesn't bother us at all anymore. It's probably because we've been shooting at 20-1 shots and none of them came in. If all the chalks win, it's simple: we get zero. I think some people are reluctant to play in tournaments because they're worried about putting their name out in public and seeing that zero on there. That's just something you have to get over."

Maury Wolff: "In the early days of playing contests, you could often tell how good the field was by looking at the leaderboard at the end of the day and seeing how many players finished with zero. The more zeros, the better the field. At least they were playing the right way."

17 The Mental Side

> *"Ninety percent of this game is half mental."*
> **– Yogi Berra**

Do you want to know what really separates the best players from the very good players? It's not their handicapping or the math skills or even how hard they are willing to work—it's what goes on between their ears. The mental side of the contest game—and the gambling world in game in general—is paramount.

Ken Massa: "The psychology of tournaments is something that you need to discuss a lot in this book, perhaps more than the nuts-and-bolts kind of strategy, because tournaments take place over a short period of time, and in that period of time, there's going to be a window of opportunity. If you latch onto it, if you're in the zone and you're in the right frame of mind, you'll catch the streak. But the majority doesn't catch it."

Eric Moomey: "Your wins will come in bunches, and there will be times when you're playing against somebody and they'll be picking all the winners. The next race comes, and damned if they don't pick the winner again. There are other times when you'll be the one picking all the winners: you go to the window to bet a 20-1 shot and the hair on the back of your neck will stand up because you know you're going to win. You've got to respect the streak."

I found it pleasantly ironic that a couple of computer guys were talking about soft factors like hot streaks. The way I look at the world, most of what people describe as hot streaks can be accounted for by the natural human desire to ascribe narrative to what are essentially random events. Does a guy like Ken Massa really believe in hot streaks?

Ken Massa: "It's not so much that a hot streak isn't a random event; it's that you tuned into it. That's the difference. Because if you get a winner, then you're going to feel in the zone a little bit, and if you start getting discouraged, if you start falling behind, and people around you are high-fiving and hitting longshots, things can really sink fast in a tournament. Psychology at the tournament is critical, and I think the most important thing to do is break the cherry right away, if you can. If you don't do that, then you start to sink, and you start to stab, and then you usually end up at zero."

Even the best players are going to go through long stretches without wins or even cashes.

Joe Scanio: "The most important thing people need to understand is that there are going to be more downs than ups in any contest. The margin for error is very, very small."

Second-guessing has been the undoing of many a contest player.

Joe Scanio: "If you go to any contest, you're going to have everyone saying to you, 'I shoulda, coulda, woulda done this or that ... I changed my mind the last minute ... ' all these sob stories. But the key to a beginner is you've got to control your emotions."

Mike Maloney: "A lot of guys get flustered. Let's say you're between horses. You bet one. The other wins and pays $30. A lot of thoughts start going through your head that don't need to be there."

Steve Wolfson, Sr.: "I get a kick out of sitting at a table with six or eight guys and you hear them say, 'If I had only done this … ' I like to quote Ogden Nash, 'If ifs and buts were candy and nuts, every day would be Christmas.' I just don't believe in looking back. If I look back, I'm done for what's coming ahead."

In other words, to paraphrase critic and author Richard Roeper, *Living in the Past* is a JethroTull album, not the way to succeed in handicapping contests. Maury Wolff really puts this issue in the proper perspective.

Maury Wolff: "Because of the solipsistic nature of human beings, we think we're the only ones who've made these mistakes. No, you're not. Everybody makes these mistakes. Ten guys in the room probably did the same thing. There's so much randomness. The guy who wins isn't some genius who should be selling his picks to the world. He's a guy who was walking around lucky for four hours."

Still, it's probably the hardest lesson to learn.

Matt Bernier: "That's probably my biggest weakness: still being very emotional with picks. I'd like to be a little more even-keeled. In a situation like we talked about before, where you were right about the winner but the odds dictated that you needed to do something different, you just have to tell yourself, 'Ultimately, you're making the right move; you were right in analyzing the race and figuring things out, but even though it won, it wasn't necessarily the right play.' But it's definitely a tough pill to swallow."

Michael Beychok believes contest psychology is of the utmost importance.

Michael Beychok: "I think psychology of handicapping is much more important than the selections. After I won the NHC, I read the book *Blink*, where Malcolm Gladwell talked about how we think about thinking, and it was a lot like reading my own journey from being an unsuccessful bettor to a winning bettor. It comes down to the old line about how when you think long, you think wrong. I used to start reading the *Form* on Thursday morning for the weekend and would just get totally lost in it, overloaded and confused.

There were times I'd tell a family member who I liked in a race and then look at the race some more and get off it. They'd win playing my selection, but I'd lose. It was nuts."

I asked him what changed, and he brought the conversation back to a familiar refrain.

Michael Beychok: "After I got enough experience, I learned to start trusting my first instinct. I'll look at a race for a few minutes, check the workout reports, check the Thorographs, and then I'll decide, 'That's the horse.' That's when I became successful, no second guessing."

I like to call it "first thought, best thought," but it's not as easy to execute as it sounds.

Michael Beychok: "I still sometimes have to remind myself to take my own advice. Get control of your own mind. Our brains can get in our own way; we should let our instincts take over. Players with experience play instinctually, look at a race in a short amount of time, and come to a decision. When you start overthinking it, that's what I call letting your brain get in the way."

Kevin Cox not only agrees but breaks out another one of his Cox-isms to rival "the illogical is the new logical."

Kevin Cox: "I call it paralysis by over-analysis. Always go with your first thought, maybe your second thought—and if you've got to go back-and-forth, you're in trouble."

DISTRACTIONS

Mike Maloney: "You need to have a game plan, avoid distractions, and keep your focus. A lot of guys are walking around socializing, being distracted, when maybe they shouldn't be."

There are times in your life when you're just going to be in a better state of mind to play the horses. Michael Beychok, who should probably write his own book about the psychology of playing the horses, touched on this earlier. There's no doubt that a distracted player isn't going to be the best player. While I was working on this book, I had a little baby to take care of during many of my non-writing hours. I had to laugh because I recorded this quote from Ken Massa just before I took a zero in the Saratoga '13 tournament.

Ken Massa: "Distractions are a key thing. In the last tournament I played, I was very distracted, talking to a lot of people. I had business on my mind; I was networking so I couldn't really keep my mind on it. I was hungry; I had a headache. Your general health, your general attitude, what's going on in your life are going to reflect on how you're thinking. If you've got all those other things on your mind, you've got a book on your mind, a new baby on your mind, then you're not going to probably do very well in tournaments."

I've learned a lot over the years, both from books and from players like the ones in this book, about how to improve my handicapping and my betting. I haven't heard much about how to improve my mental toughness.

Michael Beychok: "If you do make a mistake, and you will, you have to let it go. Let's say you were going to play that 8-1 and you didn't. It's easy to just say, 'Forget about it,' but as difficult as it is, that's what you need to do. The winning player will be able to flush the loss quickly. If you don't, it will invade your handicapping. You can't hold on to one of those in a tournament, under any circumstances, because you are forced immediately to go into the next one, make another decision, within minutes. All decisions need to be spot-on."

Notice how in many of the quotes in this chapter our players are focused on decisions as opposed to outcomes? That might be the single most important characteristic shared by successful gamblers. They know the difference between a good decision and a good outcome.

Michael Beychok: "After a contest, I'll look back and say, 'Did I make good decisions? Am I putting myself in a position to win?' It's not just about what happened in those races on that day; it's about making good decisions. As long as you are making good decisions, you are going to win."

Let's look at an example. It's early in the NYRA contest and there is an intriguing cap horse in a two-turn turf race at Saratoga. Maybe he's got an angle or two, but he definitely requires a leap of faith, as all cap horses do. The favorite looks strong, but he's no sure thing and he's 5-2. Player A takes the longshot; Player B takes the favorite, just looking to get some points on the board as we discussed back in Chapter 6.

You're watching the race, and Player A's longshot is loaded as heads are turned for home, but he's stuck behind a wall of horses. Player B's favorite has been guided to the outside, which makes sense because he's got the best paper in the race, and has a clear run. The tiring speed horse backs up into Player A's longshot, causing him to check, and he doesn't get a clear run until Player B's favorite has swept to the lead. The favorite is shortening his stride late, but the longshot doesn't have the ground to get up, and the favorite wins. Okay, who made the better decision, Player A or Player B? Player B got a great outcome; Player A made the better decision.

So then the question becomes, how do we learn to make better decisions?

Michael Beychok: "You can build yourself into a successful handicapper by believing you are a successful handicapper. By spending enough time and believing you are a successful handicapper, you will start doing things that most successful handicappers do. Demand value; don't bitch and moan about losing.

"Accept that you are going to be wrong more than you can be right. Yes, sometimes it's an external factor that caused you to be wrong, but most of the time you were just wrong, and that's okay. If you can accept that you will be wrong more than you will be right, then when you are wrong, it comes natural. 'Okay, I was wrong that time, but I will be right next time.' You can learn to have a winning outlook. But there are people who are losers who will not let themselves win."

I had this idea when Frank Scatoni and I worked on *Six Secrets of Successful Bettors* that before you learned how to win in racing, you needed to know how to lose.

Maury Wolff: "What's the worst thing you can do in a tourney? Blow a bet? You're going to be doing that all day anyway. It's not like bets are secret treasures. I'd think more about giving up an out in baseball than I would about giving up a bet in a tournament. Most of the time you're going to be wrong, and that's okay."

Racing isn't sports. Vince Lombardi's famous credo that "you can't accept losing" has no place here because it's not relevant. Losing a bet isn't the same as losing in general. Winning in gambling is something that happens over the long haul, not on an individual outcome like a sporting event. In gambling, you can still hate losing, but you also must learn to live with it.

Brent Sumja: "I go to work and even when things are going well, three out of five days I lose money. If someone playing horses for a living tells you they can do better than that, they are probably not being honest with themselves. The key to longevity as a player is keeping those losing days to a minimum and exploiting the two winning days to their fullest potential. That's what I'm hoping for, to keep the losses to a minimum."

Once you have adopted the proper mindset, the sky is the limit. Michael Beychock said something to me that suggested that he had no chance in his first few trips to the NHC. I wanted him to explain.

Michael Beychok: "I had qualified four or five times before, but the year I won was the first time when, walking in there, I felt like I could win it. Every other year, I went in there and it was overwhelming; it's huge, and I hadn't played a lot of contests and very few live ones at that. I was completely dead money those years before. The year before the win, I ended up 23rd and was in the hunt. I was in the top 15 with five or six races to go, and I threw up on myself. I didn't have a real goal, and I didn't know what to do. I passed on a horse late that would have really helped me. I did barely hold on for an in-the-money finish. The next year, however, I knew I was going to win; I walked in and knew I was going to win."

What had changed?

Michael Beychok: "One thing that worked for me at the NHC was that I visualized over and over and over again being in the hunt and what I would do. I would lie in bed the month before and go through scenario after scenario of what I would do, and I visualized myself winning. Visualization does work. It doesn't have to come true, but it does help you feel grounded in that moment."

The year Paul Shurman won the NHC Tour, he got within spitting distance of a $2 million bonus had he also won that year's NHC.

Paul Shurman: "I was lucky, actually. I had picked out 15 or 16 optional plays to make for Friday, but some bad weather took a bunch off the grass and left me pretty much with the minimum number of optional plays. I didn't do any handicapping during the tournament; I just played my picks and all my horses ran. I ended up in 30th place after day one. My goal after winning the Tour was not to be blanked in the NHC. I wanted to be in the hunt. I wanted to make them sweat a bit.

"On the second day, there was one horse at Tampa that ran second that should have gotten put up. A 20-minute blink on the top horse, but it stayed up. That would have been another $20 horse for me, and it would have changed how I played later on. But knowing what I would have probably played, I still don't think I would have won. I was a 10-1 shot out of winning and I had three shots. I could have played it safe and tried to move up in the money, but I was playing for $3 million, so I couldn't do that. I didn't love my picks in the last three races, but I had to play them. The horse I liked in the last race at Golden Gate, I couldn't play because he was too short and he lost by a nose. If my horse at Tampa had been put up, I might have played him and *that* would have been a bad beat."

I was impressed by his equanimity and asked him about this.

Paul Shurman: "I think being philosophical helps me stay calm. I don't get upset. It's just the game we play. There are bad beats and good wins, and they even out. I try not to get too excited one way or the other. It's like a test. If you're prepared for the test, you're relaxed about it. If you're not fully prepared, and you don't know what questions are coming, then you're not relaxed. The three keys to success are preparation, preparation, and preparation. You can prepare your way to a good mental state."

For more on the specifics of preparation, please refer back to Chapter 5. Part of developing a winning psychology has to do with how you carry yourself during a tournament. This is yet another area where everyone must answer the question individually.

Brian Troop: "When you see somebody in the room, and he wins a race and he's jumping up and down and screaming like an idiot, and then he loses and he's crying and all that—he's losing his composure, and that's going to affect his betting. If you win a race and you get a good price, you should forget about it because there are more races to come, and if you take a bad beat, you better forget about that, too, because otherwise you will not be successful in tournaments."

Troop's a funny example because he stays so calm all the time—even after winning the NHC!—that it kind of freaks people out sometimes.

Brian Troop: "I don't really get excited. When Jill Byrne interviewed me after I won the NHC, she said, 'You could show some excitement.' The same thing when the *Daily Racing Form* took my picture. They said to me, 'You could smile, you know.' In other words, I guess I was sort of like a dead fish. I'm not a person to jump around. I can watch a horse race on a monitor and my horse could pay $40, and I might stand there with my arms folded and nobody would know whether I had the horse. You are what you are."

Ricky Zimmer: "Randy Gallo nicknamed me 'The Quiet Assassin,' I guess because I'm not really demonstrative when I'm watching the races. I'm a low-key kind of guy."

Contrast that with the Brooklyn Cowboy, Kevin Cox.

Kevin Cox: "I'm 6-foot-4; I wear my cowboy hat; I'm easy to spot. I'm not just blending in with the crowd. I'm 'That Guy.' I've got a booming voice, and if I have a winner, everyone's going to know it. And I think that's a good idea. If you have the winner, let them know it. I'm not saying you should ever go over and intimidate a person individually, and you don't have to—the intimidation is your name on that leaderboard. Let them see your name. Walk around a little bit. Don't toot your horn or brag, just walk around a little bit. Be confident. Let people know you're there."

Another thing I love about Cox is that he has the unwavering self-confidence to match a heel in professional wrestling. Losses don't matter—they only prolong his inevitable march to victory. I once spoke to Brian Burke, who is both a statistician and a former Navy F-18 pilot. His website, www.AdvancedNFLStats.com, does for American football what Bill James did for baseball. In our conversation, Burke told me something I've never forgotten: "Every time a pilot goes on a mission, there is a chance he is not coming back. As a statistician, I know that's the truth. But the guy actually flying the plane can't think that way. In his mind, he's got to know with 100 percent certainty that the mission's success is completely within his control."

Unlike Cox, I'm not sure I'd say these following words out loud, but I do think a player who thinks this way is better off than one who is shrouded in self-doubt.

Kevin Cox: "To quote Paul Newman as Fast Eddie Felson in *The Hustler* when he plays Minnesota Fats for the first time: 'I'm the best you've ever seen, Fats, the best. Even if you beat me, I'm still the best.'"

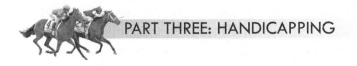

18 Finding Your Way and Finding Cap Horses

"The more you know, the more you win. That is the
allure of horse race handicapping."
— Charles Carroll, ***Handicapping Speed***

One of the biggest hurdles that new players will have in contests should be obvious to everyone: they have to learn at least some of the basics of handicapping. In this section of the book, our players will discuss various methods that they use to pick horses, especially cap horses. In some ways, this is a book in itself within the larger book, but in no way is it meant to be a definitive take on the subject. Honestly, I just thought that some of our players' ideas were too good not to share. I think experienced contest players will really enjoy hearing how their peers approach handicapping, and newer players are sure to learn something and have their curiosity piqued. For those looking for a fuller discussion of handicapping, I suggest you check out the books already mentioned by James Quinn, Brad Free, Andy Beyer, and Steve Davidowitz.

Finding one's own unique approach to handicapping can be tricky.

Brent Sumja: "You can listen to 7,000 opinions. There's a tip on every horse every day at every track. I know that from being on the backstretch, and you should always be willing to listen to what people have to say, but you definitely need to take it with a grain of salt. There are no commandments in horse racing. There is no flawless system.

There are great ideas and angles of pace, on Ragozin Sheets, and they all have their place. But if you let too many outside influences come into your thinking, you will get lost and go backwards."

Still, if you take in all the information that's out there, process it in a way that works for you, and come away making good decisions, you can win at this game. Mike Maloney believes in the power of data.

Mike Maloney: "You need to hear as many different approaches as you can, and then you find your approach somewhere in there. I've been asked a bunch of times through the years, 'Are you a speed handicapper? Are you a pace handicapper? Are you a bias guy? A Sheets guy? A Sartin guy?' Why would I want to be any one of those guys if I can be a guy made up of all those guys? If something works, I'm going to incorporate it into what I do every day. Why should I go to the golf course with one club in my bag when I can have 12? I'd take 20 clubs to the golf course if they let me; fortunately, they let you take as many as you want to the track."

There are many factors that go into the process of trying to find winners. For contest play, one of the most important exercises is how to find cap horses.

Dennis Decauwer: "One way to find a cap horse would be race flow. Does the horse look like he could be the only speed in the race? Does the horse look like he could benefit from a pace duel and make a run that perhaps he hasn't shown before?"

Eric Moomey: "When I'm looking for a cap horse, I want to know if there's any way he can get loose on the lead? A lot of times the riders will leave a longshot on the lead alone, thinking he can't make it that far. Look at Little Mike in the Breeders' Cup Turf in 2012. Sometimes odd things happen. Or you look for a race where maybe there will be a lot of speed and he can be the best closer. The big longshots that win usually fall into one of those two categories: they get loose or they have a good late kick. Those are the trends time and time again."

Garett Skiba: "Change is key for me when it comes to a longshot. Form will always be suspect for the given race or condition, otherwise the horse wouldn't be a longshot. As a handicapper, you need to isolate a certain change today that might render the poor historical performance a non-issue."

Dennis Decauwer and Ken Massa agree.

Dennis Decauwer: "One of the first things I would look for in a cap horse is something new happening that might shake up the horse. Look for a horse that's doing something different. Is the horse going from sprint to route? Is the horse going from route to sprint? Is the horse going from main track to turf, or vice versa? Is the horse putting blinkers on or taking them off? Has there been a trainer switch?"

Ken Massa: "What you want to do in a tournament is look for horses that are going to improve. Longshots aren't longshots because they look good on form or have good speed figures, or they wouldn't be longshots. The reason that they are longshots is that they look lousy on paper. In order to get them home, you need to find factors of improvement."

Mike Maloney: "I look at a lot of charts, and every chart I look at, if there's a price horse that hits the board, the first thing I'm going to do is look back and try to figure out 'Where did that come from?' All a guy has to do is hit the board twice when he shouldn't have, and then you're aware of it. And all a guy needs to do is run a bad favorite a couple of times, and you become aware of that, too."

Ricky Zimmer: "I'll go back and look at the charts of previous races from horses in that day's races, just to see: did the horse at least outrun its odds, how did the race flow go? Things like that. It really helps for finding buried horses."

Maury Wolff: "Once you know what the rules are and you know what you need, almost any rationale can be good enough to find a cap horse to bet on."

I asked Wolff to walk me through an example.

Maury Wolff: "Let's take a grass race. How many grass races do you see where there's a four-length difference from first to ninth? It happens all the time. If they run that race again, the horse that's seventh by three might go off at 20-1 and the horses that won will probably go off at 2-1, and there's just not that much difference to justify that kind of discrepancy in the prices. It doesn't take a lot of skill to play that horse. It takes more skill to pick the right horse than the wrong horse, but it takes nothing to get lucky. You see it all the time. Somebody gets through on the inside, or the best horse can't get through on the inside and the longshot that circles wins. There's an amazing amount of luck, and it's a wonderful opportunity for contests. So it can really be as simple as that: look for a horse that wasn't beaten very badly that is a big price."

I also asked our players about general handicapping approaches. What data do contest players use?

Paul Shurman: "I use everything. Years ago, when I started playing tournaments, I used the Thorograph Sheets and the *Daily Racing Form*. I thought I was pretty good. Then I met the Wolfsons, and I realized I knew nothing. Then I started getting into the breeding aspect of handicapping, using a Brisnet product called American Produce Records, and also a handicapping program called HTR that helps me visualize how a race is going to be run."

Eric Moomey: "I've done a lot of home-grown data analysis. I've tracked about 100,000 races over the last few years. You can buy information, and you can get a lot of free daily information. It's widely available. There are computer programs available that can help you analyze data. The most important thing is that whatever you use, you want to get really good at it."

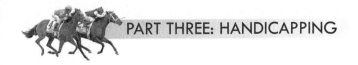

19 Using Speed Figures

Probably the most common starting point for handicappers in the modern era is speed figures. People are attracted to the idea of a single number that attempts to quantify a horse's performance. There was once a time—difficult to even imagine now—when speed figures were controversial and provided a real market edge in horse racing, almost like on-base-percentage once did in the pre-Moneyball era in baseball. But nowadays, nearly everybody uses some sort of speed figures.

Ricky Zimmer: "I use just the Beyers, which are available to everybody with a *Racing Form.* Those are solid. Everybody has access to them; they play a big part in the odds, but they are still the place I start."

Michael Beychok: "Speed figures are important, but they are not that important. They've become less important over the years because of their general availability. I still use Thorograph Sheets because I believe they are the best speed figures out there, but they aren't enough to win with alone."

Roger Cettina: "I use the Thorograph Sheet figures, but some people live and die by Sheet numbers. I don't do that. Sometimes you'll see a horse that ran a big number, and then you go and click on the chart in Formulator and see that he got an easy lead against a short field, and you can guess that's why he ran so much faster.

He's not going to run that again, and he's 3-1. Let's throw him out and go from there. It's all about how you interpret the information you have."

Proprietary speed figures like the Ragozin and Thorograph Sheets are a staple of many players' arsenals. Both products represent a horse's past performances in a visual fashion, on a graph, with one column representing one year. They take additional factors, including wind and ground loss, into effect. Lower figures are better, and they are represented in quarter-point increments. I definitely do get a better sense of a horse's trajectory looking at it in Sheet form, and it's certainly true that patterns jump off the page in a visual fashion that makes them stand out. The idea is that a horseplayer can get an idea of a horse's condition more easily—that is, his readiness to race and put forth a peak effort.

Brent Sumja: "To me, the biggest weapon to help you find bad favorites are the Sheets. Say a horse wins at Belmont in a state-bred special weight and a horse from Delaware wins an open special weight, and they show up back in the same race at Parx. I can see that the Belmont horse is actually six lengths slower, but he's 7-5 in the program. I like to look for horses that look good in the *Racing Form,* but I know, from their Sheet number, that they're not as good as they look. A lot of times the Beyer number is really reflecting what you'd see in the *Form.* I rely on the *Racing Form* but believe in the Sheets. I know the work that goes into them and I agree with the theories and premises.

"However, I differ from most Sheet readers when I say you can't take the Sheets too literally. They'll tell you, 'This is the number. Period.' I don't believe that. I've seen too many times when the front-runner on a wet track gets a ridiculous Sheet number and Beyer number, and yes, he might have been ridiculously good that day, but it's not a wet-fast track today. Some Sheets guys don't look past the number itself, but I think you have to always be willing to make your own decisions and adjustments. There's nothing in this game where you can just believe in what's written in front of you. You have to go the extra yard and look for things that work to create an edge.

"When I trained horses for the Ragozin guys, I took complete advantage of that. Those guys teaching me how to read the Sheets was like God explaining the Bible to a follower. I asked a million questions. I think it takes years and years to truly understand them and not that many people are willing to put in that time.

"Tom Amoss was the best trainer I've ever been around. When I went out on my own, he called me one day and asked me, 'Are you reading the Sheets?' I didn't know what he was talking about. He told me, 'You know how sometimes you'll be training a horse and you know he's ready to run and you take him over there and he just doesn't run? And you're determined to find a reason and you run a bunch of tests, but nothing's wrong?' I knew exactly what he meant. 'Well, that's because the horse ran a huge race that you're unaware of and you're running them back without significant rest.' It answered a lot of questions for me. It might look like the horse did it easy, or he might finish fourth beaten eight lengths. The Sheets will tell you what kind of effort that was for him and let you know not to run him back in two or three weeks."

I asked Scott Carson to talk to me about a well-kmown Sheets angle, the famed O-2-X pattern.

Scott Carson: "I'm a Ragozin Sheet player, and there are a lot of angles and patterns on the Sheets that other people can't see. A perfect example is the O-2-X. I'll usually mark a horse as playable or at least give it a second look if it's got an O-2-X pattern."

What is that exactly?

Scott Carson: "The 'O' to a Sheet player indicates when the horse has run a new top, or a career-best speed figure. Then the next race represents a regression of [within] two points of the top— the idea being that they hit the top and then they regressed two points. The 'X' means that they ran at least five points below the top, and what often happens with that 'X' race is that there is a break, usually two to three months, so that gives the horse a chance to recover so that it can run the 'O' again.

"But the thing is: the odds have gone up because the race two-back was worse than the top, and then the last race was bad, so often you get an overlay on a horse that's run an O-2-X pattern [because most people are looking at the last two poor races]. You don't always get an overlay, but it's potentially a playable horse, especially if it's a big price. Anybody who is only looking at the *Racing Form*, who is not using the Sheets, they don't see this O-2-X pattern. They might see the bad race, but they don't recognize that there's a playable pattern."

I asked Carson about any other Sheet angles that could be applied to contest play, and he mentioned one that could be used with any speed figures, really.

Scott Carson: "Another common Ragozin Sheet angle is that when a horse runs a new top as a three-year-old, and it's just a little bit better than its two-year-old top, then one or two months after that initial three-year-old top, it has a great chance to improve dramatically. Sometimes a horse like that will still be a favorite, but if it doesn't look that good compared to the other horses, then it might be a playable longshot, and the horse could still improve many lengths. In other words, it runs the small new top, and then in its next race, it's very live. But even if it runs badly in its next race, then it's even more live in the following race."

The logic behind this is that a horse that runs as well as it did at two in its first start at three is one to keep an eye on for possible contest use.

Scott Carson: "Exactly. It means it's a healthy, developing horse, and, because it hasn't raced that much, it has a lot of upside, so it's already improved a little bit on its two-year-old figure, but in time it should improve significantly over the two-year-old top. It's just a question of when. Usually, it's shortly after running through its two-year-old top. That's a pretty big angle."

While many players use the Sheets, others take a more integrated approach.

John Doyle: "I'm a believer in form-condition analysis. I'm not a slave to any one methodology. I've learned a lot from a lot of different people. I knew about the Sheets and had looked on their website, but I wasn't ever a big Sheets guy. Then Cary Fotias wrote a book called *Blinkers Off* that I read about in *The HorsePlayer Magazine*, and I thought it was really interesting. I contacted him and we became friends. I started looking at the Xtras [Fotias' proprietary performance figures], and he had some pretty interesting ideas that seemed to work. I now use his stuff in conjunction with other things, and it helps me come to my conclusions."

Fotias, one of the men to whom this book is dedicated, passed away in 2013, but his legacy lives on. The great insight of his work was to combine the cutting-edge analysis of pace handicappers with the form cycle-condition approach of the Sheets guys.

Mike Labriola: "The fastest horses win. We know that. But you can't make your handicapping solely about time, and there is definitely subjectivity in the way speed figures are made. I'll try to see if there's a longshot that has figures in the general area of the favorite. A lot of times horses will be running figures in the same range, and one will be 6-5 and another will be 12-1. That's a no-brainer. Or maybe I'll look to beat a favorite that people are betting off of one figure that might be an aberration. It's as important to be able to downgrade the contenders as it is to upgrade the longshots."

Ken Massa puts it succinctly.

Ken Massa: "Holding on to speed figures as a primary betting tool is like trying to beat football point spreads using win-loss records. Everyone sees the same thing. No edge."

20 Pace

It's a hoary old chestnut, but it's true: it's not how fast you run; it's how you run fast. Many of the longest longshots that contest players crave can be ferreted out through a careful analysis of pace. In fact, for many contest players, pace becomes the most important factor in their handicapping.

Matt Bernier: "For me, the biggest thing is the way the race sets up, trying to envision how it's going to be run before it's actually run. Obviously, there are all kinds of different things that can happen, but I'm trying to think, if the race was run a hundred times, how often is it going to go a certain way? That's pretty much how I go about pace. So if I think the two horse is going to get the lead, all by itself, 65 times out of 100, I'm banking on the two being the lone speed—and if I get the price I'm looking for, that's a horse I'm looking to play, even if maybe it doesn't look so good class-wise on paper."

I asked Bernier if he relies at all on pace figures—a corollary of speed figures available in many places, including *Daily Racing Form's* own Moss pace figures.

Matt Bernier: "I know a lot of people will use pace figures, but I only use the *Racing Form*, and I strictly go by the different running lines. If there are a whole lot of horses that look like they might go to the front, then I'll look at the fractional times as well, or see if maybe one of the runners is going from a sprint to a route, and I'll try to determine who the speed of the speed might be. I go with my own intuition, my own gut instinct."

John Conte: "When you read the *Racing Form*, it's up to you to see if there are five speed horses in the race and that logically they're going to duel with each other and set it up for a closer. Or maybe there's just one speed horse that is going to go out and win wire-to-wire. When you look at the race on paper, different scenarios unfold, and you have to figure out the right one. Look deep and see what's happening. It's also very important where the gate is set up. Sometimes it's set up right in front of the clubhouse where they go into the turn immediately, and horses from the outside don't have as good a chance as the speed horse on the inside that is going to get the jump on them."

Roger Cettina is another player who relies on having an idea of how the race will be run.

Roger Cettina: "Now more than ever, these racetracks are all geared towards speed. Another good thing that Thorograph has is something called Race Shapes, which help predict who the fastest horses will be early. They don't just look at raw times. They account for the run-up distances, which are all different. They take the wind into consideration, and they show you, on average, how fast the horses usually run, and that gives you an idea of how the race is going to shape up pace-wise. Obviously, a lot of that has to do with intent: what's in the jockey's and trainer's minds, and you can't know that. But the best thing Race Shapes do is give you an idea at a glance if this is a pace that's going to be contested or if there's just one horse that is faster than everybody else. Even if a horse doesn't look good enough to win on paper, if you think a track or turf course is favoring speed, and you think he's going to be clear after a quarter-mile and he's a price, you might as well use him."

Ricky Zimmer's approach to pace is similar, but a bit more focused on which runners are likely to have the easiest journeys (see also Trips and Track Biases in Chapter 23).

Ricky Zimmer: "I try to get an idea of how the race is going to play on paper. Especially in turf racing, I want to know who might be able to pull a good trip. In New York races, I'm pretty familiar with the horses out here, so I might remember a horse that got a bad trip or a bad setup in the past. With an out-of-town track, it's more just looking at it on paper, trying to figure out how the race is going to be run and who might benefit from how that race is going to be run."

What exactly is Zimmer looking for?

Ricky Zimmer: "Ground loss is so important, too. Pace plays a big part in whether a horse is going to be able to save ground or not. In a race without a lot of pace, I feel like horses could be more susceptible to getting caught wide, as they're trying to get position. In a race with a faster pace, they'll string out a little bit and everybody will kind of find that nice spot and not have to worry about losing too much ground. I've just seen a lot of these two-turn races, especially grass races, where horses with outside posts just get hung out there around the turn, and then when they're trying to make their moves into the slow pace, they just can't stay on."

One tool I use all the time to help me evaluate pace are the figures from a company called Racing Flow. The Racing Flow numbers aren't concerned with who is going to race where today. They focus on the past races and ascertain which horses benefitted or were hindered by a certain race flow. The numbers can be uploaded directly into your *Racing Form* via Formulator, and they can really change the picture of a certain running line.

That closer that was just plodding along? Maybe it was a race flow that really favored front-runners, and the late-running horse actually ran huge, closing into a slow pace. That speed horse that led gate-to-wire and earned a Beyer in the stratosphere in that same race? Maybe he wasn't so impressive after all, since the favorable race flow flattered his performance.

How about the closer that looked visually amazing when he swept by the entire field in the last furlong? Flow figures will give you insight into whether he might be a future graded-stakes horse or if he was simply the beneficiary of a pace meltdown. For an example of exactly how this works, check out the Applications section.

Roger Cettina: "With Racing Flow, I'm most interested in the extreme situations. Stuff like that really jumps out at me when I'm handicapping the races. If it's an extremely speed-favoring flow, and a horse comes from way back and finishes fifth, that effort might not look that good on paper, but knowing how the track was playing, that horse might be a lot better than that. For that horse, the speed figure has nothing to do with how he ran that day, and you need to know that. Maybe that horse comes back and he's 10-1 or 12-1, but maybe he would have been 4-1 or 5-1 if everybody knew what you knew."

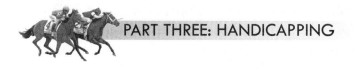

21 Form and Class

In the pre-speed figure era, class was considered the most important handicapping factor. If you were talking horses while standing around in the Belmont paddock in 1962, you wouldn't have heard anything about speed figures, and a whole lot about class. In the contest era, in my view, form and class still have an important place.

Class can be a tricky handicapping factor to describe in that it's very much inextricable from other factors, including speed and form. James Quinn defines it as "a horse's relative ability, as indicated by varying combinations of speed, stamina, and determination expressed in its races." Even if you're not a big believer in class—many Sheets players believe simply that speed is class—it's a useful concept to be aware of. It is my opinion, having watched god-knows-how-many thousands of races, that some horses were born to compete at higher levels than others, and some want to win more than others. To put it more succinctly, "Form is temporary; class is permanent." Hidden form and class angles are another terrific way for contest players to look for prices.

John Conte: "For me, the most important thing is class. If you had a fight with your two-year-old nephew, you're going to beat him up. But I want to see what you're going to do against a guy your age, your height, your weight."

Roger Cettina: "That's another great thing about Formulator. You can see what kind of Beyer numbers the other horses coming out

217

of the race usually run, and what they ran in their next start. It's an offshoot of the whole 'key race' theory, where if a race produces more than one winner next time out, maybe you want to pay a little more attention to the horses coming out of that race.

"Especially in cheaper races, looking at class can be useful. If a horse was running in a $5K claimer and maybe finished fifth, but three of the horses in front of him came back and won, that means a lot. Even if one of them came back and won, but won for $7,500, that means a lot. The strength of those races changes constantly. They're never the same from month to month. Sometimes you can look at a cheap race and see a horse that was well beaten, but maybe the winner was some Jamie Ness horse dropping down from $20K that won by a pole, and then you know that was a much tougher race than what he's facing today, even though the class level is the same in theory. It really boils down to this: you really have to do your homework."

Ricky Zimmer: "I'll try to look for a Beyer that is inflated or is low. Sometimes you'll see a race where three or four horses in that race got a lifetime best number out of nowhere, and that could be a sign that maybe the Beyer is inflated for one reason or another. The same thing is true on the other side: sometimes one will come in with a low number that just doesn't quite fit, so maybe that race will be undervalued."

Brent Sumja: "You might see that a horse is coming out of a key race from the italics in the *Form*. Now you can click on the chart and see what race he came back to win. Maybe he's a three-year-old that beat older horses, or maybe the win came in a restricted claiming race and it's not so impressive.

"Mark McGuire is a genius at betting races where the horses have all run against one another, races for older claimers on the turf. He's brilliant. He has a way of deciphering which races at the same class on the same circuit are the better ones. On the Sheets, they'll look the same to me, but he'll use Formulator to see who ended up where and how they did, and he has a real edge in those races. A lot of races that will be picked as mandatories in the contest are going to be those older claimers where the horses have run against each other 10 or 15 times."

Mark McGuire: "My specialties are horses that have run against one another over and over in basically the same types of races. It's time-consuming, hard work. It takes me almost 30 minutes a race. I'll watch films. Track biases come into play. I'll also try to find some hidden class angles. You might come up with three horses in the race, and then it just comes down to what the odds are."

But where does the edge come from?

Mark McGuire: "The public only likes to look at the last race. Even though a horse might be the best horse in the race overall, if his last race looks bad, he might be 7-1 instead of 3-1. If you're getting that kind of value, you can play that horse. Over time, that situation will play out in your favor."

Technology has made McGuire's life a lot easier.

Mark McGuire: "Formulator does in minutes what it used to take me hours to do. Back in the old days, I'd have all the tapes on VHS. I'd have to fast forward just to find the races I wanted, then I'd go back through old *Racing Forms* to find charts and make comparisons. It could take eight hours to handicap a card. With Formulator, you now have all of that stuff at your fingertips. I saw an instant pickup in my handicapping when I started using it. It's an extremely valuable tool. That's where you can find the hidden class angles.

"For example, there are three horses I like in this race, and they're supposed to be at the same class level. But now you're looking closer and asking, 'Who beat this horse?' Then you can follow along through Formulator and see who that horse was and who he's been running against, and maybe you'll see that the winning horse had been running three class levels higher. So now you know the horse in today's race is maybe a little better than he looks on paper [because he was beaten by a higher-class horse]. In some instances, a $32,000 claiming race is more like a $50,000 claiming race. Sometimes it's easy. Sometimes it's not so easy."

What did he do before Formulator?

Mark McGuire: "Back then you relied on 'refrigerator' horses. You saw something, you wrote it down, you stuck it on the fridge with a magnet, and you waited for that horse to come back and you hit him hard. There was a time a couple of decades ago when anything racing on the rail at Hollywood Park came in dead last. It went on for a whole meet and there were longshots galore. If one of those horses that raced on the rail shipped up to Bay Meadows, we would drive an hour and a half up to Santa Barbara because our local OTB wouldn't take care of it. A horse could have been beaten 30 lengths, but if he raced on the rail at Hollywood and was shipping up to Bay Meadows and dropping in class, it would win for fun. We'd get the giggles betting these things, and they won at a very high clip."

22 Trainers

Trainers are the new modern-day fundamental handicapping factor. Almost all contest players use trainers in one way or another to help them find or eliminate horses. I recently asked personal trainer (of human beings) Emily Gullikson why she thought trainers were so important in horse racing and she told me, "Because the trainer is like a coach, and without a good coach, you're not going to get the most out of what you have."

Just as some coaches can make all the difference, some trainers can improve horses mightily.

FINDING TRAINER ANGLES WITH FORMULATOR

DRF's Formulator featured prominently in our Class section, but it's a very powerful tool that has other, broader applications that cross over into a number of other topics, especially trainer angles. When it comes to contest play, I believe that trainers are just as much of a fundamental handicapping factor as speed, pace, and class. Several of our players use Formulator to find profitable trainer angles.

Mike Maloney: "Formulator is a great way for any handicapper— especially a younger handicapper—to look not just at a specific horse in a specific race, but also to take a trainer and look at what his patterns are, what his strengths are, what his weaknesses are. You're going to see things that might not necessarily show up in three-year data or five-year data. You might find something that's a little fresher, a little more recent, and maybe the stats are still not good overall in a certain category, but this more current sample is maybe a little more relevant."

John Doyle: "I look for hidden trainer angles. I hate to give this away, but I'm a nice guy, so I will. When there's a trainer who I don't know, especially at a seasonal meet like Gulfstream or Keeneland, I'll look up the trainer in Formulator, and I don't care if he's 1-for-55 on the year, all I look at are his winners. I'll look at the past performances of the winner, especially if it's a longshot, and look for the pattern the trainer used to get the horse to win. I've found some gems doing that, and it really helps take a lot of the noise out of there.

"When you see a guy who is 1-for-55, sometimes you have a knee-jerk reaction and say, 'No way.' But if you dig a little deeper, you can understand how he won that one, and possibly he can repeat that pattern. I hit a horse like that early in the NHC Qualify tournament that paid the max, and then I had a few other 5-1 type horses to carry me through to qualifying."

Scott Carson: "Has a trainer ever hit with a first-time starter? Does he hit with longshots? Are there certain workout patterns that come into play for his winners? You might also want to look into how a certain trainer does at a specific track. Not all trainers ship well, or their horses at one track maybe aren't as well-meant as at another. He would be 20 percent overall but only 5 percent at today's track.

"I also love that Formulator lets you go back over five years of data. Let's say that you see a trainer who has an 0-for-12 first-time starter record in the printed version of the *Form*. You're like, 'Really, is he that bad?' If you go into Formulator and you check his first-time starts for the last five years, maybe you find out that just two years ago he hit with three 20-1 horses, all first-time starters. You know that means that the data in the printed *Form* is incomplete [because it's based on a limited sample size].

"Formulator also lets you compare how a trainer does with first-time starters and second-time starters, and that's not a step a lot of people will take. Maybe a certain trainer is apt to give a horse a race and then fire second out. You can get a good idea from looking at the stats and his starters and look for patterns—certain jockeys, bullet works, gate works—and you can try to find winners from there. Most people in maiden races won't look beyond the Pletcher horse, but even his lose 70 percent of the time. A lot of cap horses are first- and second-time starters. I'll save the past performances of those cap horses so I know what to look for."

Maury Wolff: "First-time starters at big prices aren't a bad way to go for a player without a lot of handicapping experience. You need to find trainers who have the ability to prepare firsters. Obviously, if a horse is 20-1 first out, he's working in 1:03, not :58, but you can get lucky with that kind of horse, and all you have to do is look in Formulator. Let's suppose you have a trainer who in the last five years has won with two firsters that paid the world. Maybe he's 2-for-25 overall with firsters. That's good enough isn't it?"

What does Maury Wolff think of Formulator in general?

Maury Wolff: "Formulator is terrific, particularly for a novice player. It's a goldmine of simple, mineable longshot data. Maybe you'll see a horse with terrible paper, but he's coming off a long layoff. Some trainers are good at taking these horses that maybe ran a race or two too many and had declined, but now they've taken some time and fixed whatever issues there were, and now they're starting over. You can click on the trainer and see how he's done over the last five years with long layoffs and go through horse by horse and look at his winners. If you're looking at his overall stat line, you want to focus less on the obvious percentage of winners and more on the ROI. If he's won with a couple of $30 horses in the past, why can't he win with one today? They obviously won't win most of the time, but stranger things have happened."

THINKING LIKE CONNECTIONS

John Doyle: "Another main thing is trying to figure out trainer intention: are they trying to win this race today?"

It can be a fun and profitable exercise to go back and look at a horse's PPs in reverse order, looking at them as if you were the owner or trainer. There's a good example of this in the Applications section (Chapter 35), but several of our players, especially the ones with experience on the ownership and training side, have a lot to say about it as well. .

Mike Maloney: "Owner-trainer intent is a big thing for me. There are times when owners and trainers tip their hands, and you have to be alert to it, and if you're not, you'll miss it. I've had enough experience as an owner that I'll put myself in the shoes of the owner and trainer and ask, 'Does this move make sense?'"

I asked Maloney for an example.

Mike Maloney: "I recently saw a horse that ran in an allowance and then dropped into a claimer. He had four months off after that, back in for $25K, ran fourth, beaten a length. Now he's in for $7,500. Maybe this is too obvious of an example of a big favorite that you wouldn't want to trust. You need to ask yourself: why is the horse in the race? Why is he at Indiana Downs and not Churchill Downs? Maybe you know a certain trainer has a stable in New York and has horses at Saratoga, but this one's at Ellis Park this summer. Why?

"It might be different if it's Brad Cox or Jamie Ness or anyone who trains for Midwest Thoroughbreds, bigger outfits that are known for winning in those spots. The smaller the stable, the more powerful a negative angle that is. If a guy has four horses in his barn and the $25K horse is his big horse, which it might well be if he only has four horses, and he's going to drop that horse in for $7,500, that's like him giving up his first born. It's not going to happen unless there's a real reason.

"Even with the big trainers, those races are maybe good races to stay out of unless they're mandatories. If Mike Maker and Ken Ramsey have one like that in at Keeneland and it's 6-5, why do I want to buck those guys? Save your bullet and bet it against the guy with four horses and giving up his first-born."

Brent Sumja: "Sometimes when I'm handicapping I try to get away from my experience on the backside; it can be more of a hindrance than a help. But if I know the people, it can be a great help. Then I can be really on top of it. When I know the trainers involved, it's a little easier. Tom Amoss, who I worked for, he just wants to win all the time. I know his work pattern. I know Jerry Hollendorfer's work pattern. I know how they enter. It sticks out like a sore thumb when I see something slightly off when I know the people.

"I know a little bit too much for my own good sometimes. I'll try to put myself into that trainer/backside mode. OK, I'm the owner or trainer: 'Why are we entered in here?' If I come to a race with two huge question marks, I try to stay out of it. Every race is going to have one question mark, whatever it may be, maybe a horse dropping from $25,000 to $7,500. Does he need the drop to win or is he hurt? Are they trying to get him eligible for a starter that's in the book later? I'll keep online condition books and try to see what the connections might be thinking. Having been a trainer, I believe that you win races at 9 o'clock in the morning two, three, four days before you're running! That's when you win: at the entry booth. Connections who win enter aggressively, but not all connections are created equal. If I see a trainer who wins at 4 percent and he's entering aggressively, I get rid of those horses, but if a guy I know who is always trying to win enters aggressively, that's something I pay attention to."

Mike Maloney: "Most trainers are better at some things than other things. There are guys who train to win first out, and then there are guys like Carl Nafzger and Ian Wilkes—their game plan is not to win first out, though they'd certainly be happy if they did. But what you find with them is they'll run third or fourth at a huge price a lot of the time first time out and especially second-time out, and that can help you in the exotics. People look at the fact that their horses don't win often in their first and second starts, and then they eliminate the horses from the verticals.

"Their training style is to take those young horses back and teach them to finish. They're not sending them out of the gate to have them fight early with the horse that is maybe going to win the race. They'll use a patient rider like Calvin Borel, and it's a schooling process for the horse. If you understand that, you can look at their horses differently, and I get real interested in their horses if they're making their third or fourth starts and as the distances get longer, because they get nice horses and they take their time.

"If you get in synch with what their mindset is, you can understand a lot better about how their horses are going to perform during the race. Once they do find their running legs, they're very good betting vehicles because they're very consistent and they usually have an established running style. They become horses that I know what to expect from and can count on."

Dennis Decauwer: "I think being an owner has helped me a lot as a horseplayer in terms of knowing trainer patterns. I've had seven or eight trainers over the years and each one is a little different. Some trainers will like to work horses very fast, and I know that about them, so it doesn't really factor in if I see quick workouts from them. But it does bother me if I see that type of trainer take a horse and not run him in the morning with the usual aggressiveness; then I know there's probably an issue with that horse. Conversely, if I know a trainer, and he likes to work his horses easily in the morning and I see a fast workout, maybe accompanied by a drop in class, it seems to me that they just might be trying to get the horse claimed, and I want to stay away from that horse as well."

There's always a lot of talk on the backstretch based on how horses are working. Has former trainer Brent Sumja ever relied on this type of inside information?

Brent Sumja: "This isn't like the stock market. There is no SEC of horse racing. I can call anyone I want. I'll see a race with seven starters and I know all the trainers and I could call up each and every one of them and they would tell me the truth. It really doesn't do you any good though, because for the most part, they're all entering to win. Even if you found a spot where four of the trainers give you the idea today is not optimal and one guy says he's really ready to win, you still know how much luck is involved. There really is very little worthwhile inside information beyond first time starters or long layoff types. In the long run, you are better off doing your own work."

I've noticed that some trainers can't seem to see past the end of their own shedrows when it comes to actually handicapping races.

Brent Sumja: "Jockeys are the worst touts in the world, and the trainers are right there, too. When I was training, some people could tell how my horses were going to run not from the words I told them, but from the way I answered their questions. From that, they would know the right time to bet, so they'd just want to hear me talk. I don't even know what the cue was, but I was definitely letting them know something I didn't even really know myself, and it wasn't when I said, 'I love this horse. There's no way he'll lose.' They'd know better than me by the way I spoke about the race.

"I think there were three days when I won three in a day at the same track. Every one of those days I walked over saying to myself, 'I hope I win one today.' The days I had five or six in where I'd think, 'Today's the day! I'm going to be on the cover of the *Racing Form* tomorrow,' I'd be lucky to get one winner!"

What information would he want to know from a trainer with a horse in today's race?

Brent Sumja: "What would help is this: if I call the guy dropping the horse from 25 down to 7,500 and he lets me know if they're trying to get rid of him or if he's okay. I don't want to know anything else. They would tell me the truth because they know I would never tell anyone. Some of the guessing in those situations is being taken out of the equation with this new rule in California where if a horse is claimed and he's unsound, you can give the horse back. I think it's the greatest rule in terms of promoting the safety of the animals and also for handicappers as well. Over time, these guys are going to learn that you can't enter an injured horse because he's going to be coming back to you, anyway."

What else do our players look for in trainer angles?

Dennis Decauwer: "I'll look at trainers and jockeys and trainer-jockey combinations that are very low percentage; I'm eliminating the vast majority of those very quickly. It has nothing to do with the odds of the horse; it just has to do with the performance of the jockeys and the trainers, and the trainers and the jockeys when they work in combination with each other in different scenarios. Now, again, if I'm looking for an upset, or in a mandatory race, I may come back to one of those, but often you can find overlays in a situation with trainers and jockeys who win more frequently. I'm eliminating based on probability. If I'm dealing with a 6 percent trainer and a jockey who is 4 percent when they ride for that trainer, unless the odds are in excess of 30-1, I'm not even looking."

Maury Wolff: "Another weird one that's not a bad longshot angle at all is negative trainer changes. The crowd runs from these horses, and you can get gigantic prices. If a horse goes from Rudy Rodriguez to a guy who is 0-for-34, that horse will be an astronomical price. The market will overcompensate to death on that. You don't know what that horse has been doing. If he's in the right spot, maybe he can still win."

Brian Troop: "Trainers are very important in my handicapping. The best kind of bet you can find is a trainer like a guy we have here in Canada named Sid Attard. A lot of his horses are bet, but you'd be surprised at the number of horses you can get at 10-1 or 15-1. It's nice that there are still 20 percent trainers and you can get a good price on them still."

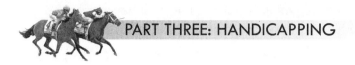

23 Trips and Track Biases

While the fundamental handicapping factors can be the backbone of your study, it can be hard to get an edge on your competition if you look at only fundamentals. When you're looking at the same things as everyone else, you're going to come up with a lot of the same horses. If you've gotten to this point in this book, you already know why that's a big problem for contest players. That's why so many successful contest players also consider more subjective handicapping factors like trips and track biases.

TRIPS

Trip handicapping is tied in closely to the art of race watching. It's never been easier than today to do trip work, via DVR or computer. Some pro players will even make their trip notes during the same race card, rewinding and writing notes on anything relevant they see. Many of our players spend a lot of time watching what they still anachronistically call "tape."

John Doyle: "What I think gives me an edge is the race replay work I do and my trip notes. That's the only thing I have that not everyone else can see; it's my subjective view of the race."

Dennis Decauwer: "I like to watch a lot of video of races, and I've noticed that sprints are won or lost either out of the gate or at the turn, so I'm looking for which horses and which riders do well out of the gate and around the turn. You have to try and visualize the race—where's this rider going to put this horse as they go into the far turn? If you haven't done anything to lose the race in one of those two places, then you greatly enhance your opportunity to win the race."

I liked this idea very much of using trip work to get a feel for what the jockeys might do in a given race. I asked Decauwer what to look for.

Dennis Decauwer: "There's a lot of feel involved, and hours and hours and hours of tape. But you certainly want jockeys who are going to give their horses a little bit of space, if at all possible. Once a rider gets out of the gate, he should either go or grab, one or the other, and too many jockeys seem to be indecisive. They'll go and then they'll grab, or they'll grab and then they'll go. You know three strides out of the gate that they were going to send, and then all of a sudden they'll grab, and now they've just totally confused the horse. I like to watch the break over and over and try to look at that head-on, and I'll focus on those jockeys and see what they're doing with their hands."

And what about on the turn?

Dennis Decauwer: "On the turn, I think a lot of it is just looking for a spot—how do they react? Where do they look for a spot? Do they try to always dive for the rail? Are they trying to get outside too soon? It all comes down to trying to identify the jockeys who will consistently put their mounts in the best positions to win."

Roger Cettina: "The unlimited replays you get with each card you buy are one of the best things about Formulator. That's a great thing. I try to look for intent in the way a horse is ridden. Sometimes a horse is off a layoff, and maybe he needs a race; he's not going to be ridden the same way as the horse that is definitely trying to win today. The people who do the trip notes don't always get everything. There are trips to be seen that aren't mentioned in there. Are they all out to win or get second? Or are they not all out? I look for things like that. If a horse isn't ridden all out, maybe he's one you'll expect to do better in his second start off the layoff.

That's an angle I like, especially when coupled with the tape work.

"Another thing you'll sometimes see on the tape is a way a maiden is ridden. Recently, I saw a race where a horse broke cleanly, and you could see he could have easily made the front, but the jockey took hold of him. The next race he came back and this time the rider sent him hard and he won. I knew from the replay that he might have more speed than it looked like by just looking at the chart."

Mark McGuire: "When you watch enough trips, you can become good at knowing what really cost a horse and what maybe didn't cost a horse so much. You can put too much stock in certain trips, but there are other trips you can notice when maybe a horse got stopped and they didn't ask for much after that because maybe they were waiting for next time. Most bad trips, the ones that get written up, are over-bet. Then you can throw the value out the window, and you have to get value for them all, because they're not all going to win."

There are other ways of attempting to do trip work that are less labor-intensive.

Mike Labriola: "I know that in the modern era, most people use film to help them understand trips, but I don't. I'm a paper guy. When I look at past performances, I can see the race in my head and envision how it's going to be run. When I look at a film, that picture is entirely different. I know people say you should get as much information as you can, but I think sometimes you can dilute what you know already works for you."

Brent Sumja: "I also watch videos. Somebody told me once, 'When you look in that end comment in the *Racing Form* and all it says is flattened out, sometimes you'll go back and see that the horse got dead stopped.' How does that happen? It happens because that guy is doing a salary job sitting in Arizona. Do you think he's going to really go and look at everything? He wants to get out of there and go home. People who just look at those end comments and the Beyer numbers—those are the people I want to play against.

I want a better number, which is what Ragozin gives me, and I want to look at the race myself. Looking at races is painful, tedious work. I do three tracks a day now. I used to do up to eight, I was killing myself, and my notes weren't as good anymore. But even watching 30 races a day from three or four tracks is a lot."

I asked Sumja if he thought race watching at this level was something teachable.

Brent Sumja: "I guess the way I look at a race can be taught, but it's tricky to explain. It's like a golfer's swing, maybe. It's maybe the one thing that we have left: your own unique interpretation of what you're seeing. I know the jockeys; I know what I used to say to the jockeys who rode for me. I never told a jockey not to win, but I certainly told jockeys 'If you're not going to get there, take care of the horse.' Don't lay him out and risk hurting him to finish fifth. If you're not going to be in the top three, I don't care. So now I look for that. I look for jockeys who are smart enough to know that they're compromised and aren't going to get there so they take care of the horse, not because they're sore, but because of next time. Being able to spot that is perhaps my biggest advantage."

Is it just as simple as seeing a jockey drop his hands in the stretch? What are we talking about here?

Brent Sumja: "It's a feel thing, and I'm certainly not always right. Sometimes they run back and I'm just wrong. You can tell a jockey whatever you want before the race. The scenario comes to fruition about one in ten times. I used to just pick the best rider I could and rather than give instructions on how to ride, I'd try to tell him/her something about the horse. This one doesn't like to be on the rail or can't take dirt. Mapping out exactly how the race will be run and telling the jockey where to be? That doesn't work. So the good jocks will realize, 'I don't have a shot today from where I am,' and they'll keep the horse buried in there until it gets to a point where maybe they'll encourage the horse to finish a little towards the end of the race. If you can see that, it's valuable information. Sometimes you'll see a horse and you can tell that he couldn't stand being on the inside. He wouldn't run up inside, but maybe next time he'll draw an outside post and run a lot better, or he'll save ground, but then when it comes time to run, the jock will take him wide and not try to run up the inside again."

What else is Sumja looking for?

Brent Sumja: "Sometimes on the tape I can see something about how a horse is travelling. Let's say a horse doesn't change leads in the stretch. Sometimes I can tell that he didn't change leads because he was sore. Another time maybe he doesn't switch because he's intimidated by the horse inside him. If you look at Easy Goer and Sunday Silence, I really believe it goes back to that pecking order in the field. There's a brilliant head-on shot of Easy Goer and Sunday Silence coming down the stretch where you can see Easy Goer's eye on Sunday Silence. In my opinion, Easy Goer had more ability. He didn't want to go by because then he couldn't see Sunday Silence. He was intimidated by him. They could have gone around again and he wouldn't have gone by. That's how horses are by their very nature and it is the essence of their class."

TRACK BIAS

Closely related to the idea of trips is the concept of track biases. Certain days at the racetrack are better for some running styles or for runners on a certain part of the racetrack.

Mark McGuire: "Track bias is important to me. In the early summer of 2013, Woodbine was probably one of the best places to bet. Weekdays, most of the time, you would see more closers there than anywhere else, but come the weekend, it was almost all speed. If it rained, it was double speed. You need to keep track of the horses running on or against the bias. That's invaluable information."

It's akin to knowing that half the numbers on the roulette wheel had no chance of winning. You won't necessarily still win if you bet, but you have a lot better chance. A track bias was partially responsible for one of my happiest days at the racetrack back in the summer of 2003 at Del Mar. The track had been playing to speed, so my friends

William Murray, Frank Scatoni, and I put together a small $48 Pick-6 ticket up in the press box, singling a couple of speed horses we liked and spreading elsewhere. It came back more than $8,000. I've been a believer in track biases ever since.

For me, once again, Racing Flow provides the bias and pace figures I use, and it has come up with a way to quantify track bias, though rating it lower than the importance of the individual race flow. Roger Cettina is a Racing Flow subscriber as well.

Roger Cettina: "Racing Flow numbers are important to me. One thing that no speed figures ever address is track bias. Thorograp will note if a horse raced on what they deemed a dead rail, and they'll add an exclamation point if the guy doing the charts for Thorograph deemed that the horse maybe didn't fully extend himself. But as far as bias goes, nobody addresses that. So you can do some of that work yourself with Formulator.

"Monmouth Park is in my backyard and a lot of days it's all speed, so if I see a day that's all speed, I can go in Formulator and make a note and that will show up for every horse that ran on that track the day that it was all speed. Racing Flow has its own bias numbers that will upload right into your PPs as well."

I asked several of our players how they look to suss out biases.

Dave Gutfreund: "I get it mostly from my own eyes and looking at past performances. Sometimes I'll go back and watch the video to see if the horse that broke from post one was actually on the rail the entire time. I keep notes and trust my instincts. The best way to follow is to watch and bet every day. If you're watching and betting every day, and you're paying the least bit of attention, you should know what's going on."

Duke Matties: "I do all of the track bias work. It's basically my job. I watch probably 50 to 100 replays a day, from around the country. I do New York, California, Florida, Kentucky. I'll take a day and I'll note in what path each horse was, if they were on the inside or the outside, and I'll compare their speed figures from that day to previous speed figures. Say the average horse that was on the rail that day ran 10 points higher than usual—that's where I come up with the idea that there was a rail bias. I'll do the same thing in reverse as well. If the outside horses ran 10 to 15 points lower, that's the same thing. I'd say the inside part of the track was better that day. It's all based on real data."

I was surprised that so much of Matties' bias work focused on inside/outside biases rather than speed/closers.

Duke Matties: "I think speed/closers isn't a bias usually. I think it's more related to the way the race is run, maybe because the pace is too slow or the pace is too fast, except for when there are really windy days. Then I think the speed/closer bias becomes more important than inside/outside."

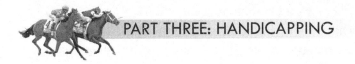

24 Breeding and Workout Information

BREEDING

Lineage is such an important part of racing that it's even referenced in the name of the sport itself: Thoroughbred racing. A knowledge of the breeding side of things is critical for contest players, because so many cap horses can be identified based on pedigree. This is partly because the races where breeding analysis is most important usually coincide with the races that have the least other information available—first-time turf, first-time starters, maiden races in general. Without information about speed and pace at its disposal, the crowd can sometimes get its market evaluations completely wrong, allowing horses who have great chances to win to go off at tremendous prices. I asked breeding expert Steve Wolfson, Sr., how he identifies horses who will like the turf.

Steve Wolfson, Sr.: "There are so many theories about why a horse will take to the grass: the size of the hoof, the angle of the pastern. My brother Gary, and I, we had our own theories and passed them on to Steve Jr., That tends to be my forte, if I have one, being able to tell if a horse will run better on the grass or dirt. That's where I can find overlays and where we found our success as a stable, Happy Valley Farm. I've always loved grass racing more. I felt I had a way of determining whether a horse would like the grass or vice versa."

Is it more something on paper or more to do with conformation?

Steve Wolfson, Sr.: "It's a combination. I had a friend who would say, 'That horse has a foot that brings tears to my eyes.' That meant you could really unload. He told us to claim a $7,500 claimer; he said this horse would love the turf. From the angle of the pastern to the size of the hoof, he rated these factors. We claimed the horse for the turf and raised it in class. Before the race, our friend said there was another horse in the same field that had better figures, and he didn't mean speed figures. Needless to say, the other horse won and we finished second, filling the exacta for $200. That's where I learned a lot. It has to do with a lot of factors: conformation, breeding, gut instinct, knowing relatives of theirs that people might not remember."

It seems that every player has his or her own method when it comes to the pedigree side of things.

Judy Wagner: "One of my other strategies is that I'm a pedigree handicapper. I love following the new sires through various websites like Equineline and The Blood-Horse. I keep notes, especially about those horses that didn't run on turf themselves but had turf in their breeding background. For example, Colonel John, he hasn't had many starters, but he's off to a great start as a turf sire."

Roger Cettina: "I like the progeny stats that come with the Thorograph figures. They'll tell you not only that the same mare had a few other foals that won, but also what numbers they ran. Did the dam's winner win a maiden claimer at Colonial or a maiden special weight at Saratoga? Thorograph tells you how fast the horses ran, and that's the information that's invaluable.

"Say you have a horse that ran at two and he hasn't run in four months, and now he's making his first start as a three-year-old. If you're looking at the progeny stats in Thorograph, it will tell you the numbers the dam's progeny ran at two and then what they ran at three. Sometimes there's a huge difference between the two, and then you can project improvement for this horse you're looking at today. You're not going to see that information anywhere else."

Every product has its own unique information. The *Racing Form* has Tomlinson ratings.

Kevin Cox: "I use the Tomlinson numbers a lot, especially for first time on the turf, and I'll go by turf Tomlinsons when I'm looking at a Polytrack race, too, because every exercise rider I've spoken to says it handles 90 percent the same as turf. I've been successful in assessing figures based on that."

Paul Shurman is another advocate of pedigree analysis.

Paul Shurman: "We love races where the pedigree information comes into play. A majority of players will pass over races with first-time starters (or just play whatever Pletcher is running) or not know how to analyze first-time grass or first time at a distance. We love those races."

What information does he use?

Paul Shurman: "You can get sibling information on Formulator, and there are other products out there that allow you to go back even further and give you more information—usually more information than most handicappers want. I am usually more interested in pedigree information from the dam side than sire stats, although in some areas, this goes against conventional theories of handicapping. There is a lot of information you can ascertain regarding class, as well as whether a horse will like the surface, distance, condition of the track, etc. Sometimes you can pick up a real gem, especially when there is little information just from a horse's siblings alone."

WORKOUT INFORMATION

Like breeding information, workout information can help take what might seem like the most tricky, chaotic races with the least amount of information and make them into an area of strength. The principle is the same. If you know more about the horses in a maiden race or a race with horses trying turf for the first time, these will be the races you choose for your optional plays. Most people sitting in a smoky room in Vegas clutching a *Racing Form* aren't going to have any clue of what's been happening out there on the track in the mornings, but you can.

Michael Beychok: "I definitely became a better contest player when I started raising the value of the workout information. *Daily Racing Form* is in that space now, giving workout reports. Racing with Bruno is something I rely on. California has been workout-centric for a long time, but the East Coast and everywhere else have not. Anytime you can get that information, I think it represents an edge. It's one of the top things that I consider when I'm making a selection."

How does he use the workout reports?

Michael Beychok: "When a player in a contest is faced with maiden races, two-year-old races, first-time starters, long layoffs, most people just reading the *Form* are not going to really know what they are looking at. In some ways, I think workout information might be the last frontier out there where you can go and get a little edge."

Brent Sumja: "Coming from the backside, I know the works can be a little ... let's say mistaken. So I have a hard time looking at the works of first-time starters and trusting that those really are the works. It's a bad thing for me, and as a result, I get lost in those races."

For me, I think workout reports are another useful tool that deserves consideration from newer players or older players looking for help in maiden races. *DRF* offers its own workout-related products, spearheaded by Mike Welsch, that can be accessed on www.drf.com.

Of course you can always take matters one step further and try to get out there yourself in the mornings and learn what's going on. It's a process that can take a lifetime to truly learn, but it's also a rewarding experience that can pay immediate dividends, and it ties in closely to the topic of our next chapter: equine body language

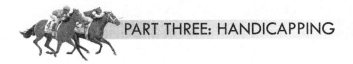

25 Body Language

I don't want you to think I'm bragging, so let me just say first off that after the pick I'm writing about in this section, I took a collar on ten races in a row in the Derby Wars $10,000 game I was playing in. But man, did the day start off right!

I was down in the corner of the paddock bar at Saratoga, watching the horses come out for the eighth race, an optional claimer that doubled as a first-level allowance. I had identified a few contenders, but the one that caught my eye was not one that made sense on paper. His neck was bowed; he looked tucked up and super fit; and his coat was full of dapples shining in the sun. His name: Sandyinthesun. He was 30-1 on the morning line; 23-1 on the board.

Sandyinthesun
Own: Ponterella Thomas and Davis Robbie G
1 Light Green, Light Blue Yoke, Sun
ARADO J (86 11 9 5 .13) 2013: (682 128 .19)

B. g. 6 (Mar)
Sire: Say Florida Sandy (Personal Flag) $2,500
Dam: In the Sun (Alleged)
Br: Tea Party Stable (NY)
Tr: Davis Robbie G(2 0 0 0 .00) 2013:(27 0 .00)

L 121

Life	21	2	0	1	$83,407	73
2013	5	0	0	0	$8,507	73
2012	11	1	0	1	$47,972	73
Sar Ⓣ	5	0	0	0	$2,128	70
D.Fst	1	0	0	0	$380	4
Wet(287)	1	0	0	0	$1,000	18
Synth	0	0	0	0	$0	-
Turf(250)	19	2	0	1	$82,027	73
DstⓉ(307)	1	0	0	0	$2,310	66

y13-6Sar	fm	1⅝ Ⓣ	:51.34	:49.83		1:00.56	3↑ⓇJohnsCall100k	**69**	7	97¼	97¾	107¼	88	812½	Lezcano A	L115 b	46.75	81-06	Hyper1211¾ Side Road1152 Quick Casablanca1213¼	Stdied 7/16,3w 3rd trn	10
																			***R-BIAS: 130 FLOW: -56 BL12: 3.2 CFR: 55**		
y13-9Bel	fm	1 Ⓣ	:24.33	:23.24	:24.53	:24.66	3↑ⓈOC 35k/N2x-N	**69**	1	48	64½	55½	59	414½	Davis J A	L122 b	15.80	75-10	AdrondckDncr1228½ *GmmCrdt*1222¼ MrRosnthl1223¾	4w 1/4p, by tired foes	6
																			***R-BIAS: 60 FLOW: 34 BL12: 5.0 CFR: 69**		
n13-8Bel	fm	1 1/16 Ⓣ	:26.46	:24.25	:23.32	:28.86	3↑ⓈOC 25k/N2x-N	**73**	2	79½	715	714	510	55	Alvarado J	L122 b	26.25	83-11	**Royal Blessing**122½ *Adirondack Dancer*122½ *Jonrah*1221¼	Outside, no factor	8
																			***R-BIAS: -24 FLOW: 65 BL12: 19.2 CFR: 71**		
n13-6Bel	fm	1¼ Ⓣ	:50.00	:48.69		:23.59	3↑OC 35k/N1x-N	**66**	7	66½	66	57	57½	57	Davis R G	L123 b	43.75	83-15	ArcAbov122no WywrdSilor1223¼ PunctulJff1221½	3-4w upper, no headway	9
																			***R-BIAS: -47 FLOW: 74 BL12: 3.5 CFR: 71**		
y13-7Bel	fm	1 Ⓣ	:25.04	:23.57	:23.34	:24.34	3↑ⓈOC 25k/N2x-N	**65**	3	76	75½	85	88¾	78¾	Davis J A	L122 b	48.00	79-12	ThThinkr122½ AdirondckDncr122nk SnkyKittn1221	Saved ground no avail	8
																			***R-BIAS: -167 FLOW: -98 BL12: 0.0 CFR: 8**		
v12-7Aqu	yl	1 1/16 Ⓣ	:24.61	:23.72	:24.37	:31.79	3↑ⓈOC 25k/N2x-N	**64**	7	98¼	96	84½	810	811¾	Davis J A	L120 b	15.70	85-03	Kharafa1195¾ Sneaky Kitten1191½ *Hear the Footsteps*120¾	Never involved	10
																			***R-BIAS: . FLOW: 291 BL12: 5.2 CFR: 100**		
t12-9Bel	yl	1 1/16 Ⓣ	:25.81	:23.95	:25.45	:31.96	3↑ⓈAlw 59000N1x	**72**	10	86¼	83¼	63½	42½	1nk	Davis J A	L121 b	17.80	62-38	Sndyinthesun121nk SleepyFrud118½ Anphylxis121½	Coaxed along, up wire	11
																			***R-BIAS: . FLOW: 75 BL12: 9.8 CFR: 76**		
t12-6Bel	gd	1 1/16 Ⓣ	:25.94	:25.66	:25.09	:30.48	3↑ⓈAlw 59000N1x	**63**	2	85½	96½	107½	1111	79½	Davis D10	L111 b	25.00	60-32	DulCitizen1211¾ GossipColumn118¾ Poliziotto121no	Squeezed st, by tired	11
																			***R-BIAS: . FLOW: -117 BL12: 5.0 CFR: 15**		
p12-6Bel	gd	1 1/16 Ⓣ	:26.34	:24.36	:23.99	:31.72	3↑ⓈAlw 59000N1x	**73**	11	76½	75½	53½	44	33¼	Davis D10	L111 b	42.25	66-33	CrbonCounty1211 NelsonAvnu1142¼ Sndyinthsun1112	3w top lane, mildly	12
																			***C-Big winds, discount flow, might have HELPED speed *R-BIAS: -89 FLOW: 90 BL12: 6.4 CFR: 65**		
p12-10Sar	fm	1 Ⓣ	:25.31	:23.19	:23.58	:23.58	3↑Alw 87000N1x	**70**	3	913	912	910	97¾	87	Davis D10	L111 b	49.75	89-03	BurntheMortgg118nk UnbridldFir1181½ *MiPoppy*118nk	2-3w turns, no rally	10
																			***R-BIAS: 60 FLOW: -133 BL12: 16.5 CFR: 16**		

KS: 2May13 AquⓉ 5f fm 1:024 B(d) *2/4* **24Apr13 Aqu 3f fst :382 B** *4/6* **15Nov12 Sar tr.t 4f fst :521 B** *11/11* **3Nov12 Sar tr.t 4f fst :522 B** *6/8* **17Aug12 Sar tr.tⓉ 4f fm :493 B(d)** *37/59* **10Aug12 Sar tr.tⓉ 4f fm :501 B(d)** *26/30*
NER: Turf(26 .04 $1.45) Routes(32 .03 $1.18) Alw(15 .07 $2.51) J/T 2012-13(1 .00 $0.00)

To me, this was a perfect contest horse. The race was wide-open on paper (the favorite was 4-1 on the morning line), and realistically any of them could win. I abandoned my previous plans and played San-dyinthesun. It was a crazy finish, with seven of them charging down the stretch, but Sandy got his nose on the line.

Boom.

Hey, I got lucky, obviously, but you're always going to have some luck involved when you pick cap horses. After the race, some troll on the contest message board started in: "Anyone who picked that horse doesn't know anything about handicapping; they were just picking a price. That horse had nothing to like on paper." Well, I guess he was half-right: what I liked wasn't on the paper. It was a straight-up looks play, and I believe that looking at horses in general might just be a new, old frontier for horseplayers in general.

One of the most frequently asked questions for me at the racetrack, just behind "What's a furlong?", is: "What are you looking for when you look at horses in the paddock?"

The answer depends on what type of race it is, how old the horses are, what the surface is, if they've been running consistently or are coming off layoffs. Basically, though, you are looking for a fit and ready runner that is well-suited to today's conditions.

What I look for the most is what I call a "controlled energy." There are many signs to indicate this. A healthy, happy look is always a plus. There is a certain energy—a little keyed up but not too much—that indicates early speed, which plays to the universal bias of dirt racing.

And then there are the specific physical attributes that indicate that the horses are doing what they want to be doing. That layoff runner, does he have a belly or is he looking tucked up and fit? That first-turf horse, does he have a big pancake of a hoof or a small hoof that's better for dirt? Is the horse close-coupled and built downhill like a sprinter? Or is he a big, long thing with a high withers and good shoul-der that looks like he'd pull a plough? That type will handle a route of ground. In a miler, I like a certain look—somewhere in between the two, a certain balance and grace. I don't mind speedy, lighter types at a mile.

I am not a conformation expert. I would never, ever think I'd have anything relevant to say when it comes to buying and selling horses. I have just been to the paddock a few thousand times and I listen carefully when the likes of The Saratoga Special's Sean Clancy and

NYRA's Maggie Wolfendale talk about what they are seeing in horses' physiques. Brent Sumja is another real body language expert with a lot to share on this topic.

Brent Sumja: "After the Sheets, the next most important part of my process is the horses' body language. I know Joe Koury, an excellent handicapper and huge reason for my quick success at tournament play from back East. I said to him twice at major contests that I had paddock picks that were over 30-1 and they both won. It happens one out of a thousand races where I'll just see a horse like that where it's almost like they are talking and saying, 'Here I am!' If you've been around them enough, that can happen. It's like a magnifying glass has hit the TV."

What is Sumja looking for?

Brent Sumja: "When you see that horse take his head and bow it down next to the pony, and he's completely within himself but ready to explode. That's a really good sign when they're going to post. Of course it doesn't help you in the second leg of a Pick-4, but if you're torn between picking a few horses in a contest, it's a great thing to see.

"People talk about the obvious things like being washy or getting agitated or taking a crap or whatever. All that stuff, I don't know much about. I look at their eyes. The one thing that a regular person who isn't around horses a lot could never understand is their eyes. To me, the washiness is only important when there is a significant amount of it between their butt cheeks, what some people call 'kidney sweat.' That to me means that they really are bothered. Sweat on a horse's shoulder when it's 90 degrees? I don't care about that unless they're just dripping."

How does Sumja's experience as a horseman help him in this regard?

Brent Sumja: "When I would put my horses on the track in the post parade, I studied them like a maniac. I ran 4,000 horses. I made notes to myself. Any athlete, any human being, who goes out on the field or up on stage nervous is not going to do as well. Nerves to me are important with anything in life. When you're calm, you do it better, period. If you can see a horse is calm and ready to go, maybe he has a little sweat or is jumping around, but if he is doing so with a calm confidence and you can spot that, it becomes a huge advantage."

What about trying to assess horses' physicality from home or from a race book?

Brent Sumja: "If I'm not playing live and I'm looking at 30 races in a day, I try to simplify the body language angles. I'm looking for ears and eyes, and I watch closely during the running of the race and can tell a lot of times at the three-eighths pole that the horse that looks like he's going to win is done. I can tell by the ears and eyes. I saw 80 horses or 160 eyes and ears a day for 15 years; I didn't need to look at the feed tub to see if the horse had eaten. I knew from the eyes. Even on the track, looking at their heads, gives you a pretty good idea where they are. It's not a major factor in any given race, maybe a 10 to 15 percent factor. But it can be a 10 to 15 percent edge that not many other people have."

And seeing this on TV is really enough for him? I know I need to be up-close and personal to really get a feel.

Brent Sumja: "TV has become sufficient. I need good views within five minutes to post. In the paddock, you can obviously get long nice looks in person, but the tack and jockey are not taking their full effect like when they're in the post parade and/or warming up in my mind. I can see what I need to more in the ears and head when they're out on the track. "Eyes" for me at this point doesn't mean physically seeing the actual eye, but paying more attention to where their eyes are focused. The focus of the eyes is more of a result of how they are carrying themselves. Are they well within themselves, yet ready for action? Are they under control but ready to explode? I think about a bad driver of a car. They seem to look right over the edge of the hood and never really see what is going on around them in the big picture.

"When I trained, one thing I demanded from every exercise rider was to take the horse on the track, stand them somewhere on the outside and let them see the big picture. Do not start their gallop until they have taken it in. The more comfortable a horse is in its surrounding, the better it will run, the more it will be willing to be guided into tight spots. I need to see them a few minutes before post to get a sense of whether they are really present in the moment or not."

How else does body language factor into his contest play?

Brent Sumja: "The body language question you have to ask, especially in cheaper races, but really any time you're dealing with horses with established form is: 'Is that normal for that horse?' For these horses with established form, it's not important to know what they look like today if you don't know what they usually look like. Okay, so he has kidney sweat. Well, maybe he has kidney sweat every time. Then it's insignificant. To really do it right, you have to keep notes like a maniac."

Fortunately, between folks like Maggie Wolfendale, who takes detailed notes at the NYRA tracks, or Southern California's Tom Quigley doing his live paddock reports on Twitter, that kind of information is available to some degree. It's also possible to take one's own notes more easily than ever in Formulator. They will pop up right in your PPs.

Does Sumja use body language in other ways?

Brent Sumja: "If I see a horse not wanting to load in the gate as a five- or six-year-old horse, and he did not do that in previous races, I would stay away from that horse for the rest of his running days. If it's something he always did, then it's obviously not important, but I write it down immediately because the race is about to run and this information will be lost by most or never even seen in the first place."

Mike Maloney mentioned earlier in the book that he does his best work when he gets to see the horses on the track. I asked him to elaborate.

Mike Maloney: "I'm not the male [equine body language expert] Bonnie Ledbetter by any means, but from all these years of observations, I've noticed that when horses do certain things, they tend to overperform or underperform. Every trainer I've had over the years has had to stand with me at the rail and listen to my low-level questions about how the horses look and why they do such and such. I haven't been able to get to a high level with body language, but I know a few little things that work for me, and I'm confident when I see them: the usual Ledbetter stuff, the rocking horse, looking at ear position; on the negative side, kidney sweat. But you have to be careful because horses are individuals and some have kidney sweat every time. Don't fall into traps like that."

I asked for some advice on how newer players might learn to read equine body language. Experience is the key.

Brent Sumja: "It's difficult to learn. When I was working for Tom Amoss and we'd stand there in the paddock, he would endlessly point things out to me, 'This one has a knee; that one is walking on egg shells.' At first, I just didn't get it, but after standing there a thousand times, just when I thought I was never going to see it, all of a sudden I started to. So to teach somebody else, I'd have to stand at a TV screen or in the paddock for months, every race, every day. After a while, they'd see it, but it's not something you can learn from a book."

No, I suppose not, but maybe this book can inspire a few future NHC champions to get out there to the racetracks and start looking at some horseflesh. I find it one of the most fun and satisfying aspects of the game. It appeals to two very different aspects of my appreciation of racing: animal lover and degenerate. You get to be close to these beautiful animals and also get an edge few other people have.

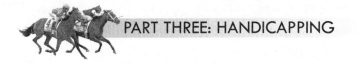

26 Computer Programs

How does one cope with the tremendous amount of information available when it comes to handicapping? How do you take it all in and process it in an elegant way? It's a very tricky process, one that every player must answer individually through years of experience, but increasingly, there is another, simpler way. Just as in other industries and other sports, computers have revolutionized the way horseplayers play. Nowhere is this more evident than on the contest scene.

Paul Shurman: "At Aqueduct a few years ago, my group came in on Saturday and sat down at our table with probably six computers among the four of us. A guy sitting at the table behind us started making fun of us. He said, 'Hey, look at those guys with their fancy computers! Who do they think they are kidding?' Another person sitting at that same table said to the guy, 'I wouldn't make fun of those guys ... they are pretty good.' Not only did Wolfson Jr., win that contest, but my brother, who flew in from California, took second. I think that guy went out the next day and bought a laptop."

Of course, it's important to know that despite some promises you might read, there are no "black box" solutions. There is still a lot of work involved, even if you're relying on a computer to do some of the work, but computer programs give handicappers a whole new arsenal of weapons to do battle in a tournament. In addition to the obvious advantages—like having a computer simulate thousands of races to make your own handicapping more efficient—computer programs can also force a certain objectivity in a game where all subjectivity can be disconcerting.

Eric Moomey: "Sometimes the more I know about the horses in a race, the harder it is for me to find a longer price. If I know all about the horses in a race, say in the Kentucky Derby, I have a really hard time convincing myself that a 20-1 shot can win. I didn't think there was any way Mine That Bird could win, but he won. So for contests, the more I know about the horses, the worse I do. Let's say a 20-1 shot wins. I'll go back to the past performances and try to convince myself that he's the winner. A lot of the time you can't do it on paper. What that tells me is that there's something else going on that can't be seen on paper."

This is exactly what a program like HTR (Handicapping Technology and Research) is trying to help you find: hidden reasons that a horse might show improvement.

Ken Massa: "What I decided to do with HTR was say, 'Show me what this horse has done since his last start.' I know he ran lousy last time, or he looks lousy on form—was there anything to tell me that he's going to turn it around? Is there anything to tell me he's going to move up? Is there anything that's going to portend improvement? And there are. There are lots of factors that can do that. As we accumulate those factors, in combination, then we can make almost a better assessment. So the more you have, the better. So if he's been gelded, he suddenly works sharp, he's getting blinkers, and he has a new trainer, then he may be a brand-new horse, especially if he's a two- or three-year-old. At that point, the paper becomes irrelevant."

Ideally, with the help of a computer, you'll keep your brain more nimble for the kind of strategic decisions you need to make along the way.

Ken Massa: "The first thing you have to do when you're playing in a tournament is to handicap the races themselves, and we've identified certain types of races as being more prolific for longshots. The key to that is what we call the VI, or Volatility Index, which is in the header for every single screen in HTR, so no matter where you are looking, you'll see in the header something called the VI. The lower that number is, the more likely a longshot will win.

The purpose of the VI rating in the header was to simulate the likely probability of the favorite winning, but it turns out it's actually a real good prognosticator for how wide-open or chaotic the race may be.

"So the VI ranges anywhere from 15 to 50. If you see a VI under 20, for example, it's usually going to be a large field—turf sprint, grass, something like that—that will have a lot of longshots, and a lot of them will have a good shot. If you see a very high VI number like 45, chances are the favorites are going to win the race. So we start out by organizing the races according to how likely it is we're going to see a longshot, and then we throw out the ones that are going to be chalky. That's how I start the process. We're trying to get you to fish in the right pond because if you do that, eventually you are going to catch one."

Some players who enjoy looking at the HTR data—including myself—don't see it as a replacement for the *Racing Form*, but rather as a complementary tool to help augment their own handicapping.

Judy Wagner: "I use HTR, but I also use the *Racing Form*. I like to have the *Racing Form* in front of me, but I take information from the HTR program and write it in on my *Form*. Many of the people who use HTR have a level of computer sophistication that I certainly don't have. They can take the statistics and export them, using Excel and various database programs to essentially crunch the numbers. I am not one of those. The first thing I look at on HTR is the workout ratings. Especially, I like to zero in on a first-time starter or a horse going to a new surface—turf, dirt, whatever. HTR has a wealth of information as far as that is concerned.

"It also has a lot of trainer and jockey statistics that are current. This information is available in the *Form*; however, it can be delayed to a certain degree. HTR can be up to the minute for the things that I look for. For example, is this a 30 percent trainer on turf compared to a well-known trainer who may only be 9 percent on turf?"

I asked Massa for a little more background on how HTR works.

Ken Massa: "I believe in reverse handicapping. Reverse handicapping refers to looking at running lines in the past performances from the opposite viewpoint. Very few horseplayers do this. Instead of focusing on the finish of the past races, we will look at the beginning—the early pace—to extract what the horse accomplished in its races. This requires a leap of faith on the user's part. Most horseplayers have been schooled to believe that past finish position, final-time ratings, and form cycle are the foundation of handicapping, but the earning power of traditional handicapping methods has dissipated dramatically."

Eric Moomey has become a believer.

Eric Moomey: "I didn't do HTR at first, and the reason I didn't do it was that I saw a lot of other players using it. If I'm using HTR, then I can't beat them. All I can do is match them. Then it dawned on me that it would still be of great use to me. What happened was, there was a contest where I was in the lead, in a contest of 100 people, and 20 people blew past me on one result. I said to myself, if I knew who the HTR players were, and I understood who they were likely to bet, then when I'm in the lead ahead of them, that would be very helpful information to know. I could protect myself by playing their horse. Likewise, if I'm in 15th and some of them are ahead of me, well, that's also very valuable information. Now you're looking for a horse that they would never consider—one that maybe the program would downgrade. Information is power."

What does Moomey like about the program?

Eric Moomey: "HTR is a nice display of information that might easily flag something for you that you wouldn't find in another source. It's not the end-all, be-all, but it's a powerful tool. As more and more people use it, however, it becomes less and less valuable over time. It offers good information on first-time starters. It has significant knowledge of firsters that you don't find in the normal past performances. Each program has its strengths and weaknesses. Some people use a program and they use it religiously and that's it. But the point is, I might use a program for one type of race and do something completely different for another type of race. There was a firster that won last weekend, and I looked at him on paper and said, 'Man, that's just crazy.' But sure enough, for whatever reason, HTR liked the horse."

Brent Sumja had a good idea about trying to incorporate computer analysis into one's handicapping.

Brent Sumja: "Nowadays there is so much information out there that you have to be careful. I was doing well and I decided I'd try a new computer program to see what it was all about, and in following this program, I went away from my basics, and that led to a three- or four-month slump. What I learned was that you have to take your core of what you've learned from your own experience and stick with it. You can add tiny things to that as time goes on, a little at a time."

Some players have taken computer use to an even more intense level: building proprietary programs and databases they use to aid them in their handicapping.

Duke Matties: "We have our own computer program we use. It's nothing that's ever been for sale. It's based on past performances, modernized speed figures, a lot of track-bias work, a lot of trainer stats, breeding information, key race stats; it'd take me hours to explain it all."

How does it work?

Duke Matties: "The whole idea of handicapping is that you can come up with your own little theories, and then it's basically weighing the options about horses. Are they going to run better? Are they going to run worse? Are they going to run the same? The computer doesn't spit out who to bet—I do have to analyze most of the data at this point—but we still have all of the information in front of us on one page, so it's like having a *Racing Form* with a lot better information in it."

Not everyone is convinced. I mentioned HTR to my friend Emily Gullikson at one point, and she quipped, "I feel about HTR like I feel about having children. It's definitely an interesting idea, but I don't think it's for me." She's not the only one.

Dennis Decauwer: "I'm probably pretty old-fashioned in that I'm not using any software to assist me, to narrow down the scope of what races I want to look at. Having said that, I guess I'm using the old-fashioned computer—my brain."

Still, even the skeptics must admit that for some players, playing with the help of a program makes life a lot easier, particularly when you're trying to choose which ten races to play out of seven full cards of races. Computer handicapping is an avenue I'd encourage all new contest players to at least explore.

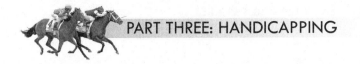

27 Other Factors

In this part of the book, we've covered our players' thoughts on the fundamentals and we've examined what they had to say on the most critical factors for contest play. We've even looked into what might be the future of playing the horses—computer play. But what about everything else? A beginning contest player in particular might want to pay close attention to a few other ways to find winners: jockeys, distance, and post position.

JOCKEYS

Maury Wolff: "Let's assume you've been reading the *Form* for six months. You're looking for stuff that is obvious but that leads to prices. I'm not a jockey guy, but there are worse angles than to notice when a good rider gets on a horse for no obvious reason and the horse is 15-1—it still might be live. It's a simple strategy, but you might catch one of those in a tournament, and it's certainly easy to look for."

Brent Sumja: "Another weakness for me in my handicapping is the jockeys. I don't give them enough credit. I don't even know who is on my horse nine out of ten times until the race is going. I know the weight, but not the jockey. I once made a mistake in a *Daily Racing Form* interview and said 'I think they should use mechanical monkeys instead of jockeys.' The next morning as the jockeys rode by me, they all were making monkey sounds and gestures. I should probably give them more credit."

I've always believed in the notion, as Maury Wolff suggested above, that it's okay to let the top jocks' agents do some of the handicapping for you; if they end up on a 10-1 shot, there might just be a reason.

Brent Sumja: "I don't disagree with that idea—the best agents win the most races—but the problem for me again goes back to having spent so much time on the backside. Sometimes the top jock ends up on that trainer's 10-1 shot because he was told he has to ride that one back to ride the Grade 1 horse next week. Sometimes the trainer and agent were in a little spat the morning of that entry. You never really know, and I don't want to get caught up in that. I don't want to read into it at all, but I definitely should be looking at it somewhat."

Dennis Decauwer: "A lot of times you'll see a jockey not ride a horse back and someone will say, 'Smith took off that horse.' Well, a lot of times, that's not the case. It's as simple as his agent didn't know the horse was going to be in that race, and he'd already made a commitment to somebody else. Some people make a big deal of it and there's nothing to it. You can't take it too literally. Sometimes it means something; sometimes it doesn't."

For me, it all comes down to price and situation. Can I easily throw a horse like this one into a Pick-4? Do I like anything at a better price in the contest the same as I like this one? Is there anything else at all to like about the horse? Then maybe I'd use the horse, but you're not going to make a proper bet on a horse based on jockey alone. It's just another piece of the puzzle.

Mark McGuire: "If I find the right race, I'm ultimately not that worried about the jockey or the trainer because ultimately the race is going to be won by the horse."

DISTANCE

Mike Labriola talked to me about an underrated handicapping factor. The distance of races can often be a major factor that's overlooked, as players fall all over themselves looking for speed and pace angles.

Mike Labriola: "One thing that I do that a lot of people don't emphasize is to really look at the distance of a race. I think distance is the lost variable of our age. People look at speed, pace, trip, but the horse could be rated best at all three of those things, and if he's a five-furlong horse, then he's not going to win going a mile and a half. That's an exaggeration, but it's a great exaggeration.

"Distance is underrated even when it's the difference between going six furlongs and six-and-a-half furlongs. People see a horse closing at five-and-a-half furlongs and think that six-and-a-half furlongs will hit him between the eyes, but it's not necessarily so. I want to see a horse that has shown me he can handle today's distances or has something that really legs him up for today's distance, like a seven-furlong bottom-builder that's maybe hidden three or four lines down."

POST POSITION

The specifics of where a horse breaks from can be important at times as well.

Kevin Cox: "One of my key bets, under the right circumstances, is outside post positions, especially in sprint races. This was one turn around the Poly, and the reason I pay extra special attention to outside post positions is that there is only one guarantee in horse racing, and it took me years to figure this out: if you're breaking from the outside, you can never get squeezed at the start. Never. You can get pushed a little, but you know what? You can get bumped, but you're not getting bumped by two horses. The horse isn't losing his breath twice if he gets bumped around; he's only losing it once, and he can still keep his stride, whereas if you have a horse that's breaking in the five hole in a ten-horse field, he can get squeezed, his legs can get tangled. So I always pay extra special attention to the outside post position in sprints.

"I also like the outside post with a speed horse because I'm a big fan of the killer crossover move. That's another thing when you have the outside post—that's the only spot where you can kick dirt in every other horse's face. You can't do that from the one hole unless you veer out to the eleven path."

Now that we've heard a lot of handicapping theory as it pertains to contest play, it's time to get to the fun part—let's take a look at how contest players, including me, have used the information discussed in this book to actually pick a few winners.

28 Roger Cettina's Second-Place Finish at the NHC

I was lucky enough to get to work with James Quinn last year as an editor of his excellent book *The Complete Handicapper*. In many ways, the book is an update of Tom Ainslie's classic, *Ainslie's Complete Guide to Thoroughbred Racing,* and whether you're a new player or an experienced veteran, I recommend reading it. I'm going to steal an idea from the Quinn book—good authors borrow, great authors steal—and present an Applications sections in this book, where we get to see some of the ideas our players have talked to us about in action.

Let's start by flashing back to Roger Cettina's second-place finish at the NHC. This is a perfect example of using speed figures—along with some additional information—to identify a horse that has a similar chance as the favorite but is ten times the price. This is the situation all contest players are looking for.

Offlee Fast	Dk. b or b. g. 3 (Apr) FTKOCT11 $7,000	Life	1	M	0	0	$310	59	D.Fst	0	0	0	0	$0	–
wn: Van Den Broeck Herman	Sire: Offlee Wild (Wild Again) $4,000								Wet(389)	0	0	0	0	$0	–
	Dam: Etch (Pioneering)	2012	1	M	0	0	$310	59	Synth	0	0	0	0	$0	–
	Br: Sierra Farm (Ky)	2011	0	M	0	0	$0	–	Turf(311)	1	0	0	0	$310	59
	Tr: Pellegrini Ronald(25 5 2 2 .20) 2012:(74 13 .18)	Gp ①	1	0	0	0	$310	59	Dst①(348)	0	0	0	0	$0	–

7Dec12-10GP fm 1⅛ ① .24³ :49² 1:13² 1:43⁴ Md 65000(75-65) 59 6 2¹ 2½ 43½ 83¾ 7⁶ Santana J Z L120 b 71.40 72– 25 Greengrssofyoming122² ShockLeder122½ McIlroy122½ Tired 5w into lane 12

RAINER: Turf(31 .10 $2.35) Routes(76 .20 $2.51) Stakes(20 .35 $2.18)

Roger Cettina: "On Saturday at the NHC in 2013, there was a horse named Offlee Fast in the ninth at Gulfstream. This year they had allowed one double bet, $4 win and place, as opposed to the usual $2 win and place. It was a maiden special weight on the grass, and I had narrowed him down as one of the main contenders on Thursday after watching the replay. He had run in a maiden claimer the first time and was moving up in class. I knew on Thursday that he'd be my max bet for Saturday. He was 20-1 morning line, and I thought he'd be every bit of that by post time.

"His last Thorograph number was nearly as good as the morning-line favorite. There was maybe a one-point difference, and the favorite was 3-1 and Offlee Fast was 30-1. I watch tons of replays on Formulator, and he just looked like the kind of horse that didn't extend himself in that first race, and I love horses moving up in class, because often the crowd underrates them. I could see from Formulator that the trainer was 33 percent at the meet. You know how it goes in racing: when barns are going well, they're going well., and when they're not, they're not. It really can't be explained; it is what it is."

Offlee Fast won and paid $59.60.

29 John Doyle and Dapper Gene

Let's take a look at a couple of more NHC examples, starting with the last race from the year John Doyle won, 2011. This is a great example of using a trainer angle on the price on the board to make the right decision at the right time.

Stoneside (Ire)
Own: Naify Marsha

B. g. 6 (Feb)
Sire: Marchand de Sable (Theatrical*Ire)
Dam: Greenstone*Ire (Green Desert)
Br: Dr B. Krief (Ire)
Tr: Canani Julio C(44 7 8 4 .16) 2010:(0 0 .00)

Life	33	5	10	8	$442,086	100	D.Fst	0	0	0	0	$0 –
2010	9	0	4	3	$60,176	96	Wet(301*)	0	0	0	0	$0 –
2009	3	0	0	1	$12,768	97	Synth	4	0	2	2	$38,550 93
Sa Ⓣ	8	1	1	3	$107,260	100	Turf(300)	29	5	8	6	$403,536 100
							DstⓉ(316)	8	2	2	2	$99,930 100

31Dec10-2SA	fm	*6½f	Ⓣ	:212 :431 1:063 1:123	3↑Clm 40000(40-35)	89	9	4	64¼	57	33½	2nk	Nakatani C S	LB122	2.40	92-08	*Sassou*nk Stoneside1¼ A Lil Dumaani½	4wd into lane,rallied	9
10Dec10-4Hol	fst	5½f	◈	:22 :444 :562 1:023	3↑OC 40k/n1x	85	1	5	42	42½	32½	26¼	Gomez G K	LB124 f	*1.60	91-10	Moonlark6¼ Stoneside½ A Lil Dumaani1¼	Came out str,up 2nd	6
11Nov10-7Hol	fm	6f	Ⓣ	:221 :442 :561 1:073	3↑OC 62k/n2x	90	8	7	73¾	95½	95½	53¾	Pedroza M A	LB120	3.90	95-01	Caracortado1¾ Cherokee Heaven1 *Amazombie*¾	3wd into str,outkicked	10
18Aug10-6Dmr	fm	5f	Ⓣ	:214 :434 :552	3↑GreenFlshH102k	95	8	7	77	78½	77	61	Rosario J	LB117	6.90	96-03	ClifornFlgno DH *QuickEnough* DH MySummerSlw½	Willingly,tight wire	8
27Jun10-7Hol	fm	6f	Ⓣ	:231 :452 :563 1:082	3↑RKKerlanMH75k	96	3	5	32	32	32	2¾	Pedroza M A	LB117	8.50	94-05	My Summer Slew¾ Stonesideno *Unzip Me*1	Rail,loomed btw,up 2nd	7
6May10-2Hol	fst	6f	◈	:224 :453 :563 1:081	3↑OC 80k/c-N	93	3	3	2½	21½	23	24½	Pedroza M A	LB120	3.50	91-13	*Cost of Freedom*4½ Stoneside1¼ M One Rifle8¼	Vied,stalked,2nd best	5
7Mar10-7SA	fst	6½f	⊗	:213 :44 1:084 1:151	4↑JHernandez60k	88	7	2	44	45½	21	31¾	Pedroza M A	LB116	5.30	87-13	Sangaree½ Gallant Son1¼ Stoneside2¼	Bid btwn,led,outkicked	7
3Feb10-3SA	fm	*6½f	Ⓣ	:21 :424 1:051 1:111	4↑Alw 55554c	95	6	4	64½	64¼	42½	3½	Pedroza M A	LB116	5.50	98-01	Victor's Cry½ Cherokee Heavenhd Stoneside1	Angle out,gamely btwn	9
2Jan10-5SA	fm	*6½f	Ⓣ	:212 :432 1:06 1:114	4↑ImprsvLckH66k	93	6	2	33½	44	42½	32½	Smith M E	LB116	3.40	93-04	Cherokee Heaven1¼ Mr. Cacht1¼ Stonesideno	Angled in hill,held 3d	8
29Nov09-7Hol	fm	6f	Ⓣ	:231 :452 :57 1:084	3↑OC 100k/c-N	96	2	6	31	2hd	1½	2nk	♦Gomez G K	LB118 b	3.10	93-07	T. D. Vancenk DH Get Funky DDH Stonesidehd	Drifted out,bump late	9
Disqualified and placed third																			

TRAINER: 61-180Days(25 .08 $0.30) Sprint(132 .15 $1.66) Stakes(47 .13 $1.16)

apper Gene
wn: Siquicros Baltazar

Dk. b or b. g. 5 (Feb)
Sire: Catienus (Storm Cat) $5,000
Dam: LIl Irene (LIl E. Tee)
Br: John T. L. Jones Jr. (Ky)
Tr: Palma Hector O(48 5 2 11 .10) 2010:(0 0 .00)

Life	23	5	2	5	$173,160	93	D.Fst	1	0	0	1	$3,960 82
2011	1	1	0	0	$20,400	89	Wet(339)	0	0	0	0	$0 –
2010	10	2	0	3	$51,600	93	Synth	11	1	1	4	$72,240 93
Sa Ⓣ	7	2	1	0	$59,960	90	Turf(278)	11	4	1	0	$96,960 90
							DstⓉ(308)	6	2	1	0	$57,960 90

Jan11-10SA	fm	*6½f	Ⓣ	:214 :44 1:062 1:122	4↑Clm c-(32-28)	89	4	6	77¼	75¼	52¼	1½	Talamo J	LB121 b	5.60	93-07	*Dapper Gene*½ *Stoneside*nk *Exclamation*1¼	3wd into lane,rallied	10
Claimed from Featherston, Jacobsen and Miller for $32,000, Mitchell Mike Trainer 2010: (375 92 71 47 0.25)																			
Dec10-2SA	fm	*6½f	Ⓣ	:212 :431 1:063 1:123	3↑Clm c-(40-35)	83	7	3	99¼	810	66	52¾	Bejarano R	LB122 fb	*1.90	89-08	*Sassou*nk Stoneside1¼ A Lil Dumaani½	Came out str,late bid	9
Claimed from Siquieros Baltazar for $40,000, Palma Hector O Trainer 2010(as of 12/31): (101 15 19 10 0.15)																			
Nov10-5Hol	fm	6f	Ⓣ	:223 :444 :563 1:083	3↑Clm 40000(40-35)	89	5	6	711	79¼	75¾	11	Bejarano R	LB120 fb	3.10	94-06	Dapper Gene1 Fandino½ Maui Mark¾	Came out str,rallied	7
Nov10-6Hol	fm	6f	Ⓣ	:233 :461 :574 1:092	3↑Clm c-(32-28)n1y	85	5	5	74¾	86¼	52¼	1hd	Bejarano R	LB124	*2.20	90-10	*Dapper Gene*hd *Sassou*no Yes It's a Cat1¼	Tight 3/8,rallied btwn	10
Claimed from Dart, Ronald, Galb, Robert, Hochman, Bruce, Dart, Gwen and West, Mary Ellen for $32,000, West Ted H Trainer 2010(as of 11/12): (49 10 10 5 0.20)																			
Oct10-7OTH	fst	6f	◈	:231 :462 :574 1:094	3↑Clm 35000(40-35)	90	1	5	51¾	42	41¼	3nk	Garcia M	LB118	3.10	88-17	Charm N Chuckno Position Ank *Dapper Gene*¾	Wait,split,rail bid	6

AINER: +180Days(13 .08 $0.46) Turf(57 .05 $0.66) Sprint(186 .10 $1.47) Stakes(17 .00 $0.00)

John Doyle: "I knew Stoneside was going to be the favorite in the race, and I didn't like him. I had played him last time and thought he had a perfect trip, and I didn't like how he finished. I had a feeling I was going to want to play the race, and depending on where

I was on the leaderboard, I wanted to have a couple of options, so I looked at a longshot, Wing Forward, who I would have played if I was more behind, and then there was Dapper Gene, a mid-priced horse that I liked best. The reason I liked him best was trainer Mike Mitchell. He claimed the horse last time out, in a race where he was only beaten two lengths by Stoneside.

"And Mitchell's just a genius. I figured going from the lower-percentage Hector Palma barn to Mitchell had to be a significant move up. I did a little Formulator analysis, and Mitchell was six-for-seven in the money first time off the claim when he turf sprints at Santa Anita, and five of those were wins. Dapper Gene was the only horse besides the favorite to have a win over the course. Also, I expected Dapper Gene to get more pace to run at than he did in his previous effort. Dapper Gene was 5-1; Stoneside was 2-1. It was an easy decision for me. Going into the last race, I knew I didn't need the longshot, and I didn't like the favorite, so that was the play."

30 John Conte and Raiding Party Land The 2009 NHC

Raiding Party is the horse that landed the NHC for John Conte. I love how he went back in the past performances and found the critical piece of information that the crowd was ignoring.

John Conte: "In the last race, there was a horse, Raiding Party, that I thought should have been 5-1—the 10 horse in the 11th race at Santa Anita. He'd done nothing on the turf, but the race had been taken off the turf and was being run on the Pro-Ride, which was like Polytrack, then I looked way, way back in the horse's past performances with my magic magnifying glass, I spotted the fact that this horse had run in Europe in '07, and he had won two out of three starts on Polytrack. So the racing gods were very good to me. The fact that the race came off the turf was a big advantage.

---

iding Party (Ire)
: Alexander Nicholas B

B. f. 4 (May)
Sire: Orpen (Lure)
Dam: Lady Angola (Lord At War*Arg)
Br: Airlie Stud (Ire)
Tr: Mitchell Mike R (147 39 24 26 .27) 2008:(0 0 .00)

	Life	7	3	0	1	$50,955	85	D.Fst	0 0 0 0	$0	–
	2009	1	1	0	0	$31,200	85	Wet(279°)	0 0 0 0	$0	–
	2008	2	0	0	1	$7,240	76	Synth	4 3 0 0	$43,715	85
								Turf(350)	3 0 0 1	$7,240	76
	Sa	1	1	0	0	$31,200	85	Dst(334)	1 1 0 0	$31,200	85

n09-11SA fst 1 ⊗ :241 :49 1:134 1:364 4↑ⒻAlw 58192n1x 85 7 11½ 11½ 11 11½ 11½ Flores D R LB119 22.30 82– 16 Raiding Party 1½ *Onebadkitty* 2½ Unusual Spirit 1 Inside, ridden out 8
g08– 7Dmr fm 1½ ① :234 :481 1:123 1:42 ⒻOC 80k/n1x -N 76 3 5³ 52½ 42 52½ 85½ Flores D R LB118 49.20 83– 09 Solar Miss ¾ Fire n' Brimstone 2¾ Lullabytime½ Lacked room rail lane 10
508– 8SA fm 1 ① :233 :473 1:112 1:351 ⒻOC 80k/n1x -N 69 3 4³ 42½ 42 32½ 33½ Flores D R LB117 15.50 85– 11 Czechers 1 Wickednwackyingrid 2½ RaidingPrty no Stalked pace, held 7
c07– 7SA fm 1 ① :23 :48 1:114 1:354 ⒻBlueNorthr85k 52 9 10 12 9 10 9 7¾ 9 10 9 15¼ Smith M E LB118 7.40e 70– 12 Gorgeous Goose 1¾ Golden Doc A 1½ Ariege hd Came out str, no rally 10
reviously trained by John Hills
07 Wolverhampton (GB) ft 6f ◇LH 1:154 Catherine Birch Nursery Hcp (polytrack) 11½ Sanders S 130 *1.50 Raiding Party 1½ Natmana 1½ Lake Sabina no 12
acing Post Rating: 78 Hcp 9200 *Handily placed in 4th or 5th, led 200y out, readily*
07 Wolverhampton (GB) ft 6f ◇LH 1:151 Median Auction Mdn Stks (polytrack) 1¹ Sanders S 124 4.00 *Raiding Party* 1 Miesko½ Just Like A Woman 3¾ 13
acing Post Rating: 74 Maiden 9100 *Trckd ldrs, 2nd hfwy, led & drifted right 150y out, ridden out*
07 Lingfield (GB) ft 6f ◇LH 1:124 Median Auction Mdn Stks (polytrack) 43¾ Quinn T R 124 50.00 Rockfield Lodge hd Sunny Sprite 1½ Alls Fair 2½ 11
acing Post Rating: 55 Maiden 6100 *Missed break, behind, mild late gain*

INER: +180Days(27 .22 $3.09) Turf/Dirt(55 .11 $0.82) Dirt(171 .20 $1.48) Routes(223 .22 $1.57) Stakes(60 .27 $1.43)

"A lot of people overlooked the horse, and a lot of people who maybe did notice that the horse had run well on Polytrack didn't have the guts to play it at 22-1. One other gentleman did play it, but he was $9 behind me, so he thought that he won when Raiding Party came in, but I knew that I had won. Maybe 29 out of 30 times, the guy who bet the even-money shot would win. But the racing gods were smiling on me."

PART FOUR: APPLICATIONS

31 Surfside with Dennis Decauwer and Luckarack

7 Luckarack		B. g. 5 (Apr)								Life	34	10	6	5	$402,410	93	D.Fst	15	6	1	3	$203,830	93

7 Luckarack
Own: Diller or Hansen or Rocks
9-2   Black, Red Chevrons On Sleeves, Black $40,000
ESPINOZA V (146 24 30 21 .16) 2013: (338 55 .16)

B. g. 5 (Apr)
Sire: Lucky Pulpit (Pulpit) $2,500
Dam: Tamarack Bay (Dehere)
Br: Mr & Mrs Larry D Williams (Cal)
Tr: Hansen Scott(10 1 1 2 .10) 2013:(14 2 .14)

L 124

Life 34 10 6 5 $402,410 93   D.Fst 15 6 1 3 $203,830 93
2013 7 0 1 3 $22,550 88   Wet(388*) 0 0 0 0 $0 –
2012 10 3 3 1 $92,090 93   Synth 13 2 3 2 $97,980 93
Hol ⑦ 3 2 1 0 $79,280 84   Turf(288) 6 2 2 0 $100,600 84
                            Dst⑦(372) 3 2 1 0 $79,280 84

16Jun13–6BHP fst 6f ◇ :22.01 :45.39 :57.77 1:10.54 3↑ Clm 40000(40-35)   87 2 8   86½ 75½ 51¾ 3¾ Puglisi I   L120 b 9.90 88–15 GutshotStright120ᵐᵏ ChpmnsPk122½ Luckrck120ʰᵈ   Came out str,late 3rd 9
17May13–5BHP fm 6f ⑦ :23.07 :45.47 :57.06 1:08.86 3↑ Clm c–(40-35)   77 4 8   86½ 64¼ 44 2³¾ Quinonez A   L120 b 3.80 88–08 Et Tu Walker120³¾ Luckarack120ʰᵈ Major Magic120ʰᵈ   Up 2nd 3wd wire 8
   Claimed from Moger Steve for $40,000, Moger Ed Jr Trainer 2013(as of 5/17): (192 22 30 38 0.11)
26Apr13–5BHP fst 6f ◇ :22.44 :45.46 :57.47 1:09.95 3↑ Clm 40000(40-35)   86 4 6   84½ 84¾ 53 3½ Quinonez A   L120 b 16.30 90–11 MasterChef120ᵐᵈ ChapmansPeak121¾ Luckarack120½   Bit awkward start 8
6Apr13–10SA fst 6½f :22.47 :45.06 1:09.23 1:15.70 4↑ OC 40k/n1x   63 6 6   85¼ 107 911 812½ Flores D R   L119 b 17.60 74–15 PointsOffthbench119½ OlvrsTlf119ⁿᵒ GonnFlyNow119¼   Steadied 3/8,4wd lane 10
14Mar13–6SA fst 6f :21.98 :44.73 :56.98 1:09.72 4↑ Clm c–(32-28)   83 1 2   87 86 84¾ 3½ Leparoux J R   L121 b 2.80 84–17 Thinking of Girls121¾ Courtside121¹ Luckarack121½   Shift out, surged late 8
   Claimed from Peter Redekop B. C., Ltd. for $32,000, West Ted H Trainer 2012: (49 6 8 8 0.12)
2Feb13–6SA fst 6f :21.47 :43.89 :56.02 1:08.47 4↑ OC 40k/n1x   88 1 4   43 44 54½ 64¾ Maldonado E   L119 b 7.10 87–15 ItlinRules123½ PointsOffthebench123½ WllDnce119²½   3wd into lane,no rally 11
6Jan13–7SA fst 6½f :21.95 :44.70 1:09.95 1:16.45 4↑ OC 40k/n1x   – 3 9   – – – – Maldonado E   L119 b *2.00 – 24 KtesEvent119½ CooCchoo123½ FlotingFthr123ʰᵈ   Stumbld strt,lost jock 9
16Dec12–8BHP fst 6f ◇ :22.25 :45.34 :57.33 1:09.89 3↑ OC 40k/n1x   92 9 1   74½ 52½ 2ʰᵈ 2ⁿᵒ Maldonado E   L124 b 4.10 92–16 ChapmansPeak124ⁿᵒ Luckarack124¹½ WllDnce122ⁿᵒ   4wd into str,willingly 9
19Oct12–2SA fst 6½f :22.56 :45.28 1:09.77 1:16.25 3↑ Clm 32000(32-28)   83 3 3   53 52½ 1½ 1½ Maldonado E   L122 b *1.30 84–20 Luckrck122½ NewfoundGold122½ SolrRocket122ⁿᵒ   Steadied 5-1/2,4wd bid 6
19Sep12–7Fpx fst 6f :22.89 :46.44 :59.57 1:11.36 3↑ Clm 20000   85 3 7   41¾ 11½ 13½ 14¾ Maldonado E   L120 b *.50 95–11 Luckarack120¾ Max Cooper120½ Mr. Cacht120¾   Kicked clear 2nd turn 8

WORKS: 6Jly13 SA 4f fst :49 H 15/44   29Jun13 SA 4f fst :49² H 23/49   8Jun13 SA 4f fst :48⁴ H 22/57   12May13 BHP ◇ 4f fst :49⁴ H 39/55   20Apr13 SA 4f fst :48¹ H 10/38   31Mar13 SA 4f fst :47⁴ H 9/42
TRAINER: TurfSprints(3 .00 $0.00) Synth/Turf(1 .00 $0.00) Turf(5 .20 $7.24) Sprint(20 .15 $2.76) Claim(4 .00 $0.00) Alw(5 .20 $7.24)

My interview with Dennis Decauwer took place shortly after the Surfside Live-Bankroll tournament in July of 2013. I asked him about an 8-1 winner he had that day, Luckarack, in a six-furlong turf sprint. His answer combined fundamental handicapping and trip work in a way I thought would be useful to share.

Dennis Decauwer: "I liked him because of his last two races. His second race back was at a similar level, also a sprint on the grass, and the horse that won that day, Et Tu Walker, is a nice horse that had just been escalating up the ladder, from being a claimer to a stakes-caliber runner. I followed Luckarack that day, and he had a little bit of trouble. He had to weave his way outside and finished very strongly, galloping out past the winner. Even though he was beaten by about three lengths, he ran very, very well, I thought.

"Last time on the synthetic, he dropped a little bit farther back than I think he wanted to be; he had to weave his way through horses. Again, he finished very, very strongly and galloped out past the winner. On the day I bet him, he was back on the turf again, with Victor Espinoza up, who I happen to love in turf sprints, and this time he got a clean run, never had to take up or anything, and there was plenty of speed to set it up. He barely got there, but he did win."

32 Frank Scatoni on Fastinov and Key to Fame

Frank Scatoni provided an interesting example of how persistence and mental toughness can pay off from the Fall Classic at the Orleans in 2013. His first bet of the day was Fastinov.

5 Fastinov — 20-1
Own: Magee Walter B
Light Green, Kelly Green Hoop, Kelly — $16,000
FRANCO M (140 11 13 18 .08) 2013: (661 75 .11)

B. g. 3 (Apr)
Sire: Bop (Rahy) $2,500
Dam: Cordesian (Lear Fan)
Br: Elkton Stable (Pa)
Tr: Magee Walter B(1 0 0 0 .00) 2013:(19 0 .00)

115^{5}

Life	11	M	0	0	$10,294	60		**D.Fst**	4	0	0	0	$4,750	29
2013	11	M	0	0	$10,294	60		**Wet(337)**	1	0	0	0	$1,740	43
2012	0	M	0	0	$0	-		**Synth**	0	0	0	0	$0	-
								Turf(332)	6	0	0	0	$3,804	60
Bel Ⓣ	3	0	0	0	$2,866	56		**DstⓉ(295)**	5	0	0	0	$3,464	58

27Sep13-9Bel	fm	1 1/16 [T]	:24^{3} :24^{2} :24^{3} :31^{1}	3↑ Md 16000	**56**	5	$1^{½}$	$1^{1½}$	$1^{½}$	2^{hd}	$4^{5¼}$	Franco M^{5}	115 b	35.75	72-23	Pentagram120^{1½} Metro120^{2½} National Buck120^{1¼}	In hand ins, weakened	10	***R-BIAS: . FLOW: 54 BL12: 11.2 CFR: 70**
28Aug13-10Sar	fm	1 1/16 Ⓣ	:25^{3} :24^{3} :24^{2} :29^{4}	3↑ Md 25000	**50**	11	8^{10}	$8^{8¾}$	$8^{6¼}$	7^{8}	$6^{10¾}$	Franco M^{5}	114	46.50	71-18	Lasso123^{2¼} *Present Course*123^{1½} Ryvit123^{1½}	Washy,3-4wide turns	11	***R-BIAS: -108 FLOW: -95 BL12: 0.0 CFR: 12**
18Aug13-10Sar	fm	1⅜ [T]	:54^{4} :52^{4} :11^{2}	3↑ Md Sp Wt 85k	**60**	7	$10^{8¼}$	9^{6}	$9^{5¼}$	$10^{7¼}$	$10^{9¼}$	Lezcano A	119	65.75	46-21	Runs Like a Kitten119^{½} Bramley118^{2½} Viva Lad119^{hd}	6w into lane,faltered	10	***R-BIAS: -19 FLOW: -220 BL12: 3.9 CFR: 2**
27Jly13-7Suf	fst	1 ⊗	:26^{1} :24^{1} :25^{1} :27^{4}	3↑ Md Sp Wt 17k	**29**	1	6^{11}	6^{11}	6^{9}	$5^{4½}$	$4^{2¼}$	Davis J A	119	4.10	74-15	Run for Cecila119^{nk} C F's Bullet119^{½} Concert Dell124^{1½}	Finished well	6	
16Jun13-10Bel	fm	1 1/16 Ⓣ	:26 :23^{2} :24^{1} :32^{1}	3↑ Md 20000	**46**	10	10^{11}	$9^{7½}$	$10^{8½}$	$5^{8½}$	$6^{10½}$	Lezcano A	119	23.70	64-19	HgAsst119^{nk} Trnngforsccss124^{5} BrndysBgGy124^{½}	Overland 2nd,lug in up	10	***R-BIAS: -109 FLOW: 60 BL12: 0.0 CFR: 55**
25May13-7Bel	my^{S}	1⅛ ⊗	:51^{1} :25^{1} :26^{1} :14	3↑ Md 20000	**43**	7	5^{4}	$7^{6¼}$	$3^{6½}$	3^{9}	$4^{14½}$	Davis J A	118	18.50	44-24	Cash YourTicket124^{8¾} **Plausibly**124^{5¾} **A.M.Mayhem**118no	4w run turn, tired	11	***R-BIAS: 38 FLOW: -29 BL12: 1.5 CFR: 45**
10May13-9Bel	fst	1⅛ ⊗	:49^{1} :24 :27^{4} :25^{3}	3↑ Md Sp Wt 73k	**–**	1	6^{12}	6^{16}	6^{16}	5^{28}	-	Lezcano A	118	34.00	- 23	ForvrThng118^{nk} Spchmkr118^{12¼} HobsonsChoc118^{15½}	Outrun early, eased	6	***R-BIAS: -16 FLOW: 45 BL12: 4.5 CFR: 65**
4May13-10Bel	fm	1 1/16 [T]	:26 :23 :24^{3} :30^{4}	3↑ Md 20000	**52**	5	7^{10}	7^{8}	$8^{5¾}$	$5^{5½}$	$4^{4½}$	Davis J A	118	3.75	73-18	UnclMitcho118^{½} LionAintEsy118^{4} BrndysBgGuy124^{no}	Tight, steadied 7/16	10	***R-BIAS: -110 FLOW: 187 BL12: 7.0 CFR: 94**

WORKS: **24Jly13 Aqu 3f fst :39^{4} B** *3/4* **10Jun13 Aqu 4f fst :51^{1} B** *5/6* **22May13 Aqu 4f fst :49^{2} B** *5/11* **29Apr13 Bel 4f fst :50 B** *20/33* **9Apr13 Bel 4f fst :51^{1} B** *4/4* **5Mar13 Bel tr.t 3f fst :36^{4} B** *2/8*
TRAINER: Turf(10 .00 $0.00) *Routes*(20 .00 $0.00) MdnClm(20 .00 $0.00) — J/T 2012-13 BEL(1 .00 $0.00) J/T 2012-13(2 .00 $0.00)

Frank Scatoni: "Fastinov was a classic case of being able to make an excuse for every one of a horse's bad races. The horse was either running against much tougher company or was parked way outside in route races. Way back on May 4, 2013, the horse was 7-2 against $20K maiden claimers and ran a very solid race. Every race after that one was a toss-out. The horse had legitimate excuses for all of those races (tougher company, off-the-turf, outside posts). Then the trainer added blinkers and dropped him to the $16K maiden-claiming level on September 27, 2013, and the horse responded with a decent effort. He showed good early speed before weakening late.

"One of my favorite unheralded angles is 'second blinkers.' Horses, like people, get better with experience. I expected Fastinov to be a lot more comfortable today, running with blinkers for the second time. On paper, it looked like there might be other speed in the race, but Fastinov's internal fractions were far superior to any of the other front-runners, so I expected him to be loose on the lead, and there is nothing more exciting than a loose-on-the-lead horse at 19-1. Usually, none of the other jocks give the longshot much of a chance to win the race, so the longshot gets away with nice, easy fractions. It also didn't hurt that the horse was being ridden by apprentice Manuel Franco, so getting a five-pound weight break on a speed horse against a weak bunch of maidens was too much to overlook.

"Fastinov set an easy pace, responded when asked, and fought hard to the wire, finishing first at 19-1. Unfortunately, he ducked out late and impeded a foe, causing his disqualification. It was a legitimate DQ, but it didn't erase the fact that the horse ran a winning race at huge odds."

To me, the key point to this story is that Scatoni didn't let being DQ'd on a capper with his first contest play get him down. He had identified a number of plays earlier in the day, and he stuck with the game plan. Jockeys need to shake it off after a DQ, and horseplayers need to do the same thing. In fact, Manuel Franco ended up winning the next race at Belmont on a 22-1 shot, while Scatoni made his next play a winning one, too, by putting $100 to win on Key to Fame at Keeneland.

10 Key to Fame
15-1
Own: Epona Racing LLC
Navy, Gold Stars, Navy Cap
$30,000
PEDROZA M (3 1 1 0 .33) 2013: (541 71 .13)

B. g. 4 (Mar)
Sire: Kela (Numerous)
Dam: All Grace (Alleged)
Br: Epona LLC (Pa)
Tr: Draper Otto(—) 2013:(33 2 .06)

121

Life	**10**	**1**	**0**	**2**	**$33,947**	**73**
2013	**7**	**0**	**0**	**1**	**$6,061**	**73**
2012	**3**	**1**	**0**	**1**	**$27,886**	**71**
Kee	**1**	**0**	**0**	**0**	**$1,503**	**71**

D.Fst	**0**	**0**	**0**	**0**	**$0**	**-**
Wet(323)	**0**	**0**	**0**	**0**	**$0**	**-**
Synth	**1**	**0**	**0**	**0**	**$1,503**	**7**
Turf(273)	**9**	**1**	**0**	**2**	**$32,444**	**7**
Dst(338)	**0**	**0**	**0**	**0**	**$0**	**-**

11Sep13-10Ind fm 1 1/16 Ⓣ :243 :24 :232 :323 3↑ Clm 15000N2L **58** 1 89¾ 87¾ 62¾ 53½ 54½ St Julien M L122 b *1.90 79-09 Lombardi Time1223 Full Disclosure1171 Rahy'sProspector122hd Bid,hung
***R-BIAS: . FLOW: 59 BL12: 13.3 CFR: 7**
3Aug13-6ElP fm 1 1/16 Ⓣ :252 :233 :234 :294 3↑ Clm 30000(30-25)N2L **64** 7 66 55½ 53 53 32¼ Mojica R Jr L122 b 6.40 84-13 Albus1181 Courtmaster1181¼ Key to Fame122nk Broke slow, 4-5 wide
***R-BIAS: . FLOW: -12 BL12: 6.0 CFR: 4**
13Jly13-5Cnl gd 1½ Ⓣ :514 :264 :493 :262 3↑ KittensJoy50k **42** 8 65½ 68½ 1216 1221 1224 Cruise G 118 b 57.80 78 - Al Qasr1181 Target Sighted118nk Amen Kitten115nk Steadied early
22Jun13-4CD fm 1⅛ Ⓣ :491 :241 :25 :12 3↑ Clm 30000(30-25)N2L **72** 5 64½ 85½ 83¾ 76½ 54¼ Pedroza M 125 b 13.70 82-12 Vindication Now1233½ Cathedro125½ *Madris*125hd 3 wide 2nd turn
***R-BIAS: . FLOW: 2 BL12: 6.0 CFR: 5**
28May13-4Ind fm 7½f Ⓣ :254 :232 :414 3↑ OC 25k/N1x-N **69** 5 10 107¼ 1010 710 710 Ouzts P W 122 11.50 67-26 UnionBowmn1223¼ RedAllOver122½ *Cllinghrdtn*1221¼ 6path 3/16, no factor
18May13-4Ind fm 7½f Ⓣ :25 :234 :41 3↑ OC 25k/N1x-N **73** 4 6 64 64½ 53½ 53 Creed B 122 3.60 75-22 *Forever Sure*1221 Prince of Time119½ Mi Chico122hd Near rail, no threat
21Apr13-6Kee fst 7f ◈ :242 :231 :243 :123 4↑ Alw 57624N1x **71** 11 11 117¾ 116½ 75 55 Lebron V 118 41.70 78-18 Dynamical118½ Googleado1181¼ **Conspiracy**118½ Off slow,7 w,late gain
***R-BIAS: 34 FLOW: 9 BL12: 3.0 CFR: 5**
Previously trained by Delacour Leigh 2012(as of 7/30): (162 38 30 22 0.23)
30Jly12-9Prx gd *1 1/16 Ⓣ :251 :26 :251 :333 3↑ Ⓢ Alw 66608N1x **69** 4 62¾ 65½ 75 43½ 32½ Garcia Luis L114 3.20 64-29 Zempat116nk Lewahdizaniwho1172¼ Key toFame114½ Came again outside
WORKS: 28Sep13 TTC 4f fst :522 B *20/23* 5Sep13 TTC 4f fst :501 B *2/12* ●15Jun13 TTC 5f fst 1:012 B *1/15* ●8Jun13 TTC 5f fst 1:003 B *1/9* 15May13 TTC 4f fst :504 B *4/17* 1May13 TTC 5f fst 1:052 B *5/5*
TRAINER: Synth(9 .11 $1.53) Turf/Synth(3 .33 $4.60) Routes(9 .00 $0.00) Claim(6 .00 $0.00) J/T 2012-13(5 .20 $8.80

Frank Scatoni: "Sometimes less is more in handicapping, and that was the case with Key to Fame. This was a $30,000 claiming race for non-winners of two races lifetime—not exactly a field of horses that have shown a will to win. I don't have any specific data to support this, but it stands to reason that favorites are always going to be vulnerable in these races. These horses haven't won twice for a reason: they lack a clear will to win. So why take a short price on a horse that is camera shy?

"Key to Fame had one simple, strong angle going for him. He had started ten times, nine of those starts coming on the turf. His one synth race? A respectable fifth-place finish at Keeneland back in April, against far superior horses in a non-winners-of-one allowance race, breaking from the 11-post, off slowly, hooked seven-wide, and gaining late. That was at seven furlongs and today's race was at nine furlongs, so I expected him to be coming strong late. His six other races after that deceptively good Keeneland effort were very blah, although you could make excuses for several of them. The interesting thing to me was that he was coming off a race at a lower claiming level, where he finished a lackluster fifth, but he was the 9-5 favorite. I didn't think the class hike was enough to warrant a horse going from 9-5 to today's 18-1 (the very opposite of a wedding/funeral scenario, and an angle I love: playing beaten favorites right back at big prices).

"If the horse was 8-1, I probably wouldn't have liked him as much, but at 18-1 against very vulnerable favorites and several no-hopers, he was a no-brainer pick to me. I thought he was the strongest closer in the race, and I expected him to get a pace to close into, which he did.

"Two last things went into my consideration: first off, the horse was moving from turf to synth, and the trainer (while only 6 percent overall on the year) had been successful with this move once before. Secondly, the trainer had legged up this jock five times over the past year, and they teamed up for a long-shot victory; considering the fact that the trainer had won only two races all year, that was a positive indicator to me that this horse was at least well-meant today."

Key to Fame won and paid $38.80; Scatoni was in seventh at the end of day two, and even though he didn't win, he ended up finishing in the money in the tournament. But if not for that DQ on day one, things might have shaken out differently.

33 The Plod Boys at Woodbine

Here is an example of how the Racing Flow figures can help you identify longshots that make great contest picks. This one comes from "The Plod Boys," Jake Jacobs and Phil Gregoire. In the nine-furlong Nijinsky Stakes at Woodbine, let's look at the two horses in the race I would consider Flow upgrades. First, So Long George:

```
4 So Long George                                  Dk.b or br g. 4 (Apr) KEESEP10 $50,000                              Life 12 5 1 0 $164,153 89   D.Fst       0 0 0 0      $0  -
  Own: Uphill Stable                              Sire: Arch (Kris S.) $40,000                                                                   Wet(456)    0 0 0 0      $0  -
-1 White, Purple Yoke And Heart, Purple Cap       Dam: Gal of Mine (Mining)                                           2013  2 1 0 0  $45,603 89   Synth       6 2 1 0 $72,453  86
LSON E (230 24 37 29 .10) 2013: (269 25 .09)      Br: Hidden Brook Farm & Jamie Corbett (Ky)                    L 117 2012  9 4 1 0 $118,161 86   Turf(300)   6 3 0 0 $91,700  89
                                                  Tr: Charalambous John(12 1 0 1 .08) 2013:(12 1 .08)                 WO(T) 6 3 0 0 $91,700  89   Dst(T)(376) 0 0 0 0      $0  -
Jun13-8WO fm 1 (T) :232 :461 1:091 1:331 3↑KngEdwd-G2 89 5 76½ 53 61¾ 41½ 4½ Pizarro T L118 34.40 97-02 Riding the River123hd Valentino Beauty117nk Hotep117nk In tight at turn 9
                                                                                       *R-BIAS: . FLOW: 58 BL12: 4.2 CFR: 71
Jun13-4WO gd 7f (T) :241 :474 1:11 1:23 3↑OC 62k/c-N 86 5 8 64 52½ 31 1¾ Wilson E L122 13.60 82-23 So Long George122¾ Danger Bay122nk Hollinger122nk Bid midstr,driving 8
                                                                                       *R-BIAS: . FLOW: -206 BL12: 7.4 CFR: 2
Dec12-11WO fst 1¾◈ 1:16 1:42 2:341 2:592 3↑Valdctry-G3 65 7 814 727 712 615 523½ Da Silva E R L116 3.90 67-15 Heathcote11512¼ Peyton1151¾ Quaesitor1155¼ Failed to menace 9
                                                                                       *R-BIAS: 62 FLOW: 4 BL12: 0.0 CFR: 63
Dec12-10WO fst 1⅛◈ :49 1:132 1:381 1:501 3↑Alw 63740N1x 86 11 119¼ 1111 116 21 11¾ Wilson E L119 5.30 94-13 SoLongGeorge1191¾ HmpstedHeth1192 Attndnt1191 Rallied,swept by,drvg 12
                                                                                       *R-BIAS: 64 FLOW: -12 BL12: 20.8 CFR: 59
Nov12-8WO fst 1 1/16◈ :244 :49 1:131 1:441 3↑Alw 69160N1x 84 2 76 79½ 64 31 21¼ Wilson E L119 6.70 90-21 Courtville1191¼ SoLongGeorge119¾ BearsTenor122¾ Off pace,rallied 6wide 8
                                                                                       *R-BIAS: 176 FLOW: -61 BL12: 9.0 CFR: 80
Sep12-10WO fm 1 1/16 (T) :231 :461 1:104 1:424 3↑Clm 37500(40-37.5)N2x 82 12 67 69½ 68 2½ 1¾ Wilson E L115 6.65 80-20 SoLongGorg115¾ RivrLmon1211¼ MontnMmoris1211¼ All out,led 16th out 13
                                                                                       *R-BIAS: . FLOW: 134 BL12: 16.7 CFR: 90
Sep12-1WO fst 1 1/16◈ :25 :494 1:14 1:452 Clm 23500(25-23.5) 73 3 43½ 42½ 41½ 32½ 1½ Wilson E L119 3.20 85-16 SoLongGeorge119½ SpcilSlction1192¾ Rockinmbby1164½ 4w,all out,up late 6
                                                                                       *R-BIAS: -100 FLOW: -118 BL12: 6.0 CFR: 8
Aug12-4WO fm 1½ (T) :513 1:17 2:073 2:323 3↑Alw 71413N1x 58 3 53½ 66 98 99 812 Wilson E L117 18.85 58-25 OjibwySignl1221¼ SeriousInded1222 RivrLmon1223¾ Rail trip,lacked rally 11
                                                                                       *R-BIAS: . FLOW: -67 BL12: 0.0 CFR: 29
Jly12-4WO fm 1 (T) :241 :483 1:124 1:37 3↑Md 47500(50-47.5) 67 9 31½ 51¾ 41 32½ 1½ Wilson E L117 3.85 75-23 So Long George117½ Street Fight119hd Galactico1191 All out,up late 12
                                                                                       *R-BIAS: . FLOW: -102 BL12: 3.4 CFR: 18
Jun12-5WO fm 1 (T) :234 :481 1:122 1:353 3↑Md 47500(50-47.5) 63 1 97¾ 95¾ 32 33½ 44¼ Ramsammy E L116 6.90 78-18 Mr. Online1182 Good Answer1182 Alphanumeric124nk Bothered,rallied 7w 12
                                                                                       *R-BIAS: . FLOW: -65 BL12: 3.2 CFR: 29
May12-3WO fst 7f ◈ :232 :463 1:104 1:233 3↑Md 37500(40-37.5) 60 3 3 64¼ 65 58½ 48 Ramsammy E 116 48.05 74-17 Bear's Tizz1237½ Fingertips118½ Alphanumeric123hd Determined drive 9
                                                                                       *R-BIAS: -110 FLOW: -53 BL12: 0.0 CFR: 18
Nov11-4WO fst 7f ◈ :231 :462 1:11 1:242 Md 32000 42 4 8 813 89 811 810¼ Ramsammy E 120 44.30 68-19 SundncSpcl120no NoLookPss1151¼ RoylFghtr1201¾ Off slw,used,no factor 8
                                                                                       *R-BIAS: 67 FLOW: 9 BL12: 3.9 CFR: 66
RKS: 13Jly13 WO ◈ 5f fst :593 B 2/59 18Jun13 WO tr.t 4f fst :504 B 3/3 26May13 WO tr.t 5f fst 1:003 B 3/22 16May13 WO ◈ 5f fst 1:014 H 27/32 8May13 WO ◈ 5f fst 1:02 H 9/26 30Apr13 WO ◈ 5f fst 1:003 H 3/29
AINER: Turf(20 .15 $2.71) Routes(34 .15 $2.06) GrdStk(2 .00 $0.00)                                                J/T 2012-13 WO(52 .19 $3.70) J/T 2012-13(52 .19 $3.70)
```

Look at the race two back: So Long George became a Racing Flow upgrade by rallying to win despite a CFR (closer favorability ratio) of just 2. The CFR can range from 1 (best for speed) to 100 (best for stretch runners). Without the Racing Flow figures, one might assume that So Long George got a perfect trip behind collapsing speed.

Not the case. The Flow figure of -205 shows that the race was extremely beneficial to horses on or near the lead and indicates that So Long George ran much better than it looks to close with a BL 12 (a measure of combined lengths beaten at the first and second pace calls) of 7.4.

So Long George failed as an upgrade (finishing fourth on 6/23) when he was bested by several of today's rivals, but he was beaten only a half-length and had a tricky trip that the comment line doesn't do justice: he was steadied when first making a run, forced to idle behind horses, then stuck in a vise as he made his move. That was enough trouble for So Long George to keep his upgrade status for one more race. So Long George had also stayed on nicely at a mile, suggesting that the extra ground in this race would be a good thing for his chances.

The Flow data and a little basic handicapping suggested that So Long George was an overlay at 10-1.

The other interesting Flow horse from the Nijinsky was Hampstead Heath:

On its face, that's good-looking paper: an improving four-year-old that is probably ready to try a step up. But what makes him a contender in my eyes are the Flow ratings in those last two races. See those CFRs? Both equal 1. That means the races rank in the top 1 percent of all races in terms of favoring speed over stretch runners. That's a screaming upgrade that prompted Jake Jacobs, Racing Flow co-founder, to tweet the following post three days before the race: "Flow player hero Hampstead Heath takes a shot at Grade 3 company at Woodbine Sunday. Be still my heart!"

Hampstead Heath went off at 22-1. In the end, So Long George got a nice stalking trip this time and scored. Hampstead Heath, despite being bounced around in the stretch, closed late to complete the massive $423.40 exacta. And the Plod Boys, Jake and Phil, walked off into the sunset.

34 Eric Moomey and D's Perfect Soul at Woodbine

As long as we're talking about Woodbine, let's look at an example of how Eric Moomey uses cash bets to hedge his position in a contest. He was in the lead going into the last race in a contest back in July of 2013, and he ended up playing D's Perfect Soul, a horse whose paper sure doesn't look like much to me. How did Moomey come up with him?

D's Perfect Soul
Own: York Tech Racing Stable

Ch. g. 4 (Apr) CANNOV09 $706
Sire: Perfect Soul*Ire (Sadler's Wells) $7,500
Dam: River City Woman (Stephen Got Even)
Br: Adena Springs & Gardiner Farms Limited (Ont-C)
Tr: Black Ian(111 17 15 6 .15) 2013:(119 17 .14)

Life	7	1	1	0	$40,733	82	D.Fst	0	0	0	0	$0	-
2013	3	1	1	0	$37,520	82	Wet(321)	0	0	0	0	$0	-
							Synth	5	0	1	0	$16,396	68
2012	4	M	0	0	$3,213	60	Turf(272)	2	1	0	0	$24,100	74
Wo Ⓣ	2	1	0	0	$24,100	74	DstⓉ(325)	1	0	0	0	$400	74

1Jly13-7WO	fm	*1	Ⓣ	:241	:48	1:114	1:35	3↑ Alw 64529N1x	**74**	4	21½	31½	53	53	73½	Wilson E	L122 b	21.85	- -	Seekingthediamond½ MobilUnit1¾ SmmyMudlin nk	Evened out deep str	9
1Jun13-10WO	gd	7f	Ⓣ	:232	:47	1:113	1:242	3↑ Md 50000(50-47.5)	**71**	9	3	32	32	2½	1no	Wilson E	L123 b	*4.70	75- 23	D's Perfect Soul no Best Bard1 *Canadian Flag* hd	Bid 16th out,all out	14
26Apr13-8WO	fst	5½f	Ⓐ	:224	:453	:572	1:033	4↑ Md Sp Wt 60k	**68**	8	1	31½	22	22½	23	Wilson E	L122 b	14.70	92- 13	Command Force3 *D's Perfect Soul* 1½ Fingertips nk	2w,determinedly	10
9Dec12-2WO	fst	7f	Ⓐ	:24	:481	1:132	1:253	3↑ Md Sp Wt 59k	**60**	6	3	31½	31	2½	54	Wilson E	L120 b	30.45	68- 24	StrongDefence nk UnbridledWr¾ StormyRevenge2½	Failed bid,fltnd out	8
21Nov12-1WO	fst	1 1/16	Ⓐ	:242	:491	1:14	1:453	3↑ Md 32000(32-30)	**40**	4	32½	43	41½	86¼	816¼	Callaghan S	L121 b	19.75	68- 16	[D]Big Daddy Bill½ Political Fever1 Will He Won't He3	Chased turn,tired	9
4Nov12-7WO	fst	7f	⊗	:23	:454	1:103	1:231	3↑ Md Sp Wt 66k	**60**	6	1	82¾	115½	96½	108¼	Callaghan S	120	103.75	76- 15	Justin's Tapit1 Conserve no Stormy Revenge4½	6w top str,no threat	11

TRAINER: Sprint/Route(48 .10 $0.73) Turf(86 .15 $1.90) Routes(156 .17 $1.66) Stakes(44 .07 $0.42)

Eric Moomey: "Rather than looking at what was special about D's Perfect Soul, my logic was slightly different. I always exclude non-winners instead of picking winners. Let me explain.

"I was only vulnerable to horses with 8-1 odds or higher (five of the nine horses), so I threw out horses 1, 2, 3, and 4 due to their low odds (if they had won, I'd win the contest anyway). I wanted to make at least $5,000 cash if I 'got beat' in the contest by a longshot, because $5,000 is how much I value the NHC seat. Of the five longshot horses I was vulnerable to, I threw out the 6, 8, and 10

because they didn't look good on any of the computer-based data that I use.

"I was left with the 9 (Command Force, 8-1) and the 7 (D's Perfect Soul, 17-1). Do I pick the 7 or the 9 for my contest play? For me, it was simple economics: if I played the 7 in the contest and hedged the 9, my hedge costs were $555 because that's how much I needed to make my $5,000 goal. If, instead, I played the 9 and hedged the 7, my cost was only $277. Because of the longer price, I'd be able to risk less on the hedge. If the 7 wins, I would still be quite happy with $5,000 cash in lieu of an NHC seat. If a favorite wins, I get my NHC seat at a relatively low hedge cost. If the 6, 8, or 10 wins, I lick my wounds and try again another day.

"So it's not really that I 'liked the 7 horse' and decided to wager on him. I was vulnerable to him. He had the higher odds of 17-1. He was supported by the computer data I use and had a good final fraction (at least better than the 6 horse). If I was on the outside looking in, I would have chosen the 7 horse in the contest to ensure I earned enough to make it in without getting blocked. When the 1 and 7 horses finished in a photo, I kept asking myself which I would prefer, cash or an NHC seat. Either way I'd be satisfied, but today I am happy leaving with the cash."

35 Hank Seaman and Closing Range at Del Mar

In Chapter 22 on trainers, we had a little subhead that talked about trying to think like connections. It can be a profitable angle for discovering longshots. Hank Seaman, an excellent contest player who has had a lot of success on PublicHandicapper.com, provided me with a good example.

Let's look at Del Mar's fifth race from Saturday, July 20, 2013. It was a one-and-one-sixteenth-mile turf race. Let's look at Closing Range's paper:

osing Range
n: St. George Farm Racing LLC (Banwell)
Dk. b or b. f. 4 (Apr)
Sire: After Market (Storm Cat) $5,000
Dam: Subeen*GB (Caerleon)
Br: St. George Farm LLC (Ky)
Tr: Oliver Philip J(0 0 0 0 .00) 2013:(49 7 .14)

Life	9	4	1	0	$154,896	88		D.Fst	0	0	0	0	$0	–
2013	3	0	0	0	$4,998	77		Wet(285)	1	1	0	0	$20,401	63
								Synth	0	0	0	0	$0	–
2012	6	4	1	0	$149,898	88		Turf(373)	8	3	1	0	$134,495	88
Dmr Ⓣ	0	0	0	0	$0	–		DstⓉ(357)	2	1	0	0	$22,798	78

reviously trained by Oliver Victoria 2013(as of 6/15): (40 0 5 5 0.00)
un13-4Ind fm 1 Ⓣ :232 :464 1:1041:35 4↑ⒻGrlShlbyC106k 77 11 109 109 1/2 95 3/4 74 1/2 54 Mojica O L118 f 7.10 90-04 Frontside1 3/4 Kune Kune3/4 Artemus Kitten3/4 3-4wide,belated gain 11
reviously trained by Oliver Philip J 2012: (88 18 13 10 0.20)
ar13-9GP fm 1 1/2 Ⓣ :4731:121 2:232 4↑ⒻOrchid-G3 76 2 11 11 1/2 31 1/2 83 1/2 108 1/2 Trujillo E L121 f 28.20 99-05 Regalo Mia2 Angegreenno Irish Mission1 1/4 Rail, nothing left 10
eb13-8GP gd 1 3/8 Ⓣ :4821:133 1:3832:18 4↑ⒻVeryOne-G3 60 5 21 21 32 1/2 611 617 1/4 Trujillo E L121 f 8.50 51-29 Starformer3 1/4 Angegreen3/4 *Beijoca*3 1/2 Chased 2 w, tired 8
ov12-7Crc fm 1 1/2 Ⓣ :4931:15 2:0332:272 3↑ⒻLaPvyteH-G3 88 2 11 11 11 12 1/2 12 3/4 Trujillo E L116 f 19.90 101-09 Closing Range2 3/4 Ciao Bella1 1/4 Havanthd Firm rate,stayed clear 6
ct12-7Kee fm 1 1/16 Ⓣ :233 :482 1:1411:443 ⒻVllyView-G3 74 1 42 62 3/4 62 1/4 73 86 Court J K L118 f 22.70 75-20 Angel Terraceno Miss Cato2 *Zapper Belle*2 1/2 Got through, faltered 12
un in divisions
g12-9Mth fm 1 1/8 Ⓣ :5021:15 1:3821:494 ⒻTwinLights60k 83 4 11 1/2 11 11 1 1/2 1no Decarlo C P L117 f 4.70 80-24 Closing Rangeno Zucchini Flower1/2 Dancing Solo2 3/4 Determinedly inside 6
y12-7EIP fm 1 Ⓣ :251 :491 1:1421:391 3↑ⒻAlw 33000N1x 78 1 31 1/2 31 1/2 41 1/2 31 1 3/4 Mojica O L116 f *1.50 69-31 *Closing Range*3/4 Corleone3/4 Do the Charleston1/2 Split horses, in time 10
INER: Turf(86 .14 $1.87) Routes(120 .18 $2.38) Stakes(34 .18 $4.83)

Hank Seaman: "The first thing I noticed was that her breeding was equal to or superior to the others in the race. I know that just by being familiar with breeding in general and also from using Jim Mazur's Progressive Handicapping products. I also liked what Phil Oliver did with her. Unlike most trainers, Oliver did not wait for a bad race for him to give Closing Range a rest. In fact, he gave her a rest after a Grade 3 win back in November 2012 at even a longer race (one-and-one-half-miles) where she won at odds of 19-1. Fillies and mares can go south in a hurry, usually quicker than male horses, so I like that kind of careful handling.

"I also liked that Oliver did not fool around in her comeback race after her rest. Instead of entering her into an optional-claiming race for example, he had enough confidence to enter her right back in the fray of a Grade 3 at Gulfstream, at one and three-eighths of a mile in February 2013, for her first start as a four-year-old, showing two works at Payson Park. In that February 16th race, she showed her rust by tiring, but I think that effort was a great stamina builder for her, especially going so long.

"Another positive was that she showed four works after that race at Payson Park, where all the big boys seem to congregate during the winter. Payson is a beautiful training track where you must dismiss workout times because they are typically slow, but horses that train over it build stamina.

"In her next race, Oliver again shows confidence by entering her in the Grade 3 Orchid (March 30), showing again the seven-day cycle I like to see with a happy horse in training. Then she ships to Indiana Downs (June 15) to run a mile, definitely short of her best distance, but she closes respectably.

"Another thing, she has a breeder-owner (St. George Farm), which I like to see in a classy horse, and they did not hesitate to load her in the plane for a race six days after her work. It's also clear that the connections always had high expectations for her as a turf horse, which was shown when they gave no thought of keeping her on the dirt, even after breaking her maiden by ten lengths.

"Now the kicker: sometimes it pays to look for a stranger. The rest of the horses in the race all knew each other (all coming over from Hollywood), except for Closing Range (Indiana Downs) and another invader, A Time to Love (Churchill). I stayed away from A Time to Love (20-1 morning line and went off at 47-1), for this was her first time in this kind of company, and this didn't look like her distance either. So I went with Closing Range."

Closing Range won and paid $34.

36 Emily Gullikson Helps the Author Get Some Jumping Justice

I've been remiss to this point in the book in not dispensing enough small track love. In August of 2013, I was procrastinating working on this book and playing in a little online contest one Tuesday night that featured Indiana Downs (don't judge). I had just met Emily Gullikson and was impressed right away by her handicapping acumen. She seemed to me to have two areas of specialty: interpreting the works on first-time starters and coming up with interesting angles on claimers at small tracks that all looked the same to me on paper. Knowing that Gullikson's been known to stay up until the wee hours playing Australia when things get really rough, I figured she might have some clever ideas to help me out at Indiana Downs. She did indeed.

Here's the dope on Jumping Justice:

Not too thrilling at first blush, but Gullikson pointed out that a different picture emerges if you get rid of all the races that aren't sprints, which is what Tuesday night's race was. Then you have this:

Jumping Justice
Own: Woodruff Martin, Bullard, Brandon and

B. f. 3 (Apr) FTKOCT11 $4,000
Sire: Doneraile Court (Seattle Slew) $1,000
Dam: Future Answer (Copelan)
Br: Justice Farm & Greg Justice (Ind)
Tr: Fosdick Stephen V(116 10 17 11 .09) 2013:(143 14 .10)

Life	11	1	1	1	$38,438	47
2013	6	1	0	1	$22,579	47
2012	5	M	1	0	$15,859	44
Ind	5	1	0	1	$22,234	47

D.Fst	6	1	0	1	$23,976	47
Wet(353)	3	0	1	0	$13,904	44
Synth	0	0	0	0	$0	–
Turf(228)	2	0	0	0	$558	47
Dst(321)	2	0	0	0	$962	24

[redacted]

8Jly13–3Ind	fst	6f	:221 :453 :58 1:111	3↑ⒻⓈClm 12500N2L	41	7	5	77¼	56	46½	310	Rossi O	L116	4.50	76–19	Disgrace8½ ComotionNdOcen1½ JumpingJustice2	2wd turn, best of rest	9
[redacted]																		
4Jun13–4Ind	fm	7½f Ⓣ	:243 :492 1:141 1:314	3↑ⒻⓈAlw 34500N1X	47	6	6	63¾	84	98½	810	Rossi O	L116	29.10	56–33	Evana1 Angels Trace1½ Oh Juliet4½	4wd turn, no factor	10
18May13–3Ind	fst	6f	:223 :461 :59 1:122	3↑ⒻⓈAlw 34500N1X	37	1	12	1110	119½	98¾	109¼	Rossi O	L118	29.50	71–20	*Platinum Blue*3 Officiallyno Blade's Edge½	Outrun, near rail	12
1May13–6Ind	fst	5½f	:221 :463 :592 1:054	ⒻⓈMd Sp Wt 32k	47	10	1	84¼	73¼	41	11¼	Rossi O	L118	*2.00	78–21	Jumping Justice1¼ Smart Kit1 Red Jammie3½	6path turn,edged clear	10
[redacted]																		
6Oct12–4Hoo	myS	5½f	:22 :46 1:043	ⒻⓈCtyOAndrsn88k	44	1	9	96	84¾	52	47½	Rossi O	L114	22.20e	77–16	Ldystrturengine1¾ BldesEdge3½ OvertheCountr2¼	Inside trn, bid, faded	11
22Sep12–7Hoo	myS	6f	:231 :481 1:003 1:134	ⒻⓈMd Sp Wt 40k	36	8	3	76½	65¼	25	27	Rossi O	L118	13.50	66–26	RivertownBelle7 JumpingJustice2½ Dingalingling8¼	Swung 5w, 2nd best	9
28Aug12–5Hoo	fst	6f	:23 :464 :592 1:123	ⒻⓈMd Sp Wt 35k	25	2	8	76	66	52¾	410	Rossi O	L118	23.90	69–20	MyBirthdyGl6¼ *RivertownBelle*1 *Ldystrturengine*2¾	Ins trn, bid, empty	10

TRAINER: 1-7Days(9 .22 $2.36) Sprint/Route(52 .12 $1.12) Dirt(277 .10 $1.72) Routes(143 .11 $1.07) Stakes(12 .00 $0.00)

A large part of contest play is finding the relevant form lines and working off those, knowing that people don't like to go too far back or look too thoroughly at dirty-looking PPs. Once we do this exercise, something becomes very clear. Keeping in mind that the three favorites in this race had just run Beyer Speed Figures of 36, 37, and 22, Jumping Justice becomes an obvious contender, doesn't she?

Well, get this: she was 13-1 and would have been a proper cap horse if not for a late scratch. Makes you want to look a little harder at Indiana Downs, doesn't it? The gates opened, a duel emerged, and there went Jumping Justice zooming on the outside to hack up by four-plus lengths. As my friend Jeff Sotman was fond of saying, "Contest over!"

37 Don Marr with a Dangerous Lad at Saratoga

Back in Chapter 5 of this book, Michael Beychok says something along the lines of "Maybe you can find a cap horse by coming up with a creative story." To me, this is a wonderful example of that.

10 Dangerous Lad
Own: Cahalan Eugene P
15-1 Yellow And Black Quarters, Black
ORTIZ I JR (109 7 12 17 .06) 2013: (879 127 .14)

Dk. b or br g. 4 (Apr) KEESEP10 $32,000
Sire: Bob and John (Seeking the Gold) $6,000
Dam: Buttercup's Song (Unbridled's Song)
Br: B & B Thoroughbreds Inc & Marty Hughes (Ky)
Tr: Brown Bruce R(28 1 4 4 .04) 2013:(210 25 .12)

L 121

Life	9	2	0	2	$63,059	80
2013	3	0	0	2	$9,840	74
2012	4	1	0	0	$32,420	80
Sar Ⓣ	0	0	0	0	$0	-

D.Fst	4	0	0	0	$3,410	56
Wet(390)	1	1	0	0	$30,600	80
Synth	1	1	0	0	$19,209	72
Turf(294)	3	0	0	2	$9,840	74
DstⓉ(357)	2	0	0	1	$2,640	71

Previously trained by Weaver George 2013(as of 7/14): (104 18 13 13 0.17)																					
14Jly13-6Bel	fm	6f	Ⓣ	:224	:461	:572	1:091	3↑OC 25k/N1x-N	**74**	4	5	54	45	34½	32½	Ortiz I Jr	L122 f	6.60	89-07	Palace122½ Abra1222 Dangerous Lad1224¼ 4w upper, mild kick	6
2Mar13-6GP	fm	1	Ⓣ	:232	:463	1:103	1:344	4↑OC 25k/N1x-N	**61**	3	63½	74½	64½	86	86¾	Castellano J J	L119	3.00	76-19	Perfect Tay119nk Buzz the Deputy119nk Lemon View1191 Very rough trip	11
7Feb13-7GP	fm	1	Ⓣ	:242	:48	1:113	1:352	4↑Clm 25000(30-25)N3L	**71**	11	1210	128	73½	62½	3nk	Castanon J L	L117	16.90	80-14	RunawayJim117no SugrRyn112nk DngerousLd117½ Lunged, checked start	12
Previously trained by Terranova John P II 2012(as of 6/3): (89 11 12 10 0.12)																					
3Jun12-3Bel	fst	6f		:224	:451	:564	1:092	OC50k/SAL50k	**56**	2	4	56½	58	614	614¼	Ortiz I Jr	L118	13.30	78-16	Readytodefer1205 ForeverFithful1184¼ GintIndin1181½ Never in the hunt	6
6May12-2Bel	fst	6½f		:222	:45	1:091	1:153	3↑Alw 72000N1x	**53**	5	5	54	55	69½	616¼	Ortiz I Jr	L116	18.10	78-14	PowerWorld1163¼ ObviouslyTusdy1214¼ HowDoIWin1161 4w 1/2pl, folded	7
17Mar12-9Lrl	fst	1		:234	:471	1:12	1:373	PrivatTrms76k	**53**	7	21½	21½	21½	713	715¾	Castellano A Jr	L116	7.20	72-12	Raconteur118hd Hakama1161¾ Brimstone Island1162¾ Rank 5/8, faltered	7
27Jan12-8Aqu	myS	6f	⊡	:222	:46	:584	1:121	OC50k/SAL50k-N	**80**	6	2	31½	31	11½	14¼	Ortiz I Jr5	L113	*1.50	80-25	DngrosLd1134¼ PrsonlAssstnt1201¾ DnsGold118nk Lunge st,4w,vie w/ duo	6
15Dec11-8Aqu	fst	170	⊡	:234	:483	1:141	1:443	OC 75k/N1x-N	**45**	5	12	1½	1hd	54	513¼	Garcia Alan	L120	4.30	66-21	Speightscity1201¾ Holiday Promise1222¾ *Festive Spirit*1221¼ Pulled, faded	5
Previously trained by Nixon Justin 2011(as of 11/20): (81 15 7 10 0.19)																					
20Nov11-1WO	fst	7f	◈	:23	:452	1:101	1:232	Md 50000	**72**	7	7	21½	21½	11	13¾	Pinto M	L120	4.30	83-17	Dangerous Lad1203¾ Wonderbear120¾ Thursday120½ Bid top str,rdn out	8

WORKS: **Aug5 Sar tr.tⓉ 4f fm :463 B(d)** *2/58* **Jly29 Sar tr.tⓉ 5f fm 1:00 B(d)** *3/27* **Jly5 Sar tr.tⓉ 4f fm :492 B(d)** *16/27* **Jun21 Sar tr.tⓉ 4f fm :491 B(d)** *18/38* **Jun15 Sar tr.t 3f fst :363 B** *2/22* **Jun8 Sar tr.t 3f sly :39 B** *1/1*

TRAINER: 1stW/Trn(78 .08 $0.91) 2Off45-180(72 .17 $1.77) Sprint/Route(78 .05 $0.39) Turf(201 .10 $0.98) Routes(277 .09 $0.70) Alw(97 .14 $1.32) J/T 2012-13 SAR(2 .00 $0.00) J/T 2012-13(33 .09 $0.60)

Don Marr: "August 10, 2013, at Saratoga, there was a horse named Dangerous Lad. He looked okay in the race relative to the par—that is, he'd run within seven points of the average winning figure at the class level, 87, which you can see in your *Racing Form*. So he didn't look too bad, but there were definitely more obvious contenders.

"Looking at his history, he had a couple of nice wins, including one with the same jockey who was on that day, Irad Ortiz, Jr., then he faltered and took a long time off. He came back at a mile on the turf and ran pretty well with some trouble, third by a neck. The next race, a mile on the turf, he showed a little more speed, but he stopped, the comment line reading, 'Very tough trip.' Then he had another layoff, almost four months. He came back with aluminum pads and front bandages.

"Now everything I've read about first-time aluminum pads and front bandages suggests you should run—not walk—the other way when you see them, but I saw in the PPs that Dangerous Lad actually improved with them; he ran back to his old good form. I have an athletic background—boxing, running, various martial arts—and sometimes because of the various aches and pains I've gone through over the years, I feel I can relate to the horses. I could relate to Dangerous Lad. I wear compression like crazy everywhere on my body when I run. That's the human version of front bandages, and they work: your muscles stay warmer; you feel more comfortable; you move better. Then after that race with front bandages for the first time, I noticed he started training better also on the turf, really good works.

"All I could picture in my head was this horse tearing around the turf course, happy as a pig in shit now, loving his new shoes, loving his compression, loving Saratoga. I've gone for runs in Saratoga in new shoes with my compression and felt great! So I could relate to that. So I knew that this horse was ready to dance in Saratoga, and he did. And I danced right along with him, watching on TV. He paid $48.40 to win and place in the contest."

38 Show Some Lovin for the Author

Here's a fun example of using endgame strategy in a head-to-head I played in, but the thought process applies in any endgame scenario, really. I was in the lead going into the last by a dollar or two. It was a $25K maiden claimer, sprinting on the grass, and fortunately, I hated the favorite, Hoboken Joe.

10	**Hoboken Joe**	Ch. g. 3 (May) FLZDIS11 $15,000		

Own: Falcone Robert
Sire: Van Nistelrooy (Storm Cat) $5,000
Dam: Victory's Sister (Cryptoclearance)
Br: Flying Zee Stables (NY)
Tr: Schettino Dominick A (18 2 4 2 .11) 2013:(144 19 .13)

$25,000
3-1 Black, Yellow Ball, Black 'Jr,' Yellow
STELLANO J J (169 31 30 34 .18) 2013: (988 211 .21)

L 119

Life 5 M 2 2 $28,900 66 | D.Fst 0 0 0 0 $0 –
2013 5 M 2 2 $28,900 66 | Wet(291) 1 0 0 0 $300 19
2012 0 M 0 0 $0 – | Synth 0 0 0 0 $0 –
Sar 1 0 0 1 $7,000 64 | Turf(305) 4 0 2 2 $28,600 66
Dst 1 0 0 1 $7,000 64

ug13–4Sar fm 5½f :22.31 :41.04 3+Md Sp Wt 70k 64 2 4 43½ 43½ 3½ 3¾ Castellano J J L119 *1.45 85–14 GreeleyPck123½ Slimshdy119nk HobokenJoe11½²¼ Bump after brk, 3w 1/4 10
un13–6Bel fm 6f :22.81 :22.68 :12.00 :12.53 3+Md Sp Wt 60k 64 3 6 3³ 2¼ 3nk 2² Castellano J J L119 3.00 88–08 DeferredAsset11½² HobokenJoe11½² GentleJim11½² Jostled st, 3w pursuit 8
*R–BIAS: 65 FLOW: 43 BL12: 8.0 CFR: 73
ay13–4Bel fm 6f :23.36 :23.13 :11.73 :12.45 3+Md c–25000 66 9 2 53½ 3² 2² 2² Velasquez C L118 3.25 81–17 Bairn12⁴² Hoboken Joe11½² Dendrite124½ Put in pocket 3/8 11
Claimed from Bruce Golden Racing for $25,000, Jacobson David Trainer 2013 (as of 5/27): (287 68 50 48 0.24)
*R–BIAS: –13 FLOW: –3 BL12: 0.0 CFR: 48
ay13–2Bel fm 6f :23.33 :23.25 :11.80 :12.09 3+Md 25000 60 5 9 75 64½ 5³ 33½ Velasquez C L118 3.90 81–15 HerComsDrz119no Downgosfrzir124¾½ HoboknJo118¾½ Bump 2x after start 10
*R–BIAS: 6 FLOW: 23 BL12: 7.7 CFR: 59
pr13–2Aqu my⁵ 6f :23.40 :24.57 :13.61 :14.53 3+Md c–25000 19 3 7 4⁵ 4⁴ 7¹⁰ 7¹7¼ Velasquez C L118 3.45 61–17 Treblemker118²½ BetoftheDrum182½ QuietMircle111¼ Hit gate, used early 7
*R–BIAS: –37 FLOW: 126 BL12: 0.0 CFR: 88
RKS: 22Jly13Sar tr.t①4f fm :48 B(d) 12/50 23Jun13Bel 4f fst :48² B 13/45 16Jun13Bel 4f fst :49² B 34/75 15May13Aqu 4f fst :53¹ B 7/8 6Apr13Aqu 5f fst 1:03⁴ B 13/17 30Mar13Aqu 5f fst 1:03 B 17/31
AINER: TurfSprints(24 .17 $3.18) Turf(154 .15 $2.78) Sprint(132 .21 $2.23) MdnClm(48 .19 $1.74) J/T 2012-13 SAR (5 .20 $3.24) J/T 2012-13 (19 .26 $2.58)

The negatives were two-fold for me. One, he had a "hang-y," pack animal look on his paper, but he had the figures, to be sure, to be bet pretty hard. But the real negative was that the crowd interpreted Hoboken Joe as a dropper, since technically he was going from maiden special weight to the maiden-claiming ranks. However, the MSW was restricted to New York-breds, and this was open company, making it much more of a lateral move. I had zero interest in him. If I chose not to play him and my opponent did and he won, that would have been just the way that one went.

Ignoring Hoboken Joe freed me up to be creative. There were four other horses that figured, and I was able to simply pick the one I liked best. He happened to be the second choice, Show Some Lovin. I knew I was giving myself multiple outs in the process.

The angles for me were just the obvious ones—a big flow upgrade coming from a race at a higher level, and he'd already shown he could act on grass. It was also certainly notable to see top rider John Velazquez showing up for a lower-profile but always dangerous outfit.

Even though I didn't like Hoboken Joe, my opponent would likely assume I was betting him and pick someone else. The MOTO ("master of the obvious") play would be the second choice. By playing the second choice, I had a healthy chance, maybe 25 percent, of blocking him and winning that way. The fact that I actually liked Show Some Lovin best made the decision very easy.

There was no way this was ever going to be a sweat. For one thing, Show Some Lovin looked the winner every yard and won going away, but that didn't even matter. My opponent was beat before the gates opened because he'd bet Show Some Lovin as well. How's that for a kick in the teeth? You pick an open lengths winner in the last and still lose. Such are the perils of drawing stone cold dead.

PART FOUR: APPLICATIONS

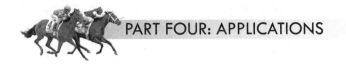

39 Brian Nadeau and the 2013 Huddie Contest

I wrote earlier about the no-cap, Saratoga-meet-long Huddie contest, and after it was over, I had a chance to interview the winner, my friend Brian Nadeau. His observations about two of his key Huddie winners speak to the power of trip handicapping.

Here's the paper on Ready Signal:

Ready Signal
Own: Tarrant Amy
1 Cream, Forest Green Diamond Hoop, Green
ADO E S (76 4 14 10 .05) 2013: (531 73 .14)

Ch. f. 4 (Feb) OBSMAR11 $190,000
Sire: More Than Ready (Southern Halo) $60,000
Dam: Marwood (Marlin)
Br: Gulf Coast Farms LLC (Ky)
Tr: Tarrant Amy(7 0 0 1 .00) 2013:(36 2 .06)

L 121

Life	13	1	1	1	$53,354	81
2013	4	0	0	0	$1,864	77
2012	5	0	0	1	$8,040	81
Sar Ⓣ	1	0	0	0	$274	53

D.Fst	2	0	0	0	$850	42
Wet(336)	0	0	0	0	$0	–
Synth	0	0	0	0	$0	–
Turf(301)	11	1	1	1	$52,504	81
DstⓉ(310)	5	1	0	1	$38,235	81

y13-9Sar	fm	5½f	Ⓣ	:21.67	:44.75	:56.27	1:02.37	3↑ⒻOC 25k/N1x-N	53	1	4	33	32	54¼	913	Cohen D	L122	24.50	78–09	ToMyVlentine1184 TizTeres117hd SwtNDiscrt1171½	Left pocket, 3w upper	11
y13-8Bel	fm	7f	Ⓣ	:22.85	:46.19	1:09.92	1:21.99	3↑ⒻOC 25k/N1x-N	77	2	3	42	52	51¾	62	Prado E S	L122	14.50	92–06	MlibuHolidy122¾ ShzHrtbrkr122hd StrtgcMssl122hd	Never fully clear lane	7
r13-9GP	fm	1	Ⓣ	:23.14	:46.25	1:09.80	1:33.09	4↑ⒻOC 25k/N1x-N	69	7	32	32	52	76½	88¾	Trujillo E	L119	77.70	83–06	Formative1191 *Kibosh*1191½ Parranda119¾	3 wide, faded	10
b13-9GP	gd	1 1/16	Ⓣ	:23.88	:47.46	1:12.22	1:43.58	4↑ⒻAlw 43500N1x	49	9	42½	32	105¼	1114	1116	Trujillo E	L119	37.30	64–26	Free as a Bird119nk Transgression1192¼ Lady's Lunar Luck1191¼	Faded	11
g12-8Mth	fm	1 1/16	Ⓣ	:24.71	:48.93	1:12.48	1:42.42	+3↑ⒻAlw 42000N1x	65	11	72¾	52½	52½	89¾	99¾	Santiago V	L118	22.60	73–18	*Pearl Keys*1202½ Quinichette116hd *Peggy Joyce*1161½	Between foes, tired	11
y12-8Mth	gd	1 1/16	Ⓣ	:24.62	:49.11	1:13.11	1:43.69	+3↑ⒻAlw 52080N1x	70	8	95¾	107	94¼	73¾	65½	Decarlo C P	L115	7.40	71–29	*Chrmingmegn*120½ PeggyJoyce1161 IndyAnnstsi115½	Off bit slow, no rally	12
y12-8Mth	fm	1	Ⓣ	:22.91	:46.49	1:10.12	1:33.79	3↑ⒻAlw 42000N1x	81	10	32	31	2½	21	31	Rocco J S Jr	L115	27.20	87–14	PeacePreserver115nk PricklyPear117¾ ReadySignl115½	Bid 3w, outkicked	11
y12-11Mth	fm	1	Ⓣ	:22.12	:45.55	1:10.08	1:34.66	ⒻLitlSilver65k	40	1	1½	1½	3½	97¾	1021	Lopez P	L117	8.70	62–21	*DancingSolo*1171½ GlamourNGlory1172½ SenatorBeck117¾	Inside,gave way	10
n12-10GP	fm	1	Ⓣ	:23.01	:47.05	1:10.85	1:34.43	ⒻSweetChant100k	70	1	11½	11½	12½	1½	67¼	Leyva J C	L116	9.00	78–15	*Dayatthespa*1161¾ Wholelottashakin1172¼ Frolic'sRevenge1201½	Rail, tired	8
c11-8GP	fm	1 1/16	Ⓣ	:23.17	:48.01	1:12.08	1:42.84	ⒻGngrBrew60k	76	12	1½	12½	12½	2½	2nk	Leyva J C	L116	25.90	82–17	FrolicsRevenge120nk ReadySignal116½ AnnoftheDance116hd	Rail, gamely	12

RKS: 16Aug13 Sar 4f fst :47³ B *3/43* **22Jly13 Sar 3f fst :36⁴ B** *5/29* **●1Jly13 Sar tr.t 3f fst :35² B** *1/41* **●23Jun13 Sar tr.t 5f fst :59² B** *1/12* **13Jun13 Sar tr.t 4f fst :48 B** *6/52* **19May13 NJF 5f gd 1:03 B** *1/2*

NER: Sprint/Route(13 .15 $5.11) Turf(52 .08 $1.08) Routes(76 .11 $1.79) Alw(25 .04 $0.29) J/T 2012-13 SAR(1 .00 $0.00) J/T 2012-13(10 .20 $3.52)

Brian Nadeau: "I had a big trip note on that filly two races back, when she was going seven furlongs at Belmont. At Horse Player Now, where I work giving out picks, we strictly watch race replays and give out horses based on trip notes, the idea being, 'Why do the work when we'll do the work for you?' This filly was the perfect example of that. In her race on July 5, my notes read: 'Rail stalk, had some room, didn't seem enamored with coming up in-

side of horses, never asked for a thing but hardly whipped.' To the chart caller's credit, he was right on it with a 'never fully clear lane' comment. As a guy who watches literally hundreds of races a week, I'm quick to point out just how poor chart callers can be sometimes, so it's only fair if I give this one some props.

"So I filed that note in my *DRF* Stable Mail, and Ready Signal popped up early in the meet. I gave her out as a five-star play for our customers on July 26, but in hindsight, it was a bad tout because she was cutting back to five and one-half furlongs, which was way too short. It was no real surprise that she got run off her feet after chasing early, and that was that. Oh, well.

"But, as you know, you have to trust your eyes. For me personally, if I start questioning my eyes and decide not to give out trip horses I've found just because they don't look good on paper, I miss a lot of nice-priced winners. Generally speaking, all 25-1 shots have one thing in common: they don't look like much on paper. So, when you're trip handicapping and looking for bombs, it pays to be creative and forgiving.

"So I wasn't too worried about that last race, especially since she had the classic excuse of running at the wrong distance. When Ready Signal showed up going a flat mile Sunday, with Edgar Prado back up, who was aboard for the original note I made on the July 5th race, she was a no-brainer pick for me. Of course, it didn't hurt that she was going to be a huge price. If I missed again with her, so what? I could always hit the delete button on my watch list, and she'd be out of my life forever.

"Luckily, it all came together. It's not often you get to give out a horse at 27-1 and know she's a winner the entire way around. I could get used to that feeling."

STRONG MANDATE

As we've discussed before, the best contest plays don't always have to be longshots. In a sense, the whole seven weeks of the Huddie contest came down simply to who could pick the winner of one race: the prestigious Hopeful Stakes at Saratoga.

Brian Nadeau: "It's kind of funny that it came down to the Hopeful, and I was pretty fortunate because I think somehow I was the only person out of 300 who picked Strong Mandate. It's easy to say after he ran off the screen, but I didn't really understand how that could be. In fact, I thought he was a real wise-guy horse that a lot of people would have picked. I used him as a block as much as anything else.

"I picked him for several reasons, most notably because I had a big note on the horse out of his maiden win: 'Sharp speed, well within himself, widened on cue mid-stretch, straight as a string; new horse with blinks, should only get better with more ground.'

"I had heard positive word about the runner-up in there, a nice Steve Asmussen prospect, so I knew that Strong Mandate must be kind of nice if he drilled him that easily. Plus, it was vintage D. Wayne Lukas, in that the horse didn't raise a hoof in his debut but added blinkers and ran off in his next start. Throw in a dream post in the Hopeful, good breeding for the wet, and a field, quite frankly, that I didn't think was very strong, and Strong Mandate was a five-star tout for me."

Afterword: The Most Important Lessons

Writing this book has been an absolute labor of love. I can't imagine a more satisfying professional endeavor than getting to meet and interview all of the men and women who appear in these pages. I've often said that writing *Six Secrets of Successful Bettors* was like getting a PhD in playing the horses. Well, this experience has been a bit like spending a year abroad doing post-doctoral study. I've so thoroughly enjoyed my time away in contest land that I'm planning on adding several tournaments onto my already solidly booked annual gambling calendar. Before we part company, I wanted to make a list of 21 of the most important lessons I've either learned or had reinforced during this process.

1. Contest play and everyday play are two very different things.

2. Work backwards. The last races are the most important; do those first.

3. Preparation is just as important as picking winners; failing to prepare is preparing to fail.

4. Have a game plan. Know what score you need and devise a plan to get there.

5. Be ready to work your ass off. Yes, socializing has an important place in contest life, but when it's time to make the donuts, you better be ready to work as hard as you ever have if you want to beat these guys and girls.

6. Focus on decisions, not outcomes. The process is more important than the specifics of what happened in any given race or contest. You need to trust the process.

7. It's an information game. Get information other people don't have or learn to use the available information better than your competition.

8. Never forget the importance of being different.

9. Stay focused. There are many ways to lose and only one way to win: don't beat yourself.

10. Cap horses come in all shapes and sizes; tailor your handicapping to find them.

11. You're never as good as you feel when you're winning or as bad as you feel when you're losing.

12. Learn to let go. If your mind is stuck on something that happened in the last race, you're in trouble for the next race.

13. Mental toughness is a skill that can be learned, and experience is the best teacher.

14. If it suits your personality, it might be a major advantage to play with a partner and/or to play multiple entries. Cap horses are hard to find, so why not maximize your chances of finding them?

15. The answer to most questions is: "It depends." Be prepared to deal with contradictions; there is a time to stick to your game plan and a time to adjust, and you'll need to be able to think on your feet to know the difference.

16. You don't have to eschew all favorites, but if you're going to play them indiscriminately, you might as well stay home and rake your lawn.

17. By the same token, stabbing at longshots willy nilly—while a better plan than playing all favorites—isn't going to get you anywhere, either. Learn to identify races where longshots are likely to win.

18. You need to learn to handicap yourself—that is, develop a style that suits who you are and put yourself in positions where you have the best chance to win.

19. Study the specifics of the rules and look for ways to make them work to your advantage.

20. It's not a bad idea to save a bullet for the end.

21. Never stop learning.

As for this last point, I had a few more quotes from our players to share.

Noel Michaels: "Even though I've written a book about this stuff, I have the opinion that I have more to learn from everyone else than they have to learn from me. Some people are so egotistical, especially horseplayers. It goes with the territory to think you know everything and nobody else knows anything. What has always helped me is to know how much I have to learn from other people. I try to take the best of what other people have to offer and incorporate that into my handicapping, and I've done that my whole career as a handicapper. You are your own person, but you have to acknowledge that other people have things to teach you and be willing to learn."

Brent Sumja: "Every person who handicaps races regularly can teach you something. You have to look at what other people are betting. You can't be afraid to learn. Everyone has something to share. Every day, as a handicapper, if you don't learn something, you're going backwards."

Ken Massa: "Successful horseplayers, tournament players or otherwise, are like the top brain surgeon who goes to the brain surgery convention. He doesn't say, 'I'm going to skip it because I'm already the best'; he goes because he still wants to learn new stuff, and he wants to expand his knowledge. I think that's one of the keys with the best players: they always want to learn more."

I have this in common with the best players; I have a thirst for knowledge and I am always looking to learn new things, and, thanks to the players in this book, I've learned quite a lot. I can only hope you feel the same way about me.

For our appendices, I wanted to have a couple of our players walk us through the entirety of one of their memorable contest runs. Paul Shurman was the first to oblige.

Appendix I:

Paul Shurman and the 2013 Saratoga Contest
by Paul Shurman

We've talked about my strategy in the NYRA contests. It's the only contest where it's win, place, or show, and my fear is always that I'm going to end up going into day two with $0 on each ticket. You can win if you only get $200 or $300 the first day, but if you have zero, your odds of winning are very, very slim.

My strategy on day one was to take one ticket and play all conservative show bets, trying to build up a bankroll to $200 or $250. On the other ticket, I wanted to play my best bets. Another reason I think that strategy works well is that a lot of people who play two tickets are playing their first choice and their second choice. I'm always playing my first choice on my non-show ticket.

On Wednesday, which was day one, I hit my first eight show bets and got ticket one up to $222. At that point, I hit a 10-1 on ticket two, my non-show ticket, to get that ticket up over $200 as well. Then, with both tickets in good shape, ticket one wasn't a show ticket anymore; it was just a regular ticket, and I played it more conventionally. So on ticket one, I used my double bet on a cap horse and didn't hit. On ticket two, I loved a 3-1 shot, and I grabbed it, getting that one up past $250.

We've also talked before about how I like to handicap backwards. I start by looking at the last race first because it's the most important, and I want to make sure I have time to do it properly and make sure

I know exactly what's coming up. So I had a horse I'd picked out at Del Mar that I knew I wanted to bet, and a horse in the last race at Arlington as well.

I liked nothing for the first maybe ten races. I didn't make a bet until the fourth at Saratoga. At that point I played two horses, one for each ticket, on a 4-1 and a 9-2. Since my tickets had roughly the same amount at that point, it didn't really matter to me which horse went on which ticket. One of my horses, Wickapecko, won, so now my number one ticket was up to around $350.

At that point, I treated ticket one as my good ticket for my best plays, and on ticket two, I started taking shots on cap horses. I didn't hit any more of those, but had I done so, then I would have switched with ticket two becoming my good ticket. Of course, that strategy of switching like that doesn't always work out. The week before, at the Wynn, it all went wrong. The winner had $250 and I had $150 ... on each of my two tickets.

Then, in the sixth at Saratoga, I played a horse called Kanturk Kid, who was 5-1.

I liked him because the race was full of speed. At least three of those horses wanted or needed the lead, and I had marked Kanturk Kid as the best closer in the race. He was a little shorter price than what I wanted, but I liked him so I went with him. He came from second-to-last and won pretty easily.

Another horse I liked on day two came in the Arlington sixth race. I loved this horse, Peters Rock, because he towered on the Thorograph figures.

3 Peters Rock
Own: Joseph W O'Brien
6-1 Lime Green, Blue Sash, Lime Green Cap
GEROUX F (263 43 37 37 .16) 2013: (389 63 .16)

B. g. 6 (Apr)
Sire: Dayjur (Danzig) $3,000
Dam: Gunnison Mary (Tajawa)
Br: Dawn R Haught-Martin (Ill)
Tr: Matthews Doug(48 8 5 9 .17) 2013:(94 17 .18)

L 121

Life	27	8	2	4	$184,325	90
2013	4	1	1	0	$31,100	89
2012	11	4	0	3	$85,618	88
AP Ⓣ	6	1	0	1	$29,637	85

D.Fst	3	1	0	0	$24,222	75
Wet(304)	0	0	0	0	$0	–
Synth	12	4	2	1	$93,753	90
Turf(245)	12	3	0	3	$66,350	86
DstⓉ(346)	10	3	0	3	$63,885	86

4Jly13–2AP fst 5½f ◈ :22.85 :41.25 3↑ Clm 30000(30-25) **89** 5 1 2½ 2hd 11½ 1hd Geroux F L122 b 3.70 95 – 11 PetersRock122hd **UnclJp1226¼ GrndSnstion1221¾** Attended,edged forward 5
***R-BIAS: 46 FLOW: -157 BL12: 0.7 CFR: 8**

14Jun13–6AP gd *5f Ⓣ :24.13 :23.43 :11.91 3↑ Clm 25000(30-25) **77** 2 2 2hd 31½ 45 63 Geroux F L119 b 6.90 87 – 10 Pirates Vow124nk **Upsell1211¼** *Stig's Deputy119¾* In touch btw, empty 8
***R-BIAS: . FLOW: 65 BL12: 1.7 CFR: 73**

26May13–5AP fm 5f Ⓣ :23.29 :23.25 :11.97 3↑ Clm 30000(30-25) **83** 4 3 34 34½ 33½ 42 Geroux F L121 b 6.20 89 – 09 *PiratesVow121¾ YankeeInjunuity121½* BarrcudBy124¾ 2d flight,willngly btw 8
***R-BIAS: . FLOW: 37 BL12: 1.0 CFR: 64**

3May13–6AP fst 6f ◈ :22.99 :23.63 :11.96 :12.63 3↑ Alw 10000s **82** 5 1 1hd 1hd 2hd 22 Geroux F L122 b 3.60 90 – 11 Bug Juice1242 Peters Rock1221 Toro Grande1153½ Dueled inside, held 2d 6
***R-BIAS: 107 FLOW: -84 BL12: 3.9 CFR: 33**

15Nov12–6Haw fm 5½f Ⓣ :22.19 :42.34 3↑ Clm 18000 **78** 9 2 42½ 53 55 32½ Martinez S B L122 b *2.10 85 – 12 StigsDeputy1172½ ArtfulBee122no PtrsRock1221¼ Tracked btw, missed 2d 10
***R-BIAS: -211 FLOW: 168 BL12: 0.0 CFR: 59**

21Sep12–4AP fm *5½f Ⓣ :22.76 :42.25 3↑ Clm 27500(27.5-22.5) **82** 6 3 21½ 21 21½ 31 Geroux F L121 b *2.10 85 – 14 PirtesVow121¾ HrvestHome120nk PetersRock1212¾ Forward, missed 2nd 6
***R-BIAS: 72 FLOW: -165 BL12: 0.0 CFR: 11**

19Aug12–2AP fm 5f Ⓣ :22.86 :23.38 :11.78 3↑ Clm c-18000 **85** 10 4 43 3½ 21½ 1¾ Geroux F L124 b 2.90 91 – 09 Peters Rock124¾ Go Getem122½ LuckWithaKiss1221 3wd advance, driving 10
Claimed from Skibinski, J., Walters, D., Nicholson Thoroughbreds, Inc., Ferruzza, L. et al. for $18,000, Domenosky Tammy Trainer 2012(as of 8/19): (112 17 34 13 0.15)
***R-BIAS: . FLOW: 5 BL12: 3.7 CFR: 52**

22Jly12–2AP fst 5f ◈ :22.79 :22.88 :12.07 3↑ Clm c-18000 **85** 4 3 34 33½ 2½ 12¼ Martinez S B L122 b 3.50 96 – 09 *Peters Rock1222¼* Pirates Vow1222¼ AngelTalk122¾ Shifted 3wd, took over 5
Claimed from O'Brien Joseph W. for $18,000, Matthews Doug Trainer 2012(as of 7/22): (120 20 16 14 0.17)
***R-BIAS: 9 FLOW: 23 BL12: 7.7 CFR: 59**

10Jun12–3AP fm *5½f Ⓣ 3↑ Clm 27500(27.5-22.5) – 5 2 21½ 21 31½ 43¾ Martinez S B L121 b *2.50 - - BrrcudBy1211 AllTnkdUp120½ LuckWithKiss1212¼ Chased 3wd, weakened 7
***R-BIAS: . FLOW: . BL12: 10.9 CFR: .**

25May12–7AP fst 5½f ◈ :22.97 :42.22 3↑ Clm 27500(27.5-22.5) **88** 3 1 2½ 2hd 22 32¼ Martinez S B L122 b 5.40 89 – 19 RorinMissl120½ EvcutonRout1221¾ PtrsRock1223¾ Pressed foe, weakened 6
***R-BIAS: -146 FLOW: -101 BL12: 0.0 CFR: 7**

WORKS: 27Jly13 AP ◈ 4f fst :51 B *47/52* **19May13 AP ◈ 4f fst :48² B** *17/55* **27Apr13 Haw 4f fst :48³ Bg** *2/17* **20Apr13 Haw 4f fst :52³ B** *30/34* **13Apr13 Haw 4f gd :51 B** *26/45* **5Apr13 Haw 5f fst 1:03 B** *11/35*
TRAINER: TurfSprints(17 .18 $1.98) Synth/Turf(26 .19 $2.98) 31-60Days(76 .20 $1.75) WonLastStart(52 .19 $2.24) Turf(132 .14 $1.55) Sprint(125 .13 $1.14) J/T 2012-13 AP(65 .20 $2.57) J/T 2012-13(138 .19 $2.24)

I almost made that my double bet, but I didn't because there were storms in the area and we lost the feed from Arlington right before the race, so I didn't know what the price was going to be, but I still played him. I pulled the race up on my computer and got to see the last five seconds in the race, just in time to see him hit the wire first at 10-1. I was just as glad that I didn't use my double bet, though, because I was getting close enough to the leader at that point that a double bet on a capper would get me there.

I really like to save my double bet as long as possible, because you never know what price you're going to need at the end, and having that double bet left gives you an advantage over everybody else who doesn't have it. That can really come in handy. Not everybody uses the double bet in the last race, but the winner usually does. Most people don't think this way, but depending on where you are at the end, you might be able to play a horse to place or show using your double bet and have enough points to get where you need to be.

In the seventh race at Arlington, there was a late scratch, and that caused a delay. This was a problem for me because there was no time between a race at Del Mar and the race at Arlington. So I was standing by the machine just waiting to see what happened at Del Mar before I made my Arlington play. The other problem was that the scores weren't updated before I made my Arlington play.

The horse I wanted to play at Arlington was for me a no-brainer, English Council.

7 English Council	B. c. 3 (Mar)		Life	4 1 0 0	$9,015	63	D.Fst	1 0 0 0	$105	14
Own: Calumet Farm	Sire: English Channel (Smart Strike) $25,000						Wet(232)	1 0 0 0	$750	44
15-1 Black, Gold Chevrons, Gold Chevrons On	Dam: Supreme Council (Rahy)		2013	2 1 0 0	$8,850	63	Synth	2 1 0 0	$8,160	63
$25,000 Br: Bluegrass Hall LLC (Ky)		L 119	2012	2 M 0 0	$165	22	Turf(370)	0 0 0 0	$0	–
SANCHEZ J (156 21 23 22 .13) 2013: (313 36 .12)	Tr: Fernandez Jose(—) 2013:(1 0 .00)		AP ⊤	0 0 0 0	$0	–	Dst⊤(372)	0 0 0 0	$0	–

Previously trained by DiVito James P 2013 (as of 6/22): (99 20 17 9 0.20)
22Jun13– 5AP fst 1⅛ ◇ :25.08 :25.03 :25.52 :31.11 3+ Md 12500(12.5-10) 63 1 1¹ 1¹ 1ʰᵈ 1³ 1⁶ Sanchez J L120 b 4.90 75 – 17 English Council120⁶ Kinzig124½ Blu Cobalto120½   Pace, turned back foe 7
*R-BIAS: 75 FLOW: –75 BL12: 0.0 CFR: 37

Previously trained by Lukas D Wayne 2012: (285 26 22 30 0.09)
11Jan13– 10P gd 1⅛ :24.54 :24.29 :26.69 :38.25 3+ Md 30000(30-25) 44 4 56½ 57 45 59½ 514¼ Lebron V L118 b 33.80 39 – 42 Congenia1242¼ Bad Ronnie121²½ Mr Percussionist121³   Inside, no rally 8
*R-BIAS: –41 FLOW: 232 BL12: 8.5 CFR: 99
23Nov12– 1CD fst 1⅛ :24.78 :24.70 :26.25 :34.99 Md 40000(40-35) 14 7 6⁸ 8¹³ 8²¹ 8²⁸ 7³⁵ Court J K L120 b 46.30 54 – 12 Bourbon Pride120²¼ Revelationist120⁶ Broken Key120³¼   No factor 9
*R-BIAS: 140 FLOW: 144 BL12: 15.0 CFR: 97
17Oct12– 3Kee fst 1⅛ ◇ :25.51 :25.90 :27.44 :32.15 Md 30000 22 7 99½118 1119 9²¹ 914¼ Court J K L118 b 14.90 48 – 32 Joy to the King118½ Revelationist118ⁿᵒ Straight Town118½   Outrun 11
*R-BIAS: 42 FLOW: 10 BL12: 2.0 CFR: 61

WORKS: 4Aug13 CmF 5f fst 1:03 B 1/2 8Jun13 CmF 5f fst 1:03 B 1/1 1Jun13 CmF 4f fst :53¹ B 1/1 23Mar13 CmF 4f fst :52 B 1/1 9Mar13 CmF 3f fst :37⁴ B 1/1 8Jan13 OP 3f fst :37 B 5/24
TRAINER: 1stW/Tm(1.00 $0.00) Turf(1.00 $0.00) Routes(1.00 $0.00)

He was a son of English Channel, and it was his first time on turf. The horse had by far the highest pedigree ratings on HTR and a very high first-time turf rating. On Thorographs, he had the second-best figures behind the favorite. That was the play.

My brother had played a cap horse, which is what he needed to get him to the lead. My horse was 6-1 when I bet him and would go up to 9-1. He and I always have this reciprocal agreement where if one of us cashes, the other gets ten percent. Well, coming for home in the Arlington race, our two horses were neck and neck, and he turned to me and said, 'How about we make it 20 percent?' I said, 'Sure.'

At that point, his horse sprinted ahead, but then my horse changed leads and went on and another horse split our two. Then there was a long inquiry. I was upset that another horse had split my brother and me, because if he'd run second and I came down, at least he would have had a high cash, but now we were in danger of losing everything. Eventually, I stayed up.

I didn't think I'd won the whole thing; I was hoping for a top-three finish. I was about 23rd going in, so I figured at least one or two people in front of me would have the horse. But at that point, I still had a chance, because most people had played their doubles, so someone would not only have had to play that horse, but he or she also would have had to save the double to play that horse ... and that's what the winner did. Funny enough, the winner didn't even need his double. He could have played that as a single bet and still beat me. I was pleasantly surprised to get second. The only downside was the little 'Okay, 20 percent' cost me $3,500!

Appendix II:

The NYRA Spring 2013 Contest: A Walk-through with Winner Kevin Cox

By Kevin Cox

First bet I made was Belmont, race two. I always want to start out on a positive note, and I don't want to over-analyze, though as I'll tell you about later, that's exactly what happened to me in the end. But in this race, David Jacobson had an uncoupled entry in the race. I liked Schoolyard Dreams.

) Schoolyard Dreams
Own: Drawing Away Stable and Jacobson Davi
2 Electric Blue, Fluorescent Orange Circle **$35,000**
SARIO J (164 30 27 28 .18) 2013: (713 168 .24)

B. h. 6 (May)
Sire: Stephen Got Even (A.P. Indy) $7,500
Dam: Hear This (Prospector's Music)
Br: John E Little (Ky)
Tr: Jacobson David(120 29 18 21 .24) 2013:(348 79 .23)

L 122

Life	27	3	7	6	$310,552	96	D.Fst	20	2	5	4	$265,038 96
2013	5	0	1	1	$25,120	92	Wet(390)	4	1	0	2	$24,980 92
							Synth	0	0	0	0	$0 –
2012	5	0	3	1	$51,434	92	Turf(280)	3	0	2	0	$20,534 88
Bel	5	0	1	2	$39,920	96	Dst(363)	1	0	1	0	$12,800 91

un13–8Bel	fst	6½f		:22.44	:45.09	1:09.49	1:15.96	3↑OC 62k/N2x	**85**	8	8	53½	54	64½	54½	Velazquez J R	L122 b	20.20	89–16	Big Business124¾ N.F.'sDestiny1221 WeeFreudian1222	3 wide pursuit turn 9
ay13–8Bel	myS	7f	⊗	:22.78	:45.86	1:09.75	1:22.65	3↑OC 62k/N2x	**82**	5	6	76¾	74¼	56½	47¼	Alvarado J	L122 b	5.90	86–12	Reload1225 Escrow Kid122¾ Inflation Target1221½	Bump after brk, 4w upr 7
pr13–9Aqu	fst	7f		:23.11	:45.51	1:09.09	1:21.52	4↑OC 62k/N2x	**92**	4	5	42	42	54	34	Saez L	L118 b	6.00	92–12	*BigBusiness*1182¾ Silmte1181¼ SchoolyrdDrems1181	3w upper, no headway 6
pr13–8Aqu	fst	1		:23.61	:46.20	1:10.87	1:36.48	4↑OC 75k/N3x	**84**	4	11	11	2hd	2½	45¼	Alvarado J	L118 b	3.45	82–18	Prcusson120no SummrSnst1181¾ FddlrsAflt1183½	Beat the gate,stumbled 5
isqualified and placed 5th																					
an13–4Aqu	fst	6f	⊡	:23.12	:45.74	:57.56	1:09.88	4↑OC 50k/N2x	**91**	7	3	32	31½	21	2½	Alvarado J	L118 b	6.10	91–09	*Plsndthnkyo*111½ SchoolyrdDrms118¾ StLmsHlo1181¼	3w pursuit, willingly 7
ov12–8Aqu	gd	1	Ⓣ	:23.79	:49.17	1:14.07	1:37.17	3↑OC c-50k/N2x	**70**	1	54½	54	75	87½	99	Rosario J	L120 fb	4.20	81–12	Dominant Jeannes1201 Hangover Kid1203 *Right One*1201½	3w upper, tired 10
laimed from Fein, Eric and Mitola, Anthony for $50,000, Dutrow Richard E Jr Trainer 2012(as of 11/16): (442 109 84 66 0.25)																					
ov12–2Aqu	fst	1		:23.32	:46.52	1:10.16	1:34.40	3↑OC 50k/N2x	**91**	5	64	53	32	32½	21½	Dominguez R A	L120 fb	*1.35	95–07	BllmyBrw1201½ SchoolyrdDrms1201 Convoctn1203½	2p,snug hold to 1/4pl 6
ep12–9Lrl	fm	1	Ⓣ	:23.26	:45.81	1:09.35	1:33.30	3↑OC 32k/N3x-N	**88**	8	57½	57½	65¾	41¼	2hd	Rodriguez E D	L120 b	2.30	105–01	SintPierre120hd SchoolyrdDrems1201¼ BdDbt1201	Late,outside bid, hung 9
ly12–8Sar	fst	1⅛		:47.81	1:11.65	1:36.14	1:48.90	3↑OC 75k/N3x-N	**90**	5	21	2½	2hd	1hd	32¾	Dominguez R A	L121 fb	2.75	92–05	Cese1211¼ GoldenGulch1211½ SchoolyrdDrems1211½	Vied btwn foe 3/8–1/8 7
un12–4Bel	fst	1		:23.45	:46.66	1:10.45	1:35.48	3↑ⓇLemnDrpKid88k	**92**	1	21	42½	43	33	2½	Alvarado J	L119 b	6.20	86–16	JhnnsbrgSml121½ SchlyrdDrms1193¼ AlmdOr1211¾	Angled 4w 1/4, gd kick 5

RKS: 25Mar13 Aqu⊡ 4f fst :50⁴ B *1/2* **15Mar13 Aqu⊡ 5f fst 1:05¹ B** *3/3* **6Mar13 Aqu⊡ 4f fst :50⁴ B** *6/15* **26Feb13 Aqu⊡ 3f fst :38³ B** *6/13* **22Feb13 Aqu⊡ 3f fst :39² B** *8/9* **26Jan13 Aqu⊡ 3f fst :40 B** *5/5*

AINER: Dirt(745 .27 $1.76) Sprint(551 .26 $1.72) Claim(536 .25 $1.70) J/T 2012-13 BEL(16 .25 $2.42) J/T 2012-13(19 .26 $2.17)

He had the best last-race Beyer in the race. Some of the others there looked over-bet, and he was just the obvious choice. He was a short price, but that's okay to me at that point. You don't want to be chasing early. If it's a common-sense type horse, get on the board. See your name up there.

When I come up with what I think is a key horse in a race, I have a good idea of the Beyer figure I think he's going to run. Then I look at the other horses in the race, and I try to figure out the highest possible figure they might get. For example, if a horse is coming off a layoff, or even second or third off a layoff, I'll give five points to the figure. If there's a first-time equipment change, I'll give five points to that figure. I'll add points for projected maturity as well. I'm not using the inflated figure as a barometer of how much I think they'll win, so much as to see if they can possibly beat my horse. I want to know who could upset the applecart.

It works the other way, too. Sometimes, if I like a horse but there's a reason he might not run as well, a bad post position or something like that, I'll deduct points when I'm projecting his figure. Other people will sit there and tell you everything they like about a horse, and they'll just keep convincing themselves they can't lose. To me, when you like a horse, you still have to find out why he could possibly run badly.

I made another bet in Belmont race three. I had three horses checked off: Comes the Dream, Unitarian, and Runs Like a Kitten, at 9-5, 3-1, and 9-2, respectively. I ended up going with Runs Like a Kitten, because if I'm torn among three horses, I'll go with the longest price out of the three. Comes the Dream won instead, but that didn't bother me; I was already on the board and he was short anyway, so on to the next race.

In Belmont's fourth, I played a bomb, Hoppy Do, who ran fifth. I initially wanted to pass the race, but he was a big price, so I took a shot. No harm done.

The next bet was in Monmouth's race six, Act of Magic.

2 Act of Magic	B. g. 4 (May)		Life	3 M	1 0	$4,139	62	D.Fst	0 0 0 0	$0
5-1 Own: Joemar Racing Stables White And Blue Triangular Thirds, Blue	Sire: Hook and Ladder (Dixieland Band) $5,000 Dam: Carson City Girl (Carson City) $20,000 Br: Joemar Racing Stables LLC (NY)							Wet(320)	0 0 0 0	$0
				2012	3 M	1 0	$4,139	62	Synth	0 0 0 0	$0
SANTIAGO V (66 5 2 6 .08) 2013: (207 12 .06)	Tr: Farfan-Casarez Luis(1 0 1 0 .00) 2013:(1 0 .00)		L 124	2011	0 M 0 0		$0	–	Turf(199)	3 0 1 0	$4,139
				Mth ⊕	1 0 1 0		$3,800	62	Dst⊕(251)	1 0 1 0	$3,800

20Oct12–3Bel yl 1⅛ [T] :24.04 :49.29 1:16.10 1:48.91 3+⒮Md Sp Wt 57k 10 7 3⁵ 3⁴ 8⁵ 7¹⁶ 7³⁰ Castro E L120 b 46.25 24–46 *Rdthprospctus120⁴ PostPttrn120¹¼ SttsofForcs120⁴¾ Tracked 4 deep, wknd
15Sep12–4Bel fm 6f [T] :22.24 :45.17 :56.83 1:09.04 3+⒮Md Sp Wt 52k 45 11 3 31½ 8⁸ 9¹⁰ 9¹⁰½ Leparoux J R L120 b 10.80 79 – 12 *OldMnMeese120¹⅓ LkotFreud123ʰᵈ ChseOnHome116¹⅓ 3w until 3/8, folded
19Aug12–2Mth fm 1 ⊕ :22.95 :46.93 1:11.57 1:36.04 3+ Md 25000(25–20) 62 6 2³ 33½ 41½ 3² 23½ Santiago V L119 b 55.70 72 – 18 *Doodleman123¾ Act of Magic119⅓ Solo Approach119ⁿᵏ Mild rally outside
WORKS: 16Jun13 Mth 4f fst :50³ B 54/69 10Jun13 Mth 5f fst 1:01⁴ B 7/17 1Jun13 Mth 5f fst 1:02 B 4/11 26May13 Mth 4f fst :51² B 18/24 18May13 Mth 4f fst :51¹ B 26/29 11May13 Mth 3f fst :37⁴ B 5/8
TRAINER: +180Days(3 .00 $0.00) Turf(12 .00 $0.00) Routes(12 .00 $0.00) MdnClm(11 .00 $0.00) J/T 2012-13 MTH (8 .00 $0.00) J/T 2012-13(9 .00 $0.0

My theory about maidens is to go anywhere in their running lines and use their best number. He hadn't run in eight months. He'd made three lifetime starts, and the one eight months ago was on a yielding turf course and he ran up the track. The one before that was sprinting on the grass: up the track. The first time out of the box, ten months ago, he had a 62 Beyer, on the turf, as an early three-year-old, from the six hole. So I gave him extra points for moving in from the six to the two. I also gave him eight or nine maturity points for the growing up he'd probably done since then, so that race to me shows he might actually run like a 70 today. I write "Max Seventy" next to him because that's what I think he's eligible to run.

I thought there might be some hidden value there. I wouldn't have taken him at 3-1. If you're going back that far, that's like finding a hidden treasure. You need to get a little reward for your efforts if you're going back that far. He ended up winning at 5-1. That got me to $180, and I think the leader might've had about $280 at that point. I was in the top 20.

In Belmont's sixth, I played So Scott, another Jacobson common-sense horse. I thought he was about 50-50 to win the race, and he was 3-1.

Next up was Monmouth's eighth race. I went with Soup A' Fleet. He had speed; he was decent odds; and he was right in the race until the top of the stretch. So, at that point, that was six bets in the books. I started cooking. I took a break until Monmouth's 10th. I played the eight horse, American Kitty:

```
8   American Kitty                          Ch. f. 4 (Feb)                                         Life    15  3  2  1  $63,572  78 | D.Fst      8  1  2  1  $31,868  78
    Own: Peace Sign Stable                  Sire: Tale of the Cat (Storm Cat) $25,000              2013     1  0  0  0     $230  55 | Wet(400)   0  0  0  0       $0   -
8-1 White, Black Peace Sign, White And Black Dam: American Diva (Quiet American)             L 120  2012    13  3  2  1  $63,262  78 | Synth      1  1  0  0  $13,200  54
CAMACHO S JR (32 4 4 5 .12) 2013: (149 10 .07) Br: Move Up Breeders LLC (Ky)                       Mth(T)   3  1  0  0  $16,130  69 | Turf(278)  6  1  0  0  $18,504  69
                                            Tr: Dibona Robert S(18 2 5 1 .11) 2013:(42 5 .12)                                         | Dst(T)(370) 3 1  0  0  $14,710  69
2Jun13-2Mth fm 5½f (T) :22.61 :45.26 :57.07 1:03.10 3↑(F)Clm c-(20-18)  55 8 4 95¼ 96¾ 75½ 73½ Trujillo E  L119 4.30 87-10 Look At Me Dance119hd Angels Way119nk Sandy Key Gal1171  No factor 9
  Claimed from Lopez Daniel J. for $20,000, Lopez Daniel J Trainer 2013(as of 6/2): ( 3 0 1 0 0.00 )
  Previously trained by Iwinski Allen 2012(as of 11/18): ( 126 22 10 15 0.17 )
18Nov12-2Prx fst 6½f :23.63 :46.89 1:11.70 1:18.23 3↑(F)Alw 16000s  68 5 7 63½ 53¾ 53¾ 43½ Alvarado R Jr  L116 2.60 76-21 Lady Repent120¾ Lisa Stannard118¾ Hot Smile1132  Broke in air, angled 7
  Previously trained by Lopez Daniel J 2012(as of 10/28): ( 38 10 11 3 0.26 )
28Oct12-7Prx fst 6f :23.07 :46.92 :59.61 1:12.50 3↑(F)Alw 16000s  68 5 5 66 53½ 54 34¾ Alvarado R Jr  L116 *1.60 70-26 LovYorSml1192½ HrdRckCndy1182¼ AmrcnKtty116nk  Rail lane, mild rally 7
7Oct12-8Mth fst 6f :22.06 :45.53 :58.09 1:10.99 3↑(F)OC 22k/n1x-N  78 4 7 75¾ 73¾ 32½ 22½ Fragoso P  L118 9.00 81-23 WestCostLdy1162½ AmricnKitty1181¾ AnglDrms116½  4 wide run, willingly 10
15Sep12-7Prx fst 6f :22.70 :46.79 :59.28 1:12.31 3↑(F)Alw 16000s  75 10 7 62¾ 5¾ 44 62¾ Pennington F  L116 7.20 73-28 English Girl1201 Chinchilla Lady1201 Hot Smile118½  Wide, flattened out 12
9Aug12-7Mth fm 1 1/16 (T) :24.81 :50.03 1:14.13 1:43.69 +3↑(F)Clm 30000(32-28)B  69 7 21 21 21 33 43½ Trujillo E  L116 5.00 73-20 AllurngPowr1192 TkHrTothTop1191¼ Subpon121nk  Tracked,needed more 7
21Jly12-5Mth fm 5f (T) :21.39 :44.79 :56.83 3↑(F)Clm c-(20-18)B  69 1 7 75¾ 62¼ 3½ 11¼ Carmouche K  L117 *1.70 88-12 AmericnKitty1171¼ PreciousPul1152½ RosisRun115no  3wd btwn 3/16,clear 7
  Claimed from Calhoun W. Bret for $20,000, Calhoun William Bret Trainer 2012(as of 7/21): ( 433 99 74 65 0.23 )
23Jun12-4CD fst 7f :23.31 :47.10 1:12.21 1:24.87 3↑(F)Clm c-(15-10)N2L  65 2 3 53 32 11 13¼ Lanerie C J  L118 *1.50 81-15 AmricnKitty1183¼ SwtOnKittn1221½ SilvrProspcts1184  Split horses, cleared 8
  Claimed from 100% Racing Stable LLC for $15,000, Pitts Helen Trainer 2012(as of 6/23): ( 42 2 8 5 0.05 )
7Jun12-3CD fm 1 1/16 (T) :23.49 :47.84 1:13.20 1:43.55 (F)Clm 30000  59 7 31½ 31 31½ 42½ 55¼ Lebron V  L118 b 7.20 77-19 Paoli120hd Original Kitten1182¾ Made Up1181½  Close up 3 w, tired 7
18May12-3CD fm 1 1/16 (T) :23.61 :47.89 1:12.38 1:43.93 (F)Clm 40000  58 3 32 32 31½ 2½ 43 Lanerie C J  L118 b 6.40 77-13 Dodie Jo1181¼ Annelle1201 Original Kitten118¾  Vied 4 wide, weakened 7
WORKS: 15Jun13 Mth 5f fst 1:01² B 2/2  22May13 Mth 5f fst 1:03 B 24/27  15May13 Mth 3f fst :38 B 8/13  2May13 Mth 4f fst :50 B 16/40  ●26Apr13 Mth 3f fst :37 B 1/7  11Nov12 Prx 3f fst :36³ B 3/9
TRAINER: 1stClaim(27 .15 $1.01) 2OffOver180(2 .00 $0.00) TurfSprints(12 .25 $1.95) Turf(55 .13 $1.02) Sprint(67 .15 $0.93) Alw(10 .10 $0.56)   J/T 2012-13 MTH(3 .33 $3.47) J/T 2012-13(3 .33 $3.47)
```

It was a first-level allowance; the horse was coming from a straight claimer, 20 down to 18. I know that there are Beyer pars listed in the *Form*, but I have my own Beyer pars as well that show what every class level runs, because for a lot of the races, the *Form* doesn't list a par; it just says "NA," so I go back through all the old *Forms* and make my own pars for every single class level individually. To me, a $19,000 open claimer winner usually runs an 86 on my pars. To me, an average first-level allowance winner will run an 81. So a lot of people will look at American Kitty and say she's going up in class from a claimer to an allowance, but I feel that horse is dropping.

So I had this horse as a drop-down; it was the second start off a layoff, so I was being forgiving of the last race. I saw that back in her three-year-old year, she'd run a 69 going two turns on the turf—not that far off if you project some improvement. What also intrigued me is that even off an eight-month layoff, she was claimed first start off the layoff. That told me she must have looked good in the paddock that day; plus, she was bet like a good thing, down to 4-1, so I thought she was great value at 19-1. She was sixth at the top of the stretch; she just whistled. That put me up there, either in front or close to it.

In Arlington race eight, I bet the 11, Hasty Warrior. He was another cap horse, but I had the race as wide open, so that's why I went for a price. I had just hit a big price, but it was still early in the game and I wanted to hit another one because it was a longshot type of race. He missed all the money by three lengths.

So then I went back to Belmont, race 11. I had two bets left, including my $40 bullet. I went with the six horse, Sir Leslie.

If you look at the whole field, you'll see that in their last starts, a lot of them ran similar numbers. The favorite looked like he'd hit his ceiling to me, and meanwhile, Sir Leslie had one of the two best figures in the race, and he was 9-1. Sometimes when you see an excellent jockey at good odds, you think that you're the stooge, that you're doing something wrong; why is this horse at such good odds? But I knew this was the play. His first start off the bench was an open maiden-claimer, and to me an open maiden-claimer $35,000 is the same as a state-bred special race. Anybody who tells you that's a dropdown, going from state-bred special weight to bottom-level maiden-claimers, is wrong. That's a lateral transfer. Now the only question was whether I would use my double bet on him. I didn't, and then after the race when he won and paid $21.80, I was kicking myself in the shins.

Then it was the last race of the first day. I've heard people say you don't want to be in first place because then you have a target on your back. I don't buy it. I want to be as far ahead of everybody as possible.

I still had my $40 bullet left, and I was in fifth place. I was looking at a horse called Chas the Man:

6 Chas the Man
Own: Charles Sigrist and Del Sol Farm LLC
-1 Yellow, Yellow 'Cjs' On Black Diamonds — $25,000
RRES F C (67 3 12 8 .04) 2013: (272 18 .07)

B. c. 4 (Feb)
Sire: Congrats (A.P. Indy) $35,000
Dam: Samantha B. (Dance Brightly)
Br: Moises Yanez & Charles Sigrist (Ill)
Tr: Yanez Moises R(46 6 8 5 .13) 2013:(70 7 .10)

L 122

Life	19	1	2	2	$47,239	71	D.Fst	2	0	0	0	$200	32
2013	3	0	1	0	$4,440	59	Wet(363)	4	0	0	1	$4,520	58
2012	12	1	1	2	$41,509	71	Synth	0	0	0	0	$0	-
AP	0	0	0	0	$0	-	Turf(233)	13	1	2	1	$42,519	71
							Dst(339)	0	0	0	0	$0	-

un13-9AP	fm	*1 1/16 (T)	:24.12	:48.94	1:15.47	1:49.03	3↑ Clm 16000N2L	59	10	3^4	2^2½	1^hd	1^1½	5^3¼	Perez E E	L122 b	2.60e	63-32	HurricnElvs122½ SomwhrnTm117^1 HomsthFct122^1	4wd early, pressed foe	11
ay13-7AP	fm	*1 1/16 (T)	:23.37	:48.37	1:13.18	1:45.50	3↑ Clm 16000N2L	59	1	2^2	2^hd	1^hd	3^1	3^3½	Vigil N	L122 b	*1.70	80-14	HTHThrtysvn122¾ [D]HmGrnHr116^2¾ ChsthMn122¾	Shiftd out,pressed btw	10
Placed second through disqualification																					
ay13-7AP	gd	*1 1/16 (T)	:23.52	:47.45	1:13.46	1:47.35	3↑ Clm 25000N2L	54	6	2½	2½	2½	2^1	7^7¾	Hamilton Q	L122 b	48.70	67-23	Piralu122^1½ Tobacco Fox122^no Bethel116^hd	Forced pace, gave way	11
ec12-4Haw	sly^S	1 1/16	:24.16	:47.53	1:12.56	1:46.46	3↑ [S]Alw 33000N$Y	32	7	4^4½	5^6	5^5½	7^15	7^27¼	Hamilton Q	L119 b	14.50	48-30	MdGenius122^9 IdelAlluvil122^1½ ShmLikItHot117^no	Tracked 3-4wd, empty	7
ov12-5Haw	fm	1 (T)	:23.83	:47.87	1:12.54	1:36.59	3↑ [S]Alw 33000N$Y	60	10	2^1	1^hd	1^hd	2^2½	8^6¾	Perez E E	L119 b	19.60	84-10	ShootthLoop122^hd PrfctlyAtHom119^2¼ Brm119^2	Bumped brk,forced pace	10
ov12-5Haw	fm	1 1/16 (T)	:22.51	:47.01	1:12.56	1:44.33	3↑ Clm 25000N2L	53	2	1^1½	1^3	1^1½	2^1	6^10¾	Torres F C	L119 b	9.50	72-20	JohrIrsh119^1¼ DoctorTrottr122½ SportngHoldy122^hd	Pace inside, emptied	10
ct12-6Haw	sly^S	1 1/16 (⊗)	:24.33	:48.65	1:13.56	1:47.74	3↑ [S]Alw 31000N$Y	58	6	2^1½	2½	1^1	3^1½	3^4¾	Torres F C	L118 b	5.50	64-26	TensWild120^2¾ SahmLikeItHot122^2 ChstheMn118^hd	Stalked, pressed btw	7
ep12-9AP	fm	*1⅛ (T)	:48.29	1:14.65	1:38.48	1:50.97	3↑ [S]Alw 44000N1X	62	6	2^3½	2^8	2^1	2^4½	7^6¼	Torres F C	L122 b	4.60e	86-24	*UnoPcdor*117^1½ *ShootthLop*122^hd Lythtpstldwn120^hd	Brief bid3/8,flattened	10
ep12-8AP	fm	1 (T)				1:38.10	3↑ [S]Md Sp Wt 42k	71	9	1^3	1^4	1^4	1^5	1^3	Torres F C	L122 b	8.80	85-12	Chas the Man122^3 *Tens Wild*122½ Games Begin122½	Pace, clear, held sway	12
ug12-7AP	gd	1 (T)	:24.27	:50.34	1:16.34	1:41.10	3↑ [S]Md Sp Wt 42k	64	5	1^3½	1^1	1^1	1^1	2^1	Mena M	L121 b	22.50	69-21	CaptainMarvin121^1 *ChstheMn*121^nk GmesBegin121^hd	Pace inside, collared	11

RKS: 16Jun13 AP ◈ 4f fst :49^2 B *24/63* ●27May13 AP ◈ 5f fst 1:00^2 H *1/26* 3May13 AP ◈ 4f fst :51^2 B *27/39* 20Apr13 AP ◈ 5f fst 1:03^2 B *5/10* 13Nov12 Haw 5f fst 1:02^2 B *4/10* 16Sep12 AP ◈ 5f fst 1:00^4 B *12/48*

AINER: Synth(108 .12 $2.94) Turf/Synth(18 .11 $1.02) Routes(147 .06 $0.73) Claim(182 .07 $1.23) — J/T 2012-13 AP(8 .13 $2.45) J/T 2012-13(13 .15 $2.60)

I could see he had tactical speed, and there was not a lot of speed in the race. The way I projected the figures in the race, he wasn't that far behind. I knew I needed 11-1 or 10-1 to possibly get first place on the day and win the day money, and I needed nobody else who could finish ahead of me to have him. He opened up at 9-2 or something crazy like that, but I know the pools in Arlington are false pools, because all the money comes in late. I waited, and then with five minutes to post, he was drifting up, 6-1, 7-1. I put my $40 win bet on him, and he drifted up right to that 11-1 mark. The only other horse with any speed broke slowly, and once I got the lead, it was almost a too-good-to-be-true thing. I ended up in first place at the end of day one by a couple of bucks.

I didn't make my first bet on the second day until the fourth race at Belmont. At that point, there was still no real movement on the board, and then I missed my first seven bets, dropping down to second or third, and the bottom of the pack was closing in as well.

In race 11 at Monmouth, I liked the five horse, Street Gem.

5 Street Gem
Own: Just For Fun Stable LLC
-2 Fluorescent Pink, Fluorescent Green
A D (2 0 0 0 .00) 2013: (316 53 .17)

Ch. f. 3 (Mar) KEESEP11 $20,000
Sire: Street Boss (Street Cry*Ire) $10,000
Dam: Nesselrode (Lemon Drop Kid)
Br: Machmer Hall (Ky)
Tr: O'Connell Kathleen(13 0 2 1 .00) 2013:(273 43 .16)

L 117

Life	8	3	2	0	$46,940	81	D.Fst	1	0	1	0	$5,400	46
2013	6	3	1	0	$41,270	81	Wet(397)	1	0	0	0	$270	38
2012	2	M	1	0	$5,670	46	Synth	0	0	0	0	$0	-
Mth (T)	1	0	0	0	$1,200	81	Turf(381)	6	3	1	0	$41,270	81
							Dst(T)(434)	0	0	0	0	$0	-

ay13-10Mth	fm	1 (T)	:23.27	:47.49	1:11.06	1:35.29	(F)LitlSilver63k	81	6	8^4¾	9^3¾	8^4	3^nk	2¾	Coa D	L117 b	23.50	79-20	RustySlipper116¾ [D]StreetGem117½ ThreeHerts116^3	Bumped foe 1/8 pole	9
Disqualified and placed 5th																					
pr13-3Tam	fm	1 (T)	:23.93	:49.24	1:13.55	1:36.90	(F)Alw 21500NC	69	4	2^2	2^2½	1½	1^2½	1^3¾	Coa D	L118 b	*.80	85-18	StrtGm118^3¾ WildAboutIrn118^2½ BowtoNoOn116½	Drew off with flourish	5
ar13-10GP	fm	1 (T)	:23.63	:47.32	1:10.06	1:34.15	(F)SecretGrac55k	71	3	3^1	1^1	1^1½	1½	4^5¾	Spieth S	L116 b	14.00	81-12	[D]Swear Me In117¾ **Coarsegold**116^1 *Coffee Clique*116^4	Off rail, gave way	7
ar13-8Tam	fm	1 (T)	:24.73	:49.66	1:13.90	1:37.28	(F)OC 75k/N1x-N	71	2	2½	2½	1½	1^4½	1^3	Spieth S	L118 b	2.50	83-16	Street Gem118^3 Raven's Rockette118^3½ Brown Eyed Sue118^1	Clearly best	7
eb13-9Tam	gd	1 (T)	:23.84	:47.96	1:12.43	1:36.63	(F)OC 75k/N1x-N	71	2	2½	1^hd	1^hd	2^hd	2^2¼	Spieth S	L118 b	*1.90	84-12	LeFscintor118^2¼ *StreetGm*118^2 BrownEydSu118^2½	Vied,wknd, bested rest	10
eb13-9Tam	fm	1 (T)	:23.40	:48.91	1:13.99	1:37.25	(F)Md Sp Wt 17k	61	2	2^2	2^1	2^1	1½	1^4	Spieth S	L120 b	6.20	83-13	Street Gem120^4 Simply Spectacular120¾ Farah120¾	Won going away	10
Previously trained by Carey Charles A 2012(as of 8/31): (22 3 3 2 0.14)																					
ug12-6Mth	fst	1	:24.09	:49.02	1:15.31	1:41.13	(F)Md 50000(50-40)	46	1	1½	1^hd	1½	2^2½	2^7½	Ayuso A^5	L115	2.10	59-28	AmeliaMr118^7½ *StreetGem*115^11¼ DollyDouble120^1¾	Stumbled start, inside	7
ug12-1Mth	my	5½f	:21.77	:45.53	:58.95	1:06.12	(F)Md 50000(50-40)	38	5	5	6^7½	6^8½	6^6½	5^6¾	Camacho S^5	L115	30.50	77-16	Back to Class120^2 Rosie My Way115½ Unsighted120^2¾	3 wide turn, no rally	8

RKS: 13Jun13 Mth 4f fst :50 B *16/28* 19May13 Mth 4f fst :49^4 B *16/33* 6Mar13 Tam 4f fst :50^3 B *8/16* 23Jan13 Tam 5f fst 1:03^1 B *5/11* 31Dec12 Crc 5f fst 1:03^3 B *5/11* 16Dec12 Crc 4f fst :50^2 B *17/35*

AINER: Turf(363 .13 $1.50) Routes(537 .12 $1.34) Stakes(54 .11 $2.10) — J/T 2012-13 MTH(1 .00 $0.00) J/T 2012-13(12 .25 $1.97)

I used the "Keep It Simple, Stupid" theory. Sweet Gem had the best last race, had run in the same type of class, same post position—everything was exactly the same. The horse was coming back within a month, and I was getting value on her. Sometimes when a horse runs its best race last out like she did, you might worry about a bounce. You don't want to miss the wedding and go to the funeral, but I wasn't too worried about that because she was only a three-year-old, and sometimes when they run their best numbers, it just means they're improving, not that they're going to bounce. I was only a few dollars out of second, so I would have played her even if she was shorter, but she was 5-1, which I thought was great. She paid $12.40.

Minutes later, it was post time for the next at Arlington. I was hugging the tote machine. There's an annoying rule at NYRA that hopefully someday they'll fix, that if there's a post-time scratch, that's it, you lose your pick, whereas some contests will at least give you the post-time favorite. It's some technology issue, but it means you better be ready to put in another pick if your horse gets scratched at the gate.

At Arlington, once again, it was a "Keep It Simple, Stupid" race. The horse was Sunny Surprise.

11 Sunny Suprise
Own: David E Campbell
2-1 White, Volunteer Orange 'T', Volunteer
CASTRO E (94 10 17 14 .11) 2013: (414 42 .10)

Dk. b or br f. 3 (Feb)
Sire: Sun King (Charismatic) $10,000
Dam: Silver Suprise (Silver Charm)
Br: Tracy Farmer & Dennis Crooks (Ill)
Tr: Janks Christine K(48 2 10 3 .04) 2013:(63 3 .05)

L 120

Life	**6**	**M**	**4**	**0**	**$27,740**	**58**	**D.Fst** 3 0 2 0 $11,080
2013	**2**	**M**	**2**	**0**	**$15,400**	**58**	**Wet(307)** 0 0 0 0 $0
							Synth 3 0 2 0 $16,660
2012	**4**	**M**	**2**	**0**	**$12,340**	**56**	**Turf(299)** 0 0 0 0 $0
AP	**3**	**0**	**2**	**0**	**$16,660**	**58**	**Dst(305)** 3 0 3 0 $18,680

2Jun13–7AP fst 6½f ◈ :24.47 :48.53 1:13.15 1:19.43 3↑Ⓕ[S]Md Sp Wt 39k **58** 10 5 8^{8} $7^{4\frac{1}{2}}$ $2^{4\frac{1}{2}}$ $2^{\frac{3}{4}}$ Desormeaux K J L120 b 2.40 79–12 EllisthBoss$120^{\frac{3}{4}}$ SunnySuprs$120^{6\frac{3}{4}}$ RosMyRos120^{1} 5w advance,steady gai

12May13–1AP fst 6f ◈ :22.61 :46.69 :59.00 1:11.83 3↑Ⓕ[S]Md Sp Wt 38k **56** 6 7 $7^{9\frac{3}{4}}$ 5^{5} 3^{6} $2^{3\frac{3}{4}}$ Desormeaux K J L118 b 4.10 83–09 *SoLongforNow*$118^{3\frac{3}{4}}$ SunnySprs$118^{2\frac{1}{2}}$ *EllsthBoss*$118^{\frac{3}{4}}$ Angled 4w, late strid

26Dec12–2Haw fst 6f :22.36 :46.38 :59.15 1:12.98 ⒻMd c-(25-20) **56** 2 5 9^{12} 6^{12} $4^{9\frac{1}{2}}$ $2^{5\frac{1}{4}}$ Contreras A L L119 b 4.00 72–22 FlowrSpll$119^{5\frac{1}{4}}$ SunnySuprs119^{5} Shdrvsmptr$114^{1\frac{1}{4}}$ Saved grnd late strid

Claimed from Young, Terry and Crooks, Sue for $25,000, Young Terry R Trainer 2012(as of 12/26): (110 10 10 13 0.09)

1Dec12–5Haw fst 1 1/16 :24.92 :49.87 1:15.79 1:48.75 Ⓕ[R]Debutante116k **37** 7 7^{6} 9^{12} 9^{17} 8^{16} $7^{21\frac{3}{4}}$ Contreras A L L114 b 32.10 42–45 *My Option*$116^{4\frac{1}{2}}$ *Indygo Kiss*117^{nk} C'Mon Feet118^{4} Stumbled star

17Nov12–5Haw fst 6f :22.73 :46.71 :59.42 1:12.88 Ⓕ[S]Md Sp Wt 33k **49** 5 8 $6^{5\frac{1}{2}}$ 6^{10} $3^{7\frac{1}{2}}$ $2^{\frac{3}{4}}$ Contreras A L L119 b 9.20 76–19 CMonFeet$119^{\frac{3}{4}}$ SunnySuprise$119^{3\frac{1}{4}}$ **Nowthtsldy**$119^{1\frac{3}{4}}$ Tight brk, late strid

9Sep12–9AP fst 5½f ◈ :22.96 :46.37 :58.32 1:04.82 Ⓕ[S]Md Sp Wt 42k **43** 10 9 9^{12} 9^{10} 7^{13} 5^{11} Contreras A L^{5} L114 b 48.50 80–14 *Catafire*$119^{8\frac{1}{2}}$ *Indygo Kiss*119^{1} Seattle Train$119^{1\frac{1}{4}}$ Broke slowly,fanned 7w

WORKS: **12Jun13 AP ◈ 5f fst 1:02 B** *7/23* **26May13 AP ◈ 4f fst :49¹ B** *21/60* **5May13 AP ◈ 6f fst 1:14 H** *2/9* **25Apr13 AP ◈ 6f fst 1:14³ B** *2/3* **17Apr13 Haw 5f fst 1:03 B** *12/21* **10Apr13 Haw 5f gd 1:06⁴ B** *9/10*

TRAINER: Synth(62 .15 $1.32) Sprint(117 .13 $0.96) MdnSpWt(56 .20 $1.92) J/T 2012-13 AP(2 .50 $2.90) J/T 2012-13(2 .50 $2

Like I told you before, I like to bet the outside posts in sprints, and she had that. She was the favorite, but that's all I needed at that point in the contest. She had Castro, who I know was riding hungry out there, and another reason I liked her is that I pay attention to trainer stats. This trainer, Christine Janks, was only 4 percent on the year, but she had three separate categories in the trainer stats listed in the *Form* of 15, 13, and 20 percent. I like when a trainer is better than 50 percent over their annual stats in any of the specific stat categories listed in the *Form*, anything over 6 percent I would've been happy with, but she had excellent stats with synthetics, in sprint, and with maidens, so I knew this was the type of horse she did well with, even though her overall numbers weren't very strong. To me, this horse was a standout. She won and paid $5.00, enough to put me in the lead. I won the two races within minutes, so I was screaming at one TV, and then I went over and screamed at the other TV.

The next race was the last one in the contest. I was in contact with my friend John DaSilva during the whole day. He must have answered 30 phone calls from me, and he didn't offer me one horse for the whole weekend. He talked me off a few, but mostly we were just discussing strategy, and he was helpful, but he almost gave me a heart attack going into that last race, which was the 12th race at Monmouth. There was a heavily favored entry at 3-5, but I didn't like either horse. Going into the last race at a NYRA contest, you have to be careful because NYRA has the double bet rule, so there were people who would be betting $40 instead of the $20 that I was betting. I was $80 ahead going into the last race. That meant that if the entry won and paid $3.40, even if somebody had it for their $40 bet, they could not catch me. So that was a freebie. If either of them won, I'd win.

I called John, and told him, "I like the eight."

He told me, "You cannot bet the eight; you've got to protect yourself."

He wanted me to bet this 9-2 shot that he liked that was the second choice and the lowest odds of the horses that could beat me. I listened to him and bet my $40 on his horse. Of course, the eight horse won. I liked the winner and allowed myself to be touted off. I was mad at John, but it was really my fault for listening, because you can't protect yourself against every horse, and at the end of the contest, it's about picking winners. You can't just go by what the tote board says. I was over-thinking it when all I needed to do was bet the horse I liked. Paralysis by over-analysis. So now I'm sitting on three horses to win the contest, none of whom I actually like, and meanwhile my original bet just won; it airs under a hand ride. So now I'm sweating.

I told my wife Nicole, "Maybe I finish third." To make things worse, there was a 30-minute tote delay at Monmouth after the race. I walked around and started asking people, "How are you sitting? Are you drawing dead? Are you alive?" And everybody was like, "No, we're drawing dead," but I was still nervous because there were still about 30 people in the room. Finally, Monmouth is official. Then there was a 10 to 15 minute NYRA delay, and I'm about to puke. The cameras for the *Horseplayers* TV show were following me around, and I said to them, "John, I could strangle you to death right now."

Then finally someone says to me, "All right, you got it." Nobody had the horse. I was told later that nobody bet the horse because everyone thought I was betting the horse. I don't know if somebody overheard me talking to John or what, but if somebody sent out a spy, he got screwed because I ended up not even playing my own horse! A lot of people could have passed me, but there were a lot of ways to go in that race and no one did.

Appendix III: **Glossary**

ADW account – Advance Deposit Wagering account which allows the bettor to play from anywhere with a phone or Internet access. *DRF Bets* is a prime example.

Airs – Wins by open lengths.

All-in – When a bettor bets his whole bankroll on one horse.

Allowance race – A race which is an in-between step for better horses between a maiden race and a stakes race.

Bankroll – The amount of money a contestant can spend in a given contest.

Beards – (See also: Shills).

Beyer (Beyer numbers) – Author Andrew Beyer's popular handicapping tool, in which he correlates prevailing track conditions with each horse's running time to calculate what he terms a "speed figure." Available in *Daily Racing Form*.

Biases – Certain race surfaces are favorable to certain paths and/or running styles on certain days. These preferences are known as biases.

Blinkers – Equipment used to restrict a horse's field of vision, often promoting early speed and sometimes increased focus.

Bomb – A longshot.

Breeder's Cup Betting Challenge – The king of the live-bankroll tournaments.

Brick-and-mortar – The physical place where a contest is held.

Bullet – A contest selection.

Carryover – A situation where a certain exotic wager, usually the Pick-6, isn't hit, and the main pool rolls over into the next day, creating a jackpot.

Cash – An in-the-money contest finish.

Chalk (Chalky) – The betting favorite, passed down from the days when the odds were written on a chalkboard.

Claiming race – The most common race type, where all the horses are available to be purchased right before the race.

Colt – A male horse until he turns five, unless he has been gelded, in which case he's known as a gelding.

Dam – The mother of a racehorse.

Dapples – Differently shaded circular patches on a horse's coat; they are known to come and go throughout a horse's life; a sign of good health.

Degenerate – Term of affection used among horseplayers that mocks society's general impression of us.

Derby Wars – www.derbywars.com, website for online horse racing contests.

Dime – Gambler-speak for $1,000.

Distance race – Also called a route; in the USA, a race at a mile or longer.

Dirt – The most common racing surface in America, typically favoring horses with early speed.

Drawing dead – Being in a position in a contest with no chance at all to win—the player is either too far behind or blocked, which is when someone ahead of him has the same horse, so that even if the player wins the race, he still can't pass the person ahead of him.

Eclipse Awards – Annual awards given out to the most successful people and horses in racing.

Equine – Of or pertaining to horses.

Exacta – A bet in which the bettor must choose the top two finishers in a given race in exact order. Boxing the exacta will cover the combination in either order. The concept of boxing applies for all horizontal exotics, with the cost going up exponentially depending on the type of bet and how many runners are covered.

Favorite – The public's betting choice in a race, often the most likely winner.

Filly – A female horse until the age of five, unless she has been bred, in which case she is a mare.

Fire – To run a good race, even if the horse in question doesn't necessarily win; sometimes used while a race is in progress: "This 40-1 shot at Hawthorne is firing. "

Foal – A baby horse.

Formulator – Indispensable handicapping database software from *Daily Racing Form*.

Furlong – An eighth of a mile; now don't ask me again.

Gelding – A castrated male horse; a horse racing for the first time after being gelded often improves, bereft of other distractions.

Grass race – A race contested on turf.

Hand ride – To win without the rider using the whip.

Head-to-head – A contest between two players only.

Hedge – A bet made in which one is looking to increase one's chance of cashing in a given race or contest by betting an outcome other than the one he or she bet initially.

Horizontal exotics – Bets like the double, Pick-3, and Pick-4, in which the bettor must pick the winners of consecutive races.

Horse Player Now – A handicapping product that offers picks in the form of trip horses designated by various expert handicappers around the country.

Horse Player World Series – A big-deal contest held at the Orleans in Las Vegas.

HorsePlayersQualify.com – A contest website of note.

HTR – A powerful handicapping software program.

Huddie Contest – An informal, online betting contest, found easily on Twitter at via the hashtag huddie (#huddie).

Kidney sweat – Sweat between the upper part of a horse's hind legs. Rarely a good sign, but often no big deal.

Looks – A horse's appearance, as in "How was he on looks?"

Low-roller – A contest with a low buy-in.

Maidens – Horses that have yet to win a race.

Maiden special weight – A type of race in which the most promising horses begin their careers.

Main Track – Dirt or synthetic track, the principle racing surface at that track.

Mare – A female horse aged five and up, or a female younger than five that has been bred.

Morning line – An educated guess by a racetrack employee, expressed in the program or the *Racing Form*, as to how the public will bet in a given race.

MSW – (See also: Maiden special weight).

National Handicapping Challenge (NHC) – The most prestigious handicapping tournament of all.

Note – A written summation about a horse's journey in a given race. (See also: Trip).

NTRA – National Thoroughbred Racing Alliance, an organization dedicated to promoting racing and that helps sponsor the NHC (National Handicapping Challenge).

Outs – Results that would give a player a win; derived from poker.

Overlay – A horse that is a good bet because its chance of winning is greater than the implied odds being offered by the tote board (see implied odds on page 187 for more).

Paddock – The area where the horses go to be saddled before they race.

Paper – Shorthand for a horse's past performances.

Pick-6 – An exotic wager where the bettor must correctly pick the winner of six designated, consecutive races; if no one hits, the main pool carries over to the next day, creating a jackpot.

Place – A traditional bet in which the horse needs to finish first or second in order for the bettor to cash.

Polytrack – A synthetic racing surface.

Pony – A horse that accompanies racehorses to the starting gate, typically to help keep them calm.

PPs – Past performances, i.e., printed representations of a horse's history, past races, layoffs, workouts, breeding, jockeys, trainers, etc.

Pro-Ride – A synthetic racing surface.

Qualifier – A tournament in which contestants are competing not for money but for an entry into a larger tournament.

Quant – A data analyst focused entirely on numbers.

Quigley's Corner – A physical place at Santa Anita and Del Mar where equine body language expert Tom Quigley sets up shop—and occasionally drinks a beer with his friends. Follow Tom on Twitter at @Quigleys_Corner.

Racing With Bruno – A workout product produced by clocker Bruno De Julio.

Ragozin Sheets – A venerable and respected company that makes advanced speed/performance figures; named for company founder Len Ragozin.

Rake – (See: Takeout).

ROI – Return On Investment—the percentage of money returned by a particular gambling proposition over time, often expressed in a $2.00 format. A winning bet will produce a positive ROI, i.e., over $2.00; a losing bet will produce a negative one, i.e., less than $2.00.

Sartin – Howard Sartin was a renowned practitioner of pace analysis whose followers were legion at one time.

Shills – A person playing on behalf of another person, see also Beards.

Short field – A race without many runners. There is no established cut-off, but I feel like anything less than eight betting interests makes for a short field.

Show – A traditional bet in which the selected horse must finish first, second, or third.

Sire – The father of a horse.

Sprints – Races shorter than one mile.

Stabbing – Desperately picking a horse based solely on its price.

Stakes horse – A horse capable of competing at the highest level in racing, i.e., stakes races.

Stud – A retired male racehorse that gets to enjoy his retirement by making little horses, er, impregnating mares to produce foals, that is.

Superfecta – An exotic wager in which the bettor has to pick the first four finishers of a given race in order.

Super high-five wager – An exotic wager in which one must pick the top five finishers in a given race in order; if no one hits, the money bet carries over to the next day, creating a jackpot.

Syndicate – A group of people betting together.

Takeout – The percentage of every bet kept by the racetrack, typically around 20 percent.

Tape – Anachronistic slang for video of a horse's past races.

Thorograph – A popular company that sells speed/performance ratings and other valuable data.

Top-sheeting – The common—and foolhardy—practice of focusing too much on a horse's last race and not enough on his/her body of work.

Tote board – A physical board, usually on the infield of the track, continuously updating, listing the odds on every horse in the race. Used metaphorically to describe any list of such numbers on a TV screen, online betting site, etc.

Tourney – Shorthand for tournament or handicapping contest.

Touts – People who give opinions on who will win a race; also, the picks themselves.

Trainer – The person responsible for the care and—you guessed it—

training of a horse. Trainers are like coaches in other sports, only far more powerful for a host of reasons.

Trifecta – A bet in which one must pick the first three finishers in a race in order.

Trip – The specifics of the journey a horse gets in a race. A good trip means a race without incident; a horse that gets a bad trip was hindered in some way.

Turf – Grass racing, as opposed to dirt racing or synthetic surface racing.

Turf Tomlinson – A numerical rating of a horse's ability to run well on grass, found in the *Daily Racing Form*. There are also Tomlinsons that rate horses' abilities for off-tracks (mud, etc.) and different distances.

Underlay – A horse who is a poor bet because the implied odds of its winning are less than its actual chance.

Vertical exotics – Bets like exactas and trifectas in which bettors must select the first two or several finishers within the same race.

Washy – An adjective used to describe a sweaty horse, sometimes a negative body language signal, often meaningless (think Patrick Ewing).

Watch list – A list of horses, usually managed via computer, that a racing fan wishes to follow, usually for betting purposes. *DRF* Stable Mail is a prime example.

Win – A bet in which the horse must finish first in order for the bettor to collect.

Wise-guy horse – A horse being bet by industry insiders and/or professional gamblers.

Workout report – A report about how horses have been working/looking in the mornings; an important tool for dealing with maiden races and layoff horses.

Wynn Handicapping Challenge – A major handicapping contest held at the Wynn in Las Vegas.

Did I miss a term you'd like defined? Tweet me @loomsboldly and I'll provide the best answer I can.

ACKNOWLEDGMENTS

Where to begin? At the top: thanks in perpetuity to my wife Susan and daughter Perrin, the best family a man can have. I've done Okay in my various gambling endeavors over the years, caught a bit of luck here and there. But I've never been anywhere near as lucky as I was the day I met Susan and the day we found out little Perrin was on her way into this world.

Thanks also to every single player I interviewed for this book. Your time, patience, and insights are all very much appreciated. Without you, there would be no book.

I must single out two of the players for extra thanks: David Gutfreund, who pointed me down some fascinating avenues, was invaluable. Even if you disavow the name you'll always be the Maven to me.

It also meant so much to me that Noel Michaels consented to be a part of this project – this book wouldn't be half as good without his groundbreaking work on this subject and I stole from it liberally. Your blessing—and help—mean a lot to me.

My appreciation for Frank Scatoni's friendship, editorial insights, and gambling ability knows no bounds. Let's make some money, indeed.

My cousin, Thomas E. Harkins, has been an incredible resource during this project, researching, transcribing, editing, and generally helping keep me sane. The next rounds are on me.

Emily Gullikson should also be lauded for her help in both picking longshot winners and bringing this book to the page. We'll all be looking up at her name on the leaderboard soon enough.

Thanks to the great Harvey Pack, for writing the foreword, and for being a great friend.

Thanks to Dave Hudson and everybody from the Huddie contest, for the inspiration.

Thanks to everyone who ever stopped by The Unbearable Lightness of Betting (www.unbearablebetting.com) and liked what they read.

Thanks to Teresa Genaro, for lending her eagle eye.

Thanks to Chris Donofry and Meg Price for collectively pulling this rabbit out of a hat.

Thanks to Kevin Geraghty, Ken Kirchner, John Avello, Kathy Locke, and McKay Smith, for running great contests and helping me get things right.

To my friends at *Daily Racing Form*, including John Hartig, Todd Unger, Jordan Goldberg, David Renard, and Mark Simon. This is going to be fun.

And a special thanks to Mandy Minger and Steven Crist—you've helped my dream of getting involved in this business become a reality. I can't thank you enough.

LIST OF HORSE-RESCUE ORGANIZATIONS

There are many more Thoroughbred aftercare organizations deserving support than the ones I mention in this list, but please use these as a starting point. The next time you cash a big ticket or land a nice placing in a contest, please think of the athletes who helped you out.

Akindale Thoroughbred Rescue
www.akindalehorserescue.org

Old Friends and Old Friends at Cabin Creek (New York division)
www.oldfriendsequine.org

Thoroughbred Retirement Foundation
www.trfinc.org

New Vocations
www.horseadoption.com

ReRun Horse Rescue
www.rerun.org

One Horse at a Time
www.onehorseatatime.org